Celts and Christians

Religion, Culture and Society

Series Editors:
Oliver Davies,
Department of Theology and Religious Studies,
University of Wales, Lampeter,
and Gavin Flood,
Department of Religious Studies,
University of Stirling

Religion, Culture and Society is a series presented by leading scholars on a wide range of contemporary religious issues. The emphasis throughout is generally multicultural, and the approach is often interdisciplinary. The clarity and accessibility of the series, as well as its authoritative scholarship, will recommend it to students and a non-specialist readership alike.

Celts and Christians

New Approaches to the Religious Traditions of Britain and Ireland

Edited by

MARK ATHERTON

UNIVERSITY OF WALES PRESS
CARDIFF
2002

© The Contributors, 2002

British Library Cataloguing-in-Publication Data
A catalogue record for this book is available from
the British Library.

ISBN 0-7083-1663-8 paperback
    0-7083-1686-7 hardback

Typeset by Mark Heslington, Scarborough, North Yorkshire
Printed in Great Britain by Dinefwr Press, Llandybïe

Contents

Foreword

This volume of essays represents a further development of the work of the Centre for the Study of Christianity and Culture at Regent's Park College, Oxford. Each began life as a public lecture in the Centre during Hilary Term 1999. The lectures were convened and the collection has been edited by Dr Mark Atherton, a Fellow of the Centre, whose interests and expertise in early British and European history and literature were particularly fitted for this task. The Centre is grateful to all the contributors, many of whom based their lectures on ideas they had developed while teaching for the MA in Celtic Christianity at the University of Wales, Lampeter.

The notion of Celtic Christianity has attracted considerable attention in recent years, and apparently Celtic ideas and practices have considerable sway both within and beyond contemporary Christianity. This study is therefore timely, addressing as it does crucial questions of both identity and theology. It also expresses well the task of the Centre for the Study of Christianity and Culture, which focuses the mission of Regent's Park College in fostering the development of a 'Christian mind' across a whole range of cultural issues, both historical and contemporary.

The Centre is also grateful for this further collaboration with the University of Wales Press, which enables the life and work of the Centre to reach a wider public than our Oxford base allows. I would also like to place on record our debt to my predecessor as Director of the Centre, Dr Alan Kreider, to whose inspiration and hard work this volume, and so much of the Centre's work, owes much.

Nicholas J. Wood, Director
Centre for the Study of Christianity and Culture
Regent's Park College, Oxford
Hilary Term, 2001

Preface

At the end of the early medieval period, the writer Gerald of Wales set off on a tour of his country, a journey which he later described in his Latin work *The Journey through Wales*; he began his account as follows:

> In the year AD 1188, Baldwin, Archbishop of Canterbury, crossed the borders of Herefordshire and entered Wales. He was a man whom everyone respected, for he was well known for his learning and his piety. It was in the service of the cross, from whence cometh our salvation, that he had undertaken this journey from England to Wales.

By Ash Wednesday the party had reached Radnor, where they were met by Rhys ap Gruffydd, prince of south Wales, and by other nobles from the area. Here, the archbishop preached a public sermon on the taking of the Cross, 'and this was explained to the Welsh by an interpreter' (*The Journey through Wales*, I. 1).

Arguably this moment is a significant one, for it marks the beginning of preparations in Wales for the Third Crusade, in a period of transition, when Europe was expanding in all directions, westwards as well as eastwards, when the Western Church was becoming more unified in its customs and practices and the older traditions of Christian spirituality were developing and changing. Fortunately for those interested in studying those traditions, the observations of Gerald and others like him have been preserved. In addition we have the great literary collections such as the Black Book of Carmarthen, the Exeter Book and The Book of the Dun Cow in which the poems of early Britain and Ireland are preserved for posterity.

As we know, Baldwin in due course completed the tour, reading Gerald's book *On the Topography of Ireland* on each day of the journey (*The Journey through Wales*, I. 2). One can feel a little sympathy for Baldwin, acting out his role piously and well, but perhaps a little lost, at sea in a world that was foreign to him. The same experience is still to be had for the English speaker who approaches the older traditions of the Celtic-speaking areas for the first time, unprepared or with false expectations. It is to be hoped that the present collection of essays can act – like the Welsh interpreters of archbishop Baldwin – as a guide to the texts and mentalities of the past, and (it may be argued) also of the present.

Part I begins by raising general questions about the sense of identity: both of the people who wrote the extant poems and religious treatises and of the people who write in the same tradition, whether creatively or academically. The reason for the focus on identity is not hard to find. Perhaps more than any other movement within today's Church, the Celtic movement is inextricably linked to issues of ethnicity, location and national identity. Accordingly, the first two chapters, by Oliver Davies and Jonathan Wooding, debate the usefulness of the term 'Celtic' as a way of reading the early medieval tradition and explore the origins of the word 'Celt' in the Latin and Greek writings of antiquity. As Jonathan Wooding shows, the word 'Celt' took on new meanings in the early Modern period with the discovery by linguists of the interconnections between the various Celtic languages; more recent debates then centred on the validity, or otherwise, of the concepts of the 'insular Celt' and the 'religious Celt'. In the third chapter, Elva Johnston explores issues of gender in Irish saints' lives, issues raised by the suggestion that Celtic Christianity was 'non-sexist' in attitude; in particular she examines the way the identity of the Irish female saint was conceived and shaped by writers of the early period. The fourth chapter questions the traditional idea of conflicting notions of 'Saxon' and 'Celt' and considers ways in which the various Celtic literatures may have left their stamp on writings in the English language.

Part II approaches the issues from a very different perspective. Taking for granted that there is an issue of identity, these four contributors focus on the texts of the tradition from a theological point of view. Densil Morgan's opening paragraph sums up many of their concerns: 'a Trinitarian vision of reality, a holding together of the motifs of creation and redemption, an incarnational attitude to the material world, and a sense of community which expresses a continuity with an ancient and pre-Christian past'. But the contributors are not of exactly the same persuasion or line of thought. A. M. Allchin focuses more on the synchronic continuities of the early medieval religious world, finding, in the period up to the twelfth century, a sense of a broadly similar theology of creation and resurrection which was shared by writers as far apart as the Greek theologian Maximus the Confessor and the Welsh author of *The Loves of Taliesin*. Thomas O'Loughlin, on the other hand, is concerned with narrative theology as expressed in the thought-world of Muirchú, the biographer of St Patrick. Rather than reading the text as history or political propaganda, he sees its value as an index of Muirchú's seventh-century (rather than Patrick's fifth-century) theology of mission, a theology that centres on specific conceptions of chosen people, baptism and continuing penance. Paradoxically, Muirchú does in fact have 'a sense of community which expresses a continuity with an ancient and pre-Christian past', but this ancient past is that of the Old Testament rather than the world of the druids. In his own study, Morgan examines how these themes are worked out in the writings of a religious poet and thinker who considered his poetry as part of a tradition that extended back through 'the classical Protestant formulations of Williams Pantycelyn and the Methodist fathers' to the humanism of the fourteenth-century poet Dafydd ap Gwilym. Similarly, Mary Low is interested in the continuities of the Gaelic poetic tradition, presenting a considered and carefully argued case for the existence of an Irish 'nature poetry' with an indirect but nevertheless very real relevance to modern concepts of ecology and the spirituality of the green movement.

The idea of a collection of essays on approaches to the Celtic world was conceived by Oliver Davies, in conversation with Alan Kreider. I would like to thank them both for their efforts and hard work in organizing the series of lectures which eventually became this book. Many other colleagues assisted in the hosting of the lectures and the conversations and discussions that followed. Elva Johnston attended all the lectures and made valuable comments, while Donald Allchin was very helpful at a later stage in the arrangement and editing of the volume.

Mark Atherton
Oxford
January 2002

The Contributors

A. M. Allchin is Honorary Professor, University of Wales, Bangor.

Mark Atherton is Fellow of the Centre for the Study of Christianity and Culture, Regent's Park College, Oxford.

Oliver Davies is Reader in Systematic Theology, University of Wales, Lampeter.

Elva Johnston is Lecturer in Medieval History, University College, Dublin.

Thomas O'Loughlin is Lecturer in Theology, University of Wales, Lampeter.

Mary Low is a freelance writer.

D. Densil Morgan is Lecturer in Theology and Dean of Arts, University of Wales, Bangor.

Jonathan Wooding is Lecturer in Theology, University of Wales, Lampeter.

Introduction

MARK ATHERTON

This book is concerned with those religious traditions of Britain and Ireland that first found expression in the poetry and prose of the early medieval period. The texts of these traditions have in part had a continuous life over the centuries, and at various times have been renewed and revived. The most recent revival has brought the term 'Celtic Christianity' into vogue, and an enthusiastic following now seeks to adapt and reuse the texts of the older tradition, to make them relevant to the spiritual needs of the present-day world. A tension has developed between the interests of the scholarly world, who usually see these texts as the product of many varied historical situations, and the concerns of enthusiasts, who see this spirituality as one single breath of fresh air that will enliven the worship and theology of the present. Arguments on both sides have become polarized. Thus the 'popular' camp can speak of 'environmentally friendly' Celts, 'non-hierarchical and non-sexist'; moreover, all the texts are treated as part of one unified culture, without making any clear distinction between the various contexts in which they developed. Against this, we find serious scholars denying any connection whatsoever between the various speakers of Celtic languages other than geography, or casting doubt on suggestions that the Christian cultures of these nations had any particular connection with 'nature'. This sounds like overstatement, probably the reaction of the serious authors to the more popular surveys they had been reading. It need hardly be said that the contributors to the present volume do not present a single front on these issues, but they would nevertheless be in basic agreement over the need to qualify the more extreme statements on either side.

The general reader is now well served with introductory

overviews of the religion of the Celtic lands and it is not the purpose of this book to be yet another new survey.[1] What it does aim to provide, however, is useful signposts and guidelines for those seeking orientation or reorientation. In the rest of this introduction, therefore, four characteristic themes and issues will be marked out as a way of preparing the ground for the more detailed studies that follow. I will consider first of all the issue of language and translatability, and secondly the various ways of reading such traditional genres as the *vita* or saint's life, an important prerequisite for studying the early medieval accounts of the lives of Brigid, Patrick and other early medieval saints. Our third concern is historical: with the effects of travel and pilgrimage on the cultural life and religious writings of the period. Finally, the theological theme of creation and incarnation is explored, allowing the various contributors to be in dialogue with each other and with the texts that constitute the focus of the book.

The languages of the texts

In the year 734, the Northumbrian monk and priest Bede – almost universally regarded as the greatest historian of the early medieval period – wrote a description of Britain and Ireland as the opening chapter of his *Ecclesiastical History*.[2] On the ethnic situation of these islands, he had this to say:

> At the present time there are in Britain, in harmony with the five books of the divine law, five languages and four nations – English, British, Irish, and Picts. Each of these have their own language; but all are united in their study of God's truth by the fifth – Latin – which has become a common medium through the study of the scriptures.[3]

The reading of this passage raises two issues. It will be immediately seen that Bede does not use the word 'Celtic'. At the time of his writing, the term was no longer in use as a means of identifying a national culture or group of cultures, although the word had enjoyed long currency in the world of classical antiquity. Apart from occasional use, the word was not to be revived until the development of historical linguistics in the early modern period.[4] Secondly, Bede suggests that the faith they shared through the Latin scriptures was a unifying force. There is no talk of schism or separate 'churches'.

Despite these apparent unities, however, the native vernaculars were a divide, and the importance of the languages in which the writers of the period wrote their work should not be underestimated. In general, the language or mother tongue in which a poet or thinker expresses their ideas inevitably colours these ideas, particularly if they are rendered in a conventional metre or verse form, as part of a poetic tradition with its own culture, its own diction and vocabulary, its own register of formulaic ideas, motifs and themes. This was very clearly the case in early medieval Britain and Ireland, and in some areas the old tradition was long-lasting. Clearly, the preservation of an old literary tradition helps to foster certain cultural attitudes, certain types of thought and ways of looking at the world. This may help to explain the continuities over time in the religious literature of Wales or of Gaelic Scotland and Ireland, a case of 'taking old texts from memory and shaping them into present contexts'.[5]

A classic expression of the influence of language on thought is that of the American linguist Edward Sapir:

> The fact of the matter is that the 'real world' is to a large extent unconsciously built up on the language habits of the group. No two languages are ever sufficiently similar to be considered as representing the same social reality. The worlds in which different societies live are distinct worlds, not merely the same world with different labels attached . . . The understanding of a simple poem, for instance, involves not merely an understanding of single words in their average significance, but a full comprehension of the whole life of a community as it is mirrored in the words, or as it is suggested through overtones.[6]

This sort of thinking is apparent in Mary Low's essay in the present volume where she suggests a link between Celtic Christianity and language culture: 'If we were to apply this definition [of Celticity] to Celtic Christianity, it would become the Christianity of people whose mother-tongue is, or was, one of the Celtic languages, and/or who identify with the cultural heritage of one of these traditional language areas in a recognizable way.'[7] Oliver Davies also considers this idea carefully and makes the important point that the Celtic texts were written in difficult languages and are the product of a world that was in many ways dramatically alien to our own, a fact which 'is conveniently forgotten when the reader is presented with an attractively produced selection of texts in modern English translation'.[8]

The issue is a complex one, and depends partly on the question of translatability. To what extent can a poem (or even a theological work) be satisfactorily translated from one language to another? Bede himself raises this question during his account of how, in a dream vision, the cowherd Cædmon acquired the ability to compose religious poetry. Bede, who is writing in Latin, gives a version of 'Cædmon's Hymn' in Latin, then comments on it: 'This is the general sense but not the actual words that Cædmon sang in his dream; for verses, however masterly, cannot be translated literally from one language into another without losing something of their beauty and dignity.'[9] Cædmon's mother tongue was English, so by Mary Low's definition, he is not a Celtic poet, despite his British name and his proximity to Irish-influenced Christianity.[10]

A similar problem of translation arises in the question raised by Thomas O'Loughlin about Muirchú's story of Patrick's encounter with the old religion in Ireland. Since Muirchú is writing in Latin and drawing on Old Testament texts, O'Loughlin argues:

> we could say that Muirchú most truly got inside the message of his scriptural sources, for his story has the exact same ratio between theological tale and historical report that is to be found in the Book of Daniel (with Daniel meeting King Nebuchadnezzar) and 1 Kings (with Elijah challenging the Prophets of Baal). The Irish are ruled by an 'emperor' with a full court and a full body of religious specialists – Muirchú's lists are all drawn from the Old Testament, for example 2 Chr 33: 6, so we should avoid the word 'druid' when translating him – and, just as Herod's experts had books when they awaited the coming of Christ to their kingdom, the Irish religious experts have books which record their prophecy.[11]

We cannot be certain, but if Muirchú had written in Irish rather than Latin, this might have altered the theological emphasis of his writing. Perhaps the very use of the vernacular would have entailed the use of vernacular terms such as 'druid' which, in his Latin, he was able consciously to avoid. The fact that he wrote in Latin, however, meant that his work was available to posterity, and to a wide contemporary audience throughout Europe; this was the main motivation (as with Bede) for choosing the 'common medium' for his work.

One further linguistic complication should be considered when studying the religious traditions of Britain, Ireland and their European neighbours. This is the existence of Hiberno-Latin; a kind of Latin written by Irish scholars (at home and on the Continent) which is often identifiable by its themes, motifs and patterns of rhetoric. The reciprocal influences of the vernacular on Hiberno-Latin can be traced in the translation of set-piece themes from one language to the other. The beginning of *The Evernew Tongue*, an Irish apocryphal legend (written in Irish), tells how Philip the Apostle appears to the multitudes of the eastern world; his purpose is to speak to them of the secrets of creation, of how, in the beginning, God made heaven and earth. Here the writer lists the praises of the Lord in a characteristic theme or topos:[12]

> It was the High-King of the world, who is mightier than any king, higher than any power, more fierce than any dragon, gentler than any child, more radiant than suns, holier than any saint, more vengeful than all men, more loving than any mother, the only Son of God the Father, it was he who gave this account of the formation and creation of the world to the many nations on earth, since no one but God knew what any visible thing in the world was like, for it was as if the race of Adam had its head in a bag or lived in a dark place.

The 'mightier than any king' (more X than Y) formula is easily transferable into Hiberno-Latin. An example is the following passage from the *Collectaneum miscellaneum* of the Irish poet and scholar Sedulius Scottus, who was active at Liège on the Continent in the middle of the ninth century: 'Pater enim noster constat in excelsis, caelo altior, terra stabilior, mari profundior, aere purior, sole clarior' (For our Father remains in the heights, higher than heaven, firmer than the earth, deeper than the sea, purer than the air, brighter than the sun).[13] Sedulius, if he did not compose this himself, must have taken the extract from a Hiberno-Latin treatise and entered it into his commonplace book. A rather similar passage turns up in a different cultural context, an Old English homily of the tenth century:

> Ac hergen we and wuldrien urne dryhten on clænum geðohtum and on halgum wordum and on soðfæstum weorcum and on rihtum geleafan, for þan þe his miht is ufor þonne heofon and bradre þonne eorðe and deopre þonne sæ and leohtre þonne heofones tungel.

> But let us praise and glorify our Lord in pure thoughts and in holy words and in faithful actions and in true beliefs, since his power is

higher than heaven, wider than earth, deeper than the sea, brighter than the star in heaven.[14]

As the scholar Charles Wright has noted, this particular 'inexpressibility topos' has many analogues: from Gregory's *Moralia siue expositio in Iob*, where it may originate as a brief motif, to much lengthier elaborations on the same pattern in Irish and Hiberno-Latin texts.[15] The obvious conclusion is that the Old English homilist found his Irish motif in a book of Hiberno-Latin homilies or excerpts, which he subsequently translated and adapted to his own use. It is clear, then, that on occasions 'vernacular' thoughts could be (and actually were) rendered satisfactorily into Latin and then passed to other cultures, such as that of England. In this way, neighbouring countries did take on shared religious traits, despite the differences of culture and language.

The saint's life and theological reflection

The earlier part of our period is often called the 'age of the saints', and with good reason, since many of the most celebrated of the holy men and women of Britain and Ireland lived in the fifth and sixth centuries and their biographies, or more strictly their hagiographies, were composed in the seventh century and much later.[16] These men and women include the well-known Irish saints Patrick, the British apostle of Ireland (fifth century), Brigit of Kildare (early sixth century) and Columba,[17] the Irishman of the dominant Uí Néill tribe[18] who founded the monastery of Iona in the Western Isles of Scotland in the 560s. Other saints of Scotland are the British Ninian, who appears to have founded Whithorn (Candida Casa) in Galloway in the very early period,[19] and Kentigern, who was said to have lived at Culross on the northern (and so Pictish) side of the Forth in Fife.[20] In Wales there are the figures of Samson (fifth century), Beuno (active around 600) and David,[21] while Northumbria boasts the fame of its own Irish-influenced Anglo-Saxon saints in Oswald (the first English royal saint, killed in battle against Penda of Mercia in 642), Cuthbert (*c*.635–87) and Hilda (*c*.614–80), abbess of the double monastery for men and women at Streonæshalch (the old name for Whitby).[22]

The biography of Hild, or Hilda, has fascinated many readers.

Born *c.*614 into an Anglo-Saxon family connected with the East Anglian and Northumbrian royal houses, she was baptized by the Roman missionary Paulinus (bishop of York 625–33) after his conversion of Edwin king of Northumbria in 627. Following a long period as a laywoman, she entered the religious life, planning to become a nun at Chelles near Paris. Persuaded to stay in England by the Irishman Aidan (bishop of Lindisfarne 635–51), she became abbess of Hartlepool (between 647 and 651) remaining there until she founded the monastery at Whitby in 657. During her period as abbess (657–80), the famous Synod of Whitby took place in 664, the celebrated Old English poet Cædmon discovered his poetic gifts, and an anonymous monk wrote the first life of Pope Gregory the Great, the *Vita Sancti Gregorii*. Clearly she was a great patron, not only of the religious life but also of literary and probably political activity. As Elva Johnston suggests in her chapter in this volume, Hilda's life is broadly similar to that of Radegund in Merovingian Francia,[23] and indicates the high status that some religious women could achieve in the early medieval period. Radegund (520–87) was a Thuringian princess who became queen of the Franks and unwilling wife of King Clothair in 532. She eventually left her husband, persuaded the bishop of Soissons to make her a nun and founded a monastery dedicated to the Holy Cross at Poitiers.[24] Rather like Hilda's patronizing of Old English religious poetry, Radegund was the patron of the poet and hymn-writer Venantius Fortunatus, who wrote Latin poems in her honour[25] and later composed a prose *vita* to celebrate her life in 586. Both these powerful women bear comparison with the position attained by Brigit of Kildare in the various *vitae* written to celebrate her life and reputation.[26]

The hagiography written many years after the life of a particular saint often had the purpose of furthering the cult that had developed around the burial place or relics of that saint and providing documentary proof of their sanctity, as well as recording biographical facts and retelling the story of their life. Hagiographers followed accepted literary conventions in their work, which included a simple style to appeal to the ordinary believer, but also sophisticated allusions (or even whole incidents) taken from earlier literature, such as the Lives of St Martin of Tours, St Antony and St Benedict,[27] which the more intellectual readers would recognize and appreciate. As an example of the differences

that could occur, the two early prose lives of St Cuthbert are
instructive (one is anonymous, the other written by Bede in the
early eighth century).

The first *Life of Cuthbert* begins its main account with an event
that occurred on the playground in Cuthbert's childhood, a story
of 'how a child prophesied concerning him' that he would in later
life become a bishop. The incident is quickly told (about a page of
text in the printed edition) and parallels are briefly drawn with the
biblical Samuel and David, both 'chosen in their infancy', and
Jeremiah and John the Baptist, both 'sanctified for the work of the
Lord from their mother's womb'.[28] Appropriately, the story is
introduced with a statement of its theme and the source of the
information:

> First we record an incident of his early youth, known to us through the
> reports of many, among whom are Bishop Tumma of holy memory,
> who learnt from St Cuthbert's own lips that God's choice of him to a
> spiritual office had been predetermined, and Elias also, a priest of our
> church.

The writer or writers of this introduction are clearly local to
Lindisfarne: the incident, they say, is 'known to us', and they
name both Bishop Tumma and Elias 'a priest of our church' as
reliable witnesses. Their aim is to further the reputation of the
saint of their own monastery and locality. In the lengthier version
of the same events by Bede, however, the name Elias is removed,
probably because of its purely local significance, and in the
process of expanding the text the character of the little child
becomes more precocious. Where in the anonymous *vita* he
merely says to Cuthbert, 'O holy Bishop and priest Cuthbert,
these unnatural tricks done to show off your agility are not befit-
ting to you or your high office', in the version by Bede, he says,
'Why O Cuthbert most holy bishop and priest, do you do these
things so contrary to your nature and your rank? It is not fitting
for you to play among children when the Lord has consecrated
you to be teacher of virtue even to your elders.' Bede is clearly
writing the *vita* with a wider audience in mind, as Colgrave points
out; but although his arrangement of the events is an improvement, his omissions of names and expansions of individual scenes
do not always tally with modern tastes.[29] More interestingly for
the history of ideas, however, Bede also complicates the theologi-

cal significance of the story, expanding his version to twice the original length: he opens with a quotation from Jeremiah on bearing the yoke in youth and sitting in solitude, which he applies to Cuthbert's later life as a hermit, and he ends with the words of the psalmist, 'out of the mouth of babes and sucklings thou hast perfected praise'.[30]

The theological reading of a saint's *vita* is particularly emphasized by Thomas O'Loughlin in his study of Muirchú's seventh-century Life of Patrick in chapter 6 of this volume. In response to political interpretations by historians he argues that there certainly is a pragmatic side to a saint's life – in the case of Muirchú there is a definite bias in favour of Armagh. Nevertheless, these *vitae* were not commissioned as political propaganda but as part of a long Christian tradition of hagiography reaching back to the fourth century. Moreover, he writes, 'unless this formal religious motive is acknowledged and examined, we abuse these texts just as much as happened when they were used as factual accounts of Patrick's work in Ireland'. Partly, of course, the method he recommends is already in use: for instance, a recent study of Adomnán (*c.*628–704), the ninth abbot of Iona and author of the Life of St Columba, shows how Adomnán's citations of scripture – along with allusions to the life of the first Christian Roman emperor, Constantine – indicate and underline his particular view of Christian history and the universal work of redemption.[31] But O'Loughlin takes it a little further. His approach, which he derives from the work of Delehaye, is to study a particular hagiographic text along with its implied theology; such a theology has much more to do with the time of writing than with the named subject of the *vita*. In approaching Muirchú in this way, we can study him as a theological thinker and examine how he responded to the tradition in which he was writing.

One example will serve as illustration. The act of penance is well developed in the writings of this period and, in the implied theology of his text, Muirchú regards penance as a continuous process rather than a single act undertaken with baptism. Thus the evil brigand Macc Cuill Greccae is ordered to undertake the following penance on his conversion and baptism:

> Then Macc Cuill told the saint even more: 'I confess to you, Patrick my holy lord, that I had proposed to kill you. So judge what is the debt that

I owe for so great a crime.' Patrick replied: 'I am unable to judge, but God will judge. You must now go down to the sea, unarmed, and leave this part of Ireland. You can take none of your riches except one piece of clothing. Something poor and small which just about covers you. You are not to taste or drink any of the fruits of this island, and you shall bear this as a mark of your sin upon your head. When you arrive at the shore bind your feet with an iron fetter and throw its key into the sea. Then get into a one-hide boat and put to sea without a rudder or an oar. You can then accept wherever the wind and sea take you. In whichever place divine providence lands you, there you are to dwell and keep God's commandments.[32]

In the end, Macc Cuill is cast up on the shore of the island Euonia where he is rescued by two bishops, whom he eventually succeeds in the episcopate. As well as being illustrative of seventh-century attitudes and practices, therefore, this incident can be seen in the light of a fully developed theology of mission in the writings of Muirchú.[33]

Pilgrimage and scholarship

There are many reminiscences of Macc Cuill's voyage of penance in the historical and literary sources.[34] No less a saint than Columba himself speaks of his stay in Britain as a 'pilgrimage', and he orders others to undergo penitential exile or pilgrimage.[35] The motives for this urge to travel must have been many, but the priority was essentially devotional.[36] One famous account of *peregrinatio pro amore Dei* (pilgrimage for the love of God) is found in the Anglo-Saxon Chronicle in the annal for 891:

> In this year the Viking army went to the east, and king Earnulf, with the East Franks, Saxons and Bavarians, fought against the mounted army and put them to flight before the ships had arrived.
> And three Scots in a boat without any oars came to king Alfred from Ireland, which they left because they wanted, for the love of God, to be on pilgrimage; and they did not care where. The boat they travelled in was made of two and half hides; they took with them enough that they had food for seven nights, and after the seven nights they came to land in Cornwall, and they went from there to king Alfred. Their names were Dublasne, Machbethu and Maelmumin.
> And Swifneh died, the best teacher there was among the Scots.
> In the same year after Easter around Rogationtide, or earlier, the star

appeared that is called, in Latin, a 'cometa'. Some men say in English
that it is 'the long-haired star', because long beams of light come out of
it on one side or the other.[37]

These three 'Scots' were evidently well received at the king's
court. The king in question was Alfred the Great (871–99), that
same reformer who in 885 had summoned Asser the Welsh monk,
possibly also bishop of St David's, to spend long periods at his
court assisting in a programme of reform that included the translation of works of Latin history, theology and pastoral care.[38] As
for the three 'Scots', in more conventional spelling, they are recognized as three Irishmen: Dubslaine, Macbethath and Maelinmuin.
It is they who presumably bring the news to the court of the death
of Swifneh (Suibhne, as pronounced and spelt in the Old English
of the time),[39] a teacher who is lauded elsewhere for his literary
skills and activities.[40] Although these were not the only Irish travellers to England in the period,[41] their doings were of sufficient
import for the annalist to mention them, in an eventful year that
also saw the departure of the Vikings for the Continent, and the
appearance of a comet, juxtaposed, perhaps as a significant
portent, with the death of the great Irish teacher. Like Macc Cuill,
they also travel in a coracle, and like the famed Irish traveller
Brendan, they allow themselves to drift where wind and tide will
take them. Ultimately their goal may have been Rome, or Irish
communities in France and Germany. A possible literary product
of these Irish contacts with Anglo-Saxon culture is the undated
Old English poem 'The Seafarer', which explores the sensibilities
of a seafaring pilgrim.[42]

Another route to the Continent for pilgrims or scholars was
through Wales. Again we have a tantalizing glimpse of the arrival of
such travellers, this time at the court of Merfyn Frych in
Gwynedd. Merfyn, another successful king of the ninth century,
married Nest, of the house of Powys, in 825; their son Rhodri
Mawr (Rhodri the Great) succeeded to the throne of Gwynedd in
844 and of Powys in 855 on the death of his uncle Cyngen (who,
incidentally, was on pilgrimage in Rome). By his death in 877,
Rhodri had united Wales through diplomacy into a country that
stretched from Anglesey to Gower.[43] The evidence for Irish
pilgrims at their courts is based primarily on the story of the
'Bamberg cryptogram', a message in Greek numerals which

decoded to read: 'Mermen rex Concem salutem' (King Merfyn greets Cyngen).[44] This event, which took place at Merfyn's court, is recorded in a letter:

> This is the writing which Dubthach sent to the court of Merfyn of the Britons in order to test the Irish philosophers, since he considered himself to be the best of all the Scots and the Britons, and he thought that none of their teachers would be able to read and understand the message in the presence of king Merfyn. But we Caínchobrach, Fergus, Dominnach and Suadbar with God's help revealed the meaning of that writing . . .[45]

The letter is written by Suadbar to Colgu, his teacher back in Ireland, warning him to pass the solution on to any other Irish travellers, so that they will avoid embarrassing themselves 'in the presence of Merfyn, the glorious king of the Britons'. It seems that Merfyn enjoyed testing the skills of any Irish scholars who visited his court. The travellers then passed on their way to further scholarly employment at Continental courts and monasteries, such as St Gall; here, in the inner school, during the abbacy of Grimald (842–72) there was an Irish teacher Moengal (who changed his name to Marcellus) and here, in the great library, several manuscripts record the names of the five Irishmen mentioned in the letter to Colgu.[46] For example, a manuscript of Priscian's grammatical writings mentions Fergus, and there is even a note (*Ruadri adest*) indicating that the manuscript and its Irish user were back in Wales, in attendance at the court of Merfyn's son Rhodri.

It seems likely, therefore, that both Merfyn and his son Rhodri encouraged literary activity at their courts. A. M. Allchin, as we shall see, suggests their reigns as a likely context for a poem on creation in a ninth-century Welsh manuscript of Juvencus. Other Welsh poems which may derive from this period occur in the Black Book of Carmarthen, and they hint at connections with the Irish Culdee reform movement.[47] Whatever their ultimate origin, however, a particularly appropriate example is a poem on penitential pilgrimage known as 'Cyntefin Ceinaf Amser' or 'Maytime is the fairest season'.[48] As in the Old English 'The Seafarer', the poem contains the fine image of the mournful cuckoo, urging on the speaker to his pilgrimage at the onset of the summer.

Another Irishman abroad, already briefly referred to, is Sedulius Scottus, whose patron was Hartgar bishop of Liège. The following

Latin poem illustrates the religious sensibilities, and also the humour, of Sedulius:

> I read or write, I teach or wonder what is truth,
> I call upon God by night and day.
> I eat and freely drink, I make my rhymes,
> And snoring sleep, or vigil keep and pray.
> And very ware of all my shames I am;
> O Mary, Christ, have mercy on your man.[49]

Helen Waddell has called attention to this characteristic of Sedulius: 'the Bacchanalian verse is only the blown spray of a profound and serious scholarship'.[50] His book of excerpts, the *Collectaneum miscellaneum* mentioned above, is only one index of his breadth of learning; another is a Greek manuscript of St Paul's Epistles, now at Berne, perhaps written in Sedulius's own hand.[51] The manuscript contains the following Irish poem; although it may not be his, it expresses very precisely the dangers and rewards of pilgrimage:

> Teicht do Róim,
> mór saído, becc torbai!
> In rí chon-daigi hi foss,
> manim-bera latt, ní fogbai.[52]

> Coming to Rome,
> much labour and little profit!
> The King whom you seek here,
> unless you bring Him with you
> you will not find Him.[53]

Creation and nature

Of all the wandering scholars and poets who journeyed in this period to the court of Charles the Bald, king of the West Franks, the most famous is probably Iohannes Scottus (John the Scot) Eriugena. Well known as the author of *Periphyseon* (The Division of Nature) and other outstanding philosophical and theological writings, Eriugena was one of the few learned men in the West at the time with a thorough knowledge of Greek. He translated the Greek writings of the mystic Pseudo-Dionysius and two works by the theologian

Maximus the Confessor (*Ambigua* and *Questiones ad Thalassium*), as well as the *De imagine* of Gregory of Nyssa.[54] On his character, we have the following view in a letter written by Anastasius, the papal librarian, to Charles the Bald on 23 March 860:[55]

> It is a wonderful thing how that barbarian, living at the ends of the earth, who might be supposed to be as far removed from the knowledge of this other language as he is from the familiar use of it, has been able to comprehend such ideas and translate them into another tongue: I refer to John Scotigena, whom I have learned by report to be in all things a holy man.

It is in a context of strong royal patrons, frequent travel and many mutual influences that A. M. Allchin sees the possibility of connections between the world of Greek theology and that of early Irish and Welsh poetry. Even if the links are only indirect it is the analogues of thought and feeling that attract his theological reflections. In particular, he refers to an anonymous poem added to a Welsh manuscript of the Latin poet Juvencus, the opening verses of which read as follows:

> Almighty Creator, it is you who have made
> the land and the sea . . .

> The world cannot comprehend in song bright and melodious,
> even though the grass and the trees should sing,
> all your wonders, O true Lord!

> The Father created the world by a miracle;
> it is difficult to express its measure.
> Letters cannot contain it, letters cannot comprehend it.

> Jesus created for the hosts of Christendom,
> with miracles when he came,
> resurrection through his nature for them.

> He who made the wonder of the world
> will save us, has saved us.
> It is not too great a toil to praise the Trinity.[56]

This poem, with its Trinitarian exploration of God's work in the world in stanzas 3, 4 and 5, is then explored in the light of a passage from Maximus the Confessor:

The mystery of the incarnation of the Word bears the power of all the hidden meanings and figures of scripture as well as the knowledge of visible and intelligible creatures. The one who knows the mystery of the cross and the tomb knows the principles of these creatures. And the one who has been initiated into the ineffable power of the resurrection, knows the purpose for which God originally made all things.

A. M. Allchin's assumption is that such texts, though far apart in terms of geography and modes of expression, are all 'characteristic expressions of the late development of first millennium Christianity, a Christianity which is formed before the schism between East and West and before the development of the western Middle Ages'.

On this point Mary Low is in broad agreement, for she emphasizes the message of the Irish texts that, through the incarnation, God becomes one, 'not just with human flesh, but with the wind and air, fire, the sun and the stars, salt, bitterness, stones, the earth and flowers'. Citing the Irish apocryphon *The Evernew Tongue*, she writes that 'Every material and every element in nature' rose from the grave with him and was freed from the power of death:

> Every material and every element and every nature which is seen in the world were all combined in the body in which Christ arose, that is in the body of every human person. . . . All the world arose with him, for the nature of all the elements was in the body which Jesus assumed.[57]

One final question remains to be asked. Did such theological views of creation and incarnation die out completely with the expansion of Europe in the twelfth and thirteenth centuries and the subsequent changes that took place in the political and cultural make-up of these islands?[58] From the point of view of the Welsh poetic tradition (and probably also the Irish and Hebridean) it is possible to demonstrate, though not prove conclusively, that the older tradition preserved this characteristic doctrine of creation, in which the world is a theophany or manifestation of God. An unusual poem by the early fourteenth-century Dafydd ap Gwilym, for instance, explores the eucharistic significance of a woodland grove:

> There was raised upon a mound for us
> a perfect leaf as consecrated wafer,
> and the eloquent slender Nightingale

> from the corner of the near-by thicket
> (the valley's wandering poetess) rang out
> the Sanctus bell to the assembly, with clear whistle,
> and lifted up the consecrated Host
> to the sky above the copse
> with adoration to our Lord the Father,
> with a chalice of ecstasy and love.[59]

A similar theology rings out in the poetry of D. Gwenallt Jones, as Densil Morgan argues. In a poem entitled 'Catholigrwydd' (Catholicity), published in 1969, Gwenallt describes the person of Christ as 'imprisoned by his flesh and his Jewish bones / Within the confines of his land' but who then gives himself as a living sacrifice to the Father before being raised up anew in the miracle of resurrection:

> A mwy y mae Caerdydd cyn nesed â Chalfaria,
> A Bangor bob modfedd â Bethlehem,
> Gostegir y stormydd ym Mae Ceredigion,
> Ac ar bob stryd fe all y lloerigion
> Gael iechydwriaeth wrth odre Ei hem . . .

> And since then Cardiff is as near as Calvary
> And Bangor every inch as Bethlehem,
> The storms are stilled on Cardigan Bay,
> And in every street the afflicted
> Find healing from the touch of His hem . . .

In his comment on this passage, Densil Morgan speaks of how

flesh and spirit, the particular and the universal, the ordinary and the extraordinary are all harmonized in Christ, the incarnation of God's redemptive love, whose reality is forever known anew in the *epiclesis* or making present of the Holy Spirit. If Celtic spirituality represents a living tradition in which the eternal verities of the gospel become incarnate in the everyday lives of ordinary people in Cardiff, Bangor and on the shores of Cardigan Bay, it is to this tradition that the artistry and poetic imagination of Gwenallt belong.

Notes

[1] Of the many introductions available, the following are recommended: J. P. Mackey (ed.), *An Introduction to Celtic Christianity* (Edinburgh,

1989); Esther de Waal, *A World Made Whole: Rediscovering the Celtic Tradition* (London, 1991); Patrick Thomas, *Candle in the Darkness* (Llandysul, 1993); P. O'Dwyer, *Towards a History of Irish Spirituality* (Dublin, 1995).

2   Bede, *Ecclesiastical History of the English People*, trans. Leo Sherley-Price, revised R. E. Latham (London, 1990), (henceforth *HE*). Bede is writing from an English point of view, but he has good credentials as an accurate user of documents and a careful sifter of the facts.

3   Bede, *HE*, I. 1.

4   See Jonathan Wooding's discussion in Chapter 2. A rare use of the word is found in *Waltharius*, a Latin epic poem written in Germany in the ninth or tenth century. See David N. Dumville, 'Ekiurid's *Celtica lingua*: an ethnological difficulty in *Waltharius*', *Cambridge Medieval Celtic Studies*, 10 (1985), 39–52, reprinted in his *Britons and Saxons in the Early Middle Ages* (Aldershot, 1993), ch. 12.

5   Austin L. Becker, *Beyond Translation: Essays towards a Modern Philology* (Ann Arbor, MI, 1995), 9.

6   David G. Mandelbaum, *The Selected Writings of Edward Sapir* (Berkeley, CA, 1951), 162.

7   See Chapter 8 below.

8   See Chapter 1 below.

9   Bede, *HE*, IV. 24.

10 For more discussion, see Chapter 4 in this volume.

11 See Chapter 6 below.

12 Oliver Davies (ed.), *Celtic Spirituality* (New York, 1999). For the original text, see W. Stokes (ed.), *Tenga Bhith-Nua Annso Sis / The Evernew Tongue Here Below*, *Ériu*, 2 (1905), 96–162; Màire Herbert and Martin McNamara, *Irish Biblical Apocrypha* (Edinburgh, 1989).

13 Sedulius Scottus, *Collectaneum miscellaneum*, ed. D. Simpson, CCCM 67 (Turnhout, 1988), 135.

14 Vercelli V, ll. 194–7. The letters <þ> and <ð> both represent the same 'th' sound, pronounced initially and finally as in 'thorn' and 'bath', medially as in 'bathing'.

15 Wright, *Irish Tradition*, 246–7, n. 124.

16 N. K. Chadwick, *The Age of the Saints in the Early Celtic Church* (Oxford, 1961).

17 Columba, Irish name Colum Cille, was born *c.*521 and died on Iona in 597.

18 The Uí Néill (the descendants of Niall) were a powerful royal dynasty in Irish politics in the early medieval period, who traced their ancestry back to the legendary 'Niall of Nine Hostages' through various lineages, in particular the northern Uí Néill (in Donegal and Tyrone) to whose family St Columba belonged, and their rivals the southern Uí Néill. See Thomas Charles-Edwards, 'The origins and rise of the Uí Néill', in his *Early Christian Ireland* (Cambridge, 2000), 441–68.

19 Daphne Brooke, *Wild Men and Holy Places: St Ninian, Whithorn and the Medieval Realm of Galloway* (Edinburgh, 1994).

20 Alfred P. Smyth, *Warlords and Holy Men: Scotland AD 80–1000* (London, 1984), 34.

21 For an introduction to the lives of these Welsh saints, see Oliver Davies, *Celtic Christianity in Early Medieval Wales: The Origins of the Welsh Spiritual Tradition* (Cardiff, 1996), 7–27.

22 C. Stancliffe and E. Cambridge (eds.), *Oswald: Northumbrian King to European Saint* (Stamford, 1995); G. Bonner, D. W. Rollason and C. Stancliffe (eds.), *St Cuthbert: His Cult and his Community to AD 1200* (Woodbridge, 1989); C. E. Fell, 'Hild, Abbess of Streonæshalch', in H. Bekker-Nielsen et al., *Hagiography and Medieval Literature* (Odense, 1981), 76–99.

23 For the two *vitae* of Radegund, see F. A. C. Mantello and A. G. Rigg, *Medieval Latin: An Introduction and Bibliographical Guide* (Washington, DC, 1996), 620, 626.

24 There is a brief evaluation of her life in Peter Brown, *The Rise of Western Christendom: Triumph and Diversity AD 200–1000* (Oxford, 1996), 153.

25 Helen Waddell (ed. and trans.), *Mediaeval Latin Lyrics* (Harmondsworth, 1952), 68–71.

26 See Chapter 3 below.

27 For the *vitae* of these early hermits and saints, which were widely read and imitated in early Britain and Ireland, see Carolinne White (trans.), *Early Christian Lives* (London, 1998).

28 Bertram Colgrave (ed. and trans.), *Two Lives of Saint Cuthbert* (Westport, CT, 1968), 67.

29 See Colgrave's comments on other parallel incidents, ibid., 15.

30 Lamentations 3: 27, 28, and Psalms 8: 3.

31 The Constantinian parallels refer to St Oswald, king of Northumbria (634–42), who is presented as establishing a Christian empire after defeating a tyrant. The two original accounts of Oswald's victory over Cadwallon are in Bede, *HE*, III. 2 and Adomnán, *Life of St Columba*, I. 1. They are discussed by Jennifer O'Reilly, 'Reading the scriptures in the Life of Columba', in Cormac Bourke (ed.), *Studies in the Cult of Saint Columba* (Dublin, 1997), 80–106, at 81–5.

32 Thomas O'Loughlin (trans.), 'The Life of Patrick by Muirchú', in Oliver Davies (ed.), *Celtic Spirituality* (New York and Mahwah, NJ, 1999), 91–117, at 108.

33 For more discussion, see Chapter 6 below.

34 Thomas Charles-Edwards, 'The social background to Irish *peregrinatio*', *Celtica*, 11 (1976), 43–59.

35 Adomnán of Iona, *Life of St Columba*, trans. Richard Sharpe (London, 1991), III. 22 and II. 39.

36 For reflections on this theme, see Philip Sheldrake, *Living between Worlds: Place and Journey in Celtic Spirituality* (London, 1995), 58–69; and De Waal, *A World Made Whole*, 53–64.

37 G. P. Cubbin, *The Anglo-Saxon Chronicle: A Collaborative Edition*, vol. 6. *MS D* (Cambridge, 1996), 30.

38 Asser eventually wrote his *Life of King Alfred* in 893.

39 N. K. Chadwick, 'The Celtic background of early Anglo-Saxon England', in N. K. Chadwick (ed.), *Celt and Saxon: Studies in the Early British Border* (Cambridge, 1963), 323–52, at 347.

40 The death of 'Suibne, son of Maelumai, anchorite and excellent scribe of Clonmacnois' is recorded in the *Annals of Ulster*, for the year 890 (891). See Simon Keynes and Michael Lapidge (trans.), *Alfred the Great* (Harmondsworth, 1983), 283, n. 14.

41 Kathleen Hughes, 'Evidence for contacts between the churches of the Irish and the English from the Synod of Whitby to the Viking Age', in Peter Clemoes and Kathleen Hughes (eds.), *England before the Conquest: Studies in the Primary Sources Presented to Dorothy Whitelock* (Cambridge, 1971), 49–67.

42 For more details, see Chapter 4.

43 John Davies, *A History of Wales* (London, 1993), 81.

44 Myles Dillon and Nora K. Chadwick, *The Celtic Realms* (London, 1967), 114–17. Dáibhí Ó Cróinín, *Early Medieval Ireland 400–1200* (London, 1995), 223.

45 The Latin text is printed by R. Derolez, *Runica Manuscripta: The English Tradition* (Bruges, 1954), 98.

46 Ibid., 154–5.

47 Davies, *Celtic Christianity in Early Medieval Wales*, 28–48.

48 Ibid., 39–42; P. L. Henry, *The Early English and Celtic Lyric* (London, 1966).

49 Waddell (ed. and trans.), *Mediaeval Latin Lyrics*, 135.

50 Helen Waddell, *The Wandering Scholars* (London, 1934), 69.

51 Ibid., 68. Whitley Stokes and John Strachan (eds.), *Thesaurus Palaeohibernicus: A Collection of Old Irish Glosses, Scholia, Prose and Verse*, 2 vols. (Cambridge, 1901–3), II. xx. 290–6. The canon of Sedulius's writings is listed in Michael Lapidge and Richard Sharpe, *Bibliography of Celtic Latin Literature 400–1200* (Dublin, 1985), 177–80.

52 James Carney (ed. and trans.), *Medieval Irish Lyrics* (Dublin, 1985), no. XXXII.

53 Kenneth Hurlstone Jackson (trans.), *A Celtic Miscellany: Translations from the Celtic Literatures* (Harmondsworth, 1971), no. 121.

54 I. P. Sheldon-Williams, 'Eriugena's Greek sources', in J. J. O'Meara and L. Bieler (eds.), *The Mind of Eriugena* (Dublin, 1970), 1–15.

55 Ó Cróinín, *Early Medieval Ireland*, 228. See also J. F. Kenney, *Sources*

for the Early History of Ireland: Ecclesiastical. An Introduction and Guide (New York, 1929), 581.

56   Fiona Bowie and Oliver Davies (eds.), *Celtic Christian Spirituality* (London, 1995), 27. Oliver Davies, *Celtic Christianity in Early Medieval Wales*, 50.

57   From *Tenga Bhith-Nua Annso Sis / The Evernew Tongue Here Below*, ed. Stokes, 98–9, §11–13. For more discussion see Chapter 8.

58   For a survey, see Robert Bartlett, *The Making of Europe: Conquest, Colonization and Cultural Change 950–1350* (London, 1994).

59   Rachel Bromwich (ed. and trans.), *Selected Poems of Dafydd ap Gwilym* (Harmondsworth, 1985), no. 24.

I
Identities

1

Celtic Christianity: texts and representations

OLIVER DAVIES

It is difficult to be a Christian today – at least in the English-speaking world – without encountering in some form or other the widespread phenomenon of interest in what is known popularly as the age of 'the Celtic Church'. The extravagant lifestyles of ascetic saints with exotic names and supernatural powers have an immediate appeal for the modern cultural imagination. Theirs is a marvellous world which appears to stand outside the tiresome constraints of ordinary space and time. Such a world is memorably evoked, for instance, by Seamus Heaney in poem viii of his 'Lightenings', a retelling of an old Irish annal.[1] In this story, a ship sailing through the air from the Otherworld snags its anchors on the altar rail of the abbey church of Clonmacnoise, where the monks are holding a meeting. A crewman shins down the rope and struggles to free the anchor, but is about to drown when the abbot and monks realize his plight and rush to his aid, allowing the man to escape 'out of the marvellous as he had known it'.[2] Seen from this perspective, the age of the Celtic saints can seem to represent a different historical reality, linked intimately with our own, through place names and the common currency of Christianity, and yet still in a sense a non-place, a world beyond reach: a Christian utopia. The cultural and religious phenomena which surround the modern engagement with 'Celtic Christianity' are both complex and diverse, and include elements to do with ethnic identity, historical consciousness and popular religious impulses, as well as a more sober spirit of Christian reform, which combine and interact in ways that are not easily measured. But for all its ambiguities, the Celtic revival is a significant movement for our times, and it is one which by careful and nuanced analysis can reveal insights into some of the deep structures of religious consciousness as these manifest in the contemporary world.

The following discussion falls into four parts therefore. The first deals with the issue of ethnic identity as such, and of Celtic identity (or 'Celticity') in particular, while the second considers some of the ways in which Christianity as a religion can be seen to interact with the theme of Celticity. Thirdly, I shall examine the role of texts in the transmission of Celtic Christianity, once again seeking to set this within the context of a general discussion of orality and the written word in the Christian world. Finally, I shall consider significant distinctions to be drawn between history and tradition, and shall suggest orientation points for establishing the ethics of historical reappropriations by religious communities seeking to make use of the past.

Celticity

Human social identity is a deeply complex matter which draws together diverse factors of an ethnic and cultural kind with social and political motivations in ways which inevitably escape precise evaluation. The addition of a historical, or more properly a historiographical, perspective to identity adds further layers of personal presupposition and political motivation, which require perhaps rather different tools of analysis. But there are some basic categories which can throw light on human identities and their construction. Anthropologists for instance usefully speak in terms of 'emic' and 'etic' identities. Emic signifies an insider identity (in parallel with *phonemic*, from which it derives, signifying the semiotic properties of words which are only apparent to those who speak and understand a language), while etic (from *phonetic*) represents outsider identities (that is, purely the sound properties of words, which are apparent to all). In many cases these coincide (most citizens of France will be happy to refer to themselves as 'français' and be known to their fellow Europeans by that category). But there is no necessary correspondence between the two. In fact, one of the consequences of the temporal distanciation implied in the writing of history is the tendency for emic and etic identities to diverge, at times dramatically so. Perhaps inevitably, history is written from the perspective of specific powerful emic identities, and their satellite etic ones. In a living discourse, the occlusion of the self-description of others is colonialist and oppressive, for it generally entails an active disregard for the rights of those whose own self-description is refused in favour of a preferred descriptor by another more powerful group.[3] Where the emic identities which are being obscured occur in the past, however, and have no modern survival, then there is no one to speak for them. As an example we can take the case of the widescale appropriation of the 'Ancient Britons' (who spoke an early form of Welsh) as precursors of the Modern Britons (largely English and English-speaking). An English schoolchild might very well feel more able to identify with King Arthur (who like her or himself was a 'Briton') than with the perfidious Romans and the strangely named Anglo-Saxons. Many historians of British history may not in fact be interested in how King Arthur (if he existed) might have seen himself. A Welsh student of history on the other hand might feel an intense interest in the emic identity of King Arthur, who (if he existed at all) was surely a proto-Welshman and thus potentially her or his own ancestor. Welsh historians will resist the assimilation of Welsh history into that of England and will seek an alternative reading of history based on the emic identities of Welsh people which are set aside by the tacit modern identification of 'British' with 'English'. But it is not likely to be the case at all that a Welsh historian would deem it necessary to affirm emic identities from the past as a principle which might otherwise be lost in scandalously imperialistic renderings of history. The issue here is that an ancient identity, ignored by the modern historian, is close enough to the emic identity of a modern group to cause some kind of historiographical conflict. Irish and Welsh historians, we should note, happily apply the categories of Irish or Welsh to ancient tribal groups whose emic identities would have been quite different in kind. Even in the strange Hisperic realms, one would have to travel far before encountering people who would wish to call themselves Silurians or Uí Néill today. Historiography, then, especially of the medieval and early medieval periods, entails an eclipsing of emic identities by etic ones, set up, very often, by rereadings of cultural history by dominant self-defining discourses of the modern nation-state.

At this point a further category distinction can be usefully introduced, which is the difference between what we might call 'analytical descriptors' and 'performative descriptors'. The former are the tools of the historian, who is trying to make sense of material and might very well wish to talk about Romance cultures, for instance, Germanic or Slav peoples; or indeed about the Celts. The key thing here is that such a descriptor should be *useful* to the process of analysing the complexity of human populations. It is notable that such broad-brush descriptors often follow the contours of language groups, as indicated in the examples above, on the quite sensible grounds that culture and language are intermeshed. This too is identity: the habits of mind and belief that constitute the coherence of distinct social groups, and which can be analytically identified. This is quite different from identity in our second sense, however, as what I am calling the 'performative descriptor'. It is not a reflection upon what a particular group are like, but rather an expression of how they wish to be known. This is identity primarily in a political and perhaps personal sense. It is a statement about who one is and who one wishes to be. And it may often be performed in opposition to some attempt by others to impose something undesirable upon such a group. It is possible to trace in writings from Germany during the 1930s a deepening sense of Jewish identity amongst people who had previously thought themselves to be German first and Jewish second (if at all). Here identity can get caught up with political resistance, which may be a far cry from the more neutral categories of general historiography. Needless to say, performative and analytical identities may cross over, and they clearly stand in some kind of relation to emic and etic distinctions. Our second point then, is the introduction of these terms 'analytical and performative descriptors' and the supposition that performative identity tends towards the emic – almost by definition – while analytical identities will equally tend towards the etic.

The term 'Celtic' exhibits all the characteristics of etic identities. Its more remote origins lie in the geographical and ethnographical writings of the Greeks and Romans.[4] From the sixth to the fourth century BC, geographers such as Skylax, Avienus and Hecataeus of Miletus began to describe 'Celts' as warlike peoples pushing down to the south of Europe.[5] The evidence is, however, that the term had no precise ethnic signification and that 'Celts' merely designated those peoples who lived in the west.[6] As Colin Renfrew has put it: 'to the north were the Scythians, to the east the Persians, to the south the Libyans and to the west the Celts'.[7] The word lay dormant for many centuries until it was revived by the linguistic researches of George Buchanan (1506–82) and Edward Lhuyd (1660–1709). In his *Archaeologia Britannica* of 1707, the latter described seven languages as belonging to a distinctive 'Celtic' family (Irish, Welsh, Scottish Gaelic, Manx, Cornish and Breton, as well as Gaulish). In 1853, Johann Kaspar Zeuss published his *Grammatica Celtica*, a comparative grammar of the Celtic languages, thus creating the foundation of scientific Celtic philological studies. Gradually however the word came to take on distinctly Romantic resonances which reflected the imaginative rediscovery and reconstruction of the early culture and history of Ireland, Scotland and Wales. In 1760 James Macpherson published a collection of his own compositions with the title *Fragments of Ancient Poetry, collected in the Highlands of Scotland, and translated from the Gaelic or Erse Language.* These poems, attributed to the Gaelic bard Ossian, son of Fingal, were greatly influential outside Scotland, especially on the Continent.[8] In Wales during the same period, Iolo Morganwg's free editions of Welsh medieval texts won him great influence outside Wales.[9] Macpherson and Iolo Morganwg were part not only of a general European engagement with the early history of Germanic, Slav and Celtic peoples, driven by the powerful philo-sophical and cultural forces of Romanticism, but they can also be seen as part of the movement of conquest and centralization within the formation of the modern British state. Following the suppression of the Highlands, the Highlander became an exotic other, while Iolo Morganwg appears almost to be – creatively – playing out a Romantic and ethnic role laid down for him by the dominant English-speaking peoples among whom he liked to live.[10]

But the fusion of 'Celtic' as a linguistic term with suppressed minorities and Romantic images of the past is a phenomenon more driven by the needs of dominant English-speaking peoples to find an alternative lineage than by the sense of a common Celtic identity among the Scottish, Irish, Welsh and other origi-nally Celtic-speaking communities. As we have noted, the term 'Celtic' is modern, and was not known in the medieval period or the 'age of Celtic saints', and its use as an emic identifier is certainly not widespread today.[11] Unlike most historiographical terms, which fall either into the etic-analytic or emic-performative category, 'Celtic' appears then to be both etic and performative: those who use the term do so by choice, and almost as an explicit rejection of alternative dominant identities. Crucially, the absence of emic Celts allows the term to be appropriated by a wide range of individuals who may in fact have slight association with Ireland, Wales or Scotland, or any of the other traditionally Celtic areas. To this extent we can speak of Celtic identity as being very frequently that of an 'internalized other': it is a performative etic which expresses the desire of many English-speaking people to identify with what they perceive to be an alternative and exotic strand in their own historical evolution, otherwise suppressed by what they perceive to be other less attractive identities of a more institutionalized kind.

Celts and Christianity

Christian interest in the early Celtic world began during the Reformation period with works such as *De Antiquitate Britannicae Ecclesiae* (1572) by Matthew Parker, archbishop of Canterbury, and *A Discourse of the Religion anciently professed by the Irish and the British* (1631) by James Ussher, the Anglican archbishop of Armagh. Neither author had the word 'Celtic', of course, but both were intent upon rooting Anglicanism in an ancient and indigenous tradition which was perceived to be significantly at odds with Roman Catholicism.[12] As a historical religion, Christian renewal – at least in its formal expressions – instinctively seeks to locate itself in what are perceived to be the most ancient forms of Christianity, closest in time to the incarnation itself. A similar dynamic to that of Parker and Ussher is observable in later periods of renewal, although the Nonconformists of the nineteenth century were attracted by what they perceived to be the democratic character of Celtic Christianity, countering the social elitism of a triumphalistic Anglicanism. The Reformation and Post-Reformation engagements with early Celtic Christianity generally focused on issues to do with church order and were to that extent significantly different from the current wave of Celtic revivalism.[13] Here the issues range from outrightly pagan appropriations of druidism and nature religion to an overt Celtic Christian Romanticism, or the more moderate claim that Celtic Christianity represents an aspect of the tradition which is kinder towards the natural world, more inclined to generate or tolerate empowering images of women, more focused in the creative expressions of the religious imagination and less compromised by a body–spirit dualism. Whereas the earlier appropriations of Celtic Christianity were clerical in kind, the contemporary revival is driven by the pressure of popular religion, rooted as much in the emergence of an ecological consciousness and the reconstruction of 'earth religions' as it is in the classical forms of Christian life. It may be however that both the modern 'Celtic' pagan and Matthew Parker have in common the 'Celtic' inheritance and the internalized other, as an alternative and subversive lineage. In the case of Christianity, this issue of identity may be intensified by the notion that to become a Christian is to become part of a new *gens*. This was powerfully present in early Christianity, where the integration of the Christian into the history of Israel was perhaps more dynamically felt than it is today, but it remains residually present in the tradition.[14] It may be that for some the theme of Christian social detachment of which the Letter to Diognetus speaks finds expression in an alternative 'Celtic' identity which marks the subject out as being 'a sojourner' and 'a stranger' in their own land.[15]

Although it is important to view the current Celtic Christian revival in terms of historical precedents, there are significant ways in which the contemporary phenomenon differs from revivals of the past. In the first place, the perceived lack of ecclesiastical organization is frequently attractive not because it accords with a new form of church polity, but rather because it resonates positively with the mood of individualism and self-selection which Paul Heelas, for instance, has identified as one of the key features of the New Age.[16] Also, despite the mainstream character of many of the Christian engagements with Celtic Christianity, these cannot be regarded as being wholly detached from the widespread interest in pagan themes, since an emphasis upon the role of the feminine and the natural world are common to both. The distinctiveness of the contemporary revival is summed up in its emphasis upon *spirituality* rather than arguments surrounding the principles of church order. In historical terms the word 'spirituality' is distinctively modern in resonance and, though often vague in application, precisely reflects the modern fascination with interiority, individual religious experience and personal values. In its more popular usages, 'spirituality' can be set in opposition to doctrine and belief, largely in a Christian context, or alternatively, in a secular one, to values and lifestyle which contrast with those of overt materialism. Although at times, even in its more precise Christian usage, the word 'spirituality' can seem overburdened, it does convey the modern sense that religion must have emotional and value content for the individual. It must engage the self at all levels of our existence. The demand for what we might broadly term religious experience, therefore, fed by an acute sense of the domain of the individual which is foundational to modern Western culture, has produced a particular emphasis upon the texts of the early Celtic world. Texts feed intimacy and communicate dimensions of the inner life. They can be easily brought into the home, and they lend themselves to liturgical and more general devotional use. Unlike archaeological artefacts, for instance, many texts are easily appropriated and inscribed with new meanings. Words are the common currency of cultural exchange, and the fact that the Celtic texts were written in difficult languages, and are the product of a world that was in many ways dramatically alien to our own, is conveniently forgotten when the reader is presented with an attractively produced selection of texts in modern English translation.

The role of texts

Unlike previous renewals then, the modern Celtic Christian revival is characterized by its use of texts – particularly those of a lyric character – made available in numerous anthologies. Amongst such texts none has received more currency than the *lorica* or 'breastplate' known as the 'Deer's cry' and traditionally attributed to St Patrick. The language of the text is not earlier than the eighth century, however, and the link with the Patrick tradition is tenuous.[17] The attribution to such a prominent saint serves as a recognition of the literary and religious power of the text, however, which has guaranteed it a special place in the Irish tradition. In the section which follows, I shall present a brief analysis of this work, showing the ways in which it offers itself to be read today, and contrasting this with alternative meanings which are hidden beneath the surface of the text. To this extent 'St Patrick's Breastplate' can be seen to be a paradigm case of the appropriation of early Celtic material in the current Celtic Christian revival.

The *lorica* begins with the indexical phrase 'I rise today', which is repeated at the head of six of its eight stanzas, the other two being variants. Deixis or indexical language is language which reflects a particular spatio-temporal context and which cannot therefore be understood outside that domain of shared spatio-temporal parameters. When the speaker refers to 'today', we cannot know which day they are referring to: we know only that it is the current day for them. Indexicality works by referring reality to the one who speaks, and its meanings cannot therefore be reconstructed outside that context. It is an embodied form of discourse, suggestive of orality and presence and of reality that is shared by speaker and listener. In the case of the *lorica* therefore, the reader is invited to enter the text and to make their own the successive worlds which the speaker invokes for protection. The first such world is that of the Christian Trinity, which is linked with the Creation itself (I rise today: / in power's strength, invoking the Trinity, / believing in threeness, / confessing the oneness, of Creation's Creator.//). In the second stanza, Trinitarian theology gives way to Christology as the speaker invokes the power of 'Christ's birth and baptism, [. . .] his crucifixion and burial, [. . .] his rising and ascending, [. . .] his descending and judging.' The third stanza extends to the power of the hierarchies of Christian cosmology, from cherubim to angels and archangels, and then to the patriarchs and prophets of the Old Testament and the Apostles of the New. The first three stanzas together then have set out the order of the world from a Christian perspective, treating Trinity, Christology and Christian cosmology (and ecclesiology) as discrete units. The fourth stanza marks a significant change, however, as the speaker invokes the natural powers of the environment (I rise today: / in Heaven's might, / in Sun's brightness, / in Moon's radiance, / in Fire's glory, / in Lightning's quickness, / in Wind's swiftness, / in Sea's depth, / in Earth's stability, in Rock's fixity.//). At this point it is quite natural for the modern reader to move from a credal belief in Christian cosmology to more self-consciously metaphorical and atmospheric language. Our literary and religious traditions are permeated with natural objects as symbols and as a convenient *mise-en-scène* for human life and feeling. Both classical and Romantic literature put the natural world at the service of human sensibility through art. But in this case the speaker is interested not in the symbolic properties of natural objects, nor in their substantiality, but rather at each point hypostasizes their dynamic properties. Thus his interest (if it is a male author, as is likely) lies in the actions or effects of natural objects, that is in the powers of the natural world, rather than its symbolic value. It is not mood that we encounter in these lines therefore but rather a sense of natural forces, evocative of primal religion, which understands natural objects to be channels for the real power of controlling spirits and invisible forces. We can gloss this as a particular view of the world as embodied entity, in which what is visible and open to the senses communicates or even is animated by an invisible life, on the model of the human body itself.

Stanzas one to three and stanza four essentially convey two distinct paradigms of the world as body: the first Christian and cosmological, the second natural and dynamic, associated with the energies and acts of natural objects. But in the fifth stanza a further cohesive unity is invoked in the imagery of God's body, as the speaker calls upon God's 'eye', 'ear', mouth (as 'word') and 'hand' to protect him. With the intensification of the apotropaic character of the work, which seeks to avert evil, we can see an extension of the indexical phrase 'I rise today', which precedes the stanza, in the invocation of God's 'way before me' and God's 'shield to defend me'. Now for the first time the powers of an embodied unity (here the unity of God's 'body') are aligned with the speaker's own body as he calls – or in this case - appeals to the supernatural forces for his bodily defence. The sixth stanza recapitulates the previous five and lists the evil forces against which the speaker is invoking defence: 'Around me I gather today all these powers: / against every cruel and merciless force / to attack my body and soul, / against the charms of false prophets, / the black laws of paganism, / the false laws of heretics, / the deceptions of idolatry, / against spells cast by women, smiths and druids, / and all unlawful knowledge / that harms the body and soul.//' But in the seventh and final full stanza the alignment of the speaker's body with the supernatural bodies, in this case the body of Christ, is again made explicit. As the speaker invokes the presence of Christ around him ('Christ with me, Christ before me, Christ behind me; / Christ within me, Christ beneath me, Christ above me; / Christ to right of me, Christ to left of me;') and in his physical actions ('Christ in my lying, Christ in my sitting, Christ in my rising; /'), the indexical foundation of the work becomes ever more explicit. None of this language is understandable outside a spatio-temporal context, since the position of Christ is related at all points to the position of the speaker's own body. The presence of Christ is invoked also for those other individuals who speak with the speaker, listen to him, see him and think of him ('Christ in the heart of all who think of me, / Christ on the tongue of all who speak to me, / Christ in the eye of all who see me, / Christ in the ear of all who hear me'). Thus the whole physical environment of the speaker is brought before us, including the community of which he is a part.

The use of indexicality in such a concentrated and explicit form as we find it in this text is unusual in world literature, and is by no means the norm in Celtic material. But this is a characteristic most often of the lyric, which offers access to another's world, both in terms of inner perceptions and outward responses, and it is precisely the lyric, and texts which convey a subjective 'spirituality' which, as we have noted, are prominent in the modern Celtic revival. 'St Patrick's Breastplate' represents a text which can be entirely removed from its original context; indeed it lends itself precisely to such an appropriation. The modern reader/speaker can effectively inhabit the text and reconstruct the alignment between their own embodied existence and the corpora of cosmos and Church, the natural world, God and Christ which the successive stanzas evoke. Thus, while the character of belief in the traditional medieval cosmos and in the powers of the natural world may significantly differ between the modern and the ancient speaker, the sense of their own embodiedness, and the deeply felt need for a spiritual defence against evil from without, may remain constant.

History and tradition

I took the view at the beginning of this chapter that the case of Celtic Christianity raises some significant issues of a more general kind and I can specify those now as questions to do with historiography in general and with the use of Christian historical sources in particular. It is inevitable that the modern 'user' of the text known as 'St Patrick's Breastplate' will make of it something quite different from the original author or the 'users' whom the author might have had in view. Thus although texts themselves are itinerant forms of disjunctive awareness, which is to say they are deposited out of the fluid processes of culture in a phenomenon which Michael Silverstein has called 'entextualisation' (which entails an original decontextualization), clearly the original meanings of the text are to be preferred to meanings which are easily imposed upon them by readers whose own cultural and hermeneutical contexts are very different from those which surrounded the genesis of the text.[18] However it may be used in the present, a text constantly calls its readers back, though perhaps in a sense mutely, to the mind or minds which originally conceived it and to the worlds in which its meanings were first generated. In such a popular phenomenon as the modern Celtic Christian revival, it is inevitable that many texts will be taken up and adapted for liturgical or personal-devotional use by people who have at best an uncertain grasp of their historical contexts. The question here then is to what extent we can outline an appropriate hermeneutic for Christian reading of this kind. Should it be declared illegitimate, and such texts be confined to the learned few who alone could be said to exercise responsible and informed historical judgements regarding their original meanings? Or should we declare a free-for-all, whereby each makes of the text what they will?

The importance of this question can be judged by its extreme proximity to the parallel issue of the interaction between formal historical study of the Bible and its use in Christian practice. A rigorist view to the effect that an uninformed and non-historical reading of the Bible has no intrinsic merit might appear to imply that some 1500 years of Christian exegesis should or could be regarded as a history of error. Although there may have been no intention among patristic and medieval exegetes to flaunt the historical perspective in the modern sense (since such cannot be said to have existed prior to the post-medieval period), their understandings of Scripture were not infrequently wide of the mark when judged by modern standards and hence, on a particular historical account, were unwittingly erroneous. But such a view would be to mistake history for tradition; and it is here that we must mark the distinction between a *historical* engagement with texts and what we might call a reading of texts which takes place *within tradition*. These are not necessarily in opposition, but they need to be conceived as distinct hermeneutical operations. In the former case, that of history, the text is required to be reconstructed in its original context, in a way which shows the responsible desire of the reader to access the text in its integrity, and not simply as a deposit for purely modern concerns. A reader who lacks this knowledge cannot be said to have truly 'read' the text, from the perspective of a historical hermeneutic. In the case of readings from within tradition, however, a very different dynamic operates. Here the primary assumption is not that the text needs to be reconstructed against the background of its original genesis (although this may also be seen to be desirable), but that the text as such remains in some vital way *relevant* to the reader's own life and values. A primary Christian proclamation is that God speaks to us in his word. How he speaks, and what he is saying, is a matter for debate, which may itself be informed by the latest historical scholarship, though – as history shows – it need not be. It is a primary Christian intuition that sacred texts or texts of the tradition are still generative of truth in the modern world, despite the great diversity of interpretation (indeed, there is an argument that it is the authority granted to these texts which itself sustains such a vitality and diversity of interpretation). Although there is a clear distinction between the canonical texts of Scripture and the kind of Celtic material which forms the basis of the new revival, a similar point can be made regarding a distinction between readings of such texts as history and readings as tradition or within tradition. The Christian reader wants to discover texts from the past which appear still to speak authentically to us today, for tradition is in this sense 'historical'. More ancient Christianity is easily portrayed as being closer to the source and thus enjoying an authoritative or normative status. Actual historical interrogation of the texts may well reveal aspects of early Christianity which might be seen as bizarre or positively injurious, of course, but it is also the case that early texts can open up possibilities of Christian life, thought and experience which are intriguing, refreshing or even revolutionary in the context of modern belief and practice.

The modern Celtic Christian revival is at times precariously suspended between readings of texts in a historical mode and readings of texts which are driven by the need to find ancient validation of new insights and meanings. Christians will read texts from the past, whatever prescriptive guidelines might be given, for the belief that ancient texts still speak authoritatively to us today is perhaps the defining aspect of Christian hermeneutics, as can be seen from liturgy and the eucharist in which – paradigmatically – the written word becomes the spoken word once again.[19] Indeed, there may be a case for the view that something akin to this is one of the primary characteristics of all world religions. While recognizing that tradition is in a deep sense the attribution or discovery of contemporary relevance in ancient documents, while the historical marks a belief in the primacy of the meaning of the text in its original setting, the kind of rapprochement between tradition and history which we might wish to see, and which is generally represented in the pages of this volume, is one in which tradition remains open to and aware of the constraints of historical analysis. Only in this way can the readers 'within tradition' be sure that the voice they discern in the text, to which they attribute a living relevance and which they choose to perform, is not their own.

Notes

[1]   K. H. Jackson (trans.), *A Celtic Miscellany: Translations from the Celtic Literatures* (Harmondsworth, 1971), no. 138. A similar story occurs in the late twelfth-century writer Gervase of Tilbury; see Robert Bartlett, *England under the Norman and Angevin Kings* (Oxford, 2000), 688. Gervase of Tilbury's *Otia imperialia* is edited by G. W. Leibnitz, *Scriptores rerum Brunsvicensium*, 3 vols. (Hanover, 1707–11), i, 881–1004.

[2]   Seamus Heaney, *Seeing Things* (London, 1991), 62.

[3]   The same issue arises in the context of descriptors for ethnic minorities of course.

[4]   It was used primarily of the ancient inhabitants of Gaul, though not of Britain. See J. Rhys, 'Celtae and Galli', *Proceedings of the British Academy* (1905–6), 71–134.

[5]   H. D. Rankin, 'The Celts through classical eyes', in M. Green (ed.), *The Celtic World* (London, 1995), 21–33, especially 22–3.

[6]   See the following chapter by Jonathan Wooding.

[7]   Colin Renfrew, *Archaeology and Language* (Harmondsworth, 1987), 219. The problem of archaeology and language is discussed in more detail in Jonathan Wooding's chapter below, especially his section 'The archaeological Celt'.

[8]   For an account of the Ossian controversy and the evolution of Celtic Romanticism in general, see Malcolm Chapman, *The Celts* (New York, 1992), 120–45.

9   Gwyn A. Williams, *When was Wales?* (Harmondsworth, 1985), 159–72.

10   The tendency for peoples who speak or spoke a Celtic language to be romanticized as 'Celts' by their more urbanized neighbours is already apparent in the classical period. The early experience of the tribes they called Celts on the part both of the Romans and the Greeks was of their destructive incursions into northern Italy during the fourth century and into the Greek peninsula during the third century BC. Significantly, Aristotle and Polybius attributed the quality of *thymos* to the Celts, a word which Plato employs in the sense of 'passionate arousal' or 'excitability'; Aristotle, *Eudemian Ethics,* 1229^b 28; Polybius 2. 22; see also H. D. Rankin, *Celts and the Classical World* (London, 1987), 55–6. It was natural therefore that classical authors should also see in the Celts the image of their own uncivilized past, as when Posidonius draws a direct parallel between the reservation of the prime portion to the champion at a Celtic feast and a passage from the *Iliad.* Rankin, 'Celts through classical eyes', 28.

11   Emic identities may change, just as etic ones can. It appears that modern economic marginalization and an extension of Irish and Welsh cultural and political nationalism have created an educated middle class in those places which does have some sense of being 'Celtic', though only as a secondary identity.

12   Glanmor Williams surveys this literature in 'Some Protestant views of early British Church history', in his *Welsh Reformation Essays* (Cardiff, 1967), 207–19. Amongst the earliest occurrences of the term 'Celtic Church' are G. T. Stokes, *Ireland and the Celtic Church: A History of Ireland from St Patrick to the English Conquest in 1172* (London, 1886) and John Dowden, *The Celtic Church in Scotland* (London, 1894).

13   Ian Bradley comprehensively surveys these in his *Celtic Christianity: Making Myths and Chasing Dreams* (Edinburgh, 1999).

14   Wayne Meeks, *The Origins of Christian Morality* (New Haven, CT, 1993), 26-36.

15   Letter to Diognetus, §5. See Kirsopp Lake (trans.), *Apostolic Fathers II*, Loeb Classical Library (London, 1976), 359-361.

16   Paul Heelas, *The New Age Movement* (Oxford, 1996).

17   There may be a reference to a connection between this work and Patrick in the ninth-century Book of Armagh, though the association is first made explicitly in the eleventh-century *Liber hymnorum*, where it is said that Patrick sang the *lorica* when ambushed by King Loeguire, with the result that he and his companions took on the form of wild deer. We can speculate that the name 'Deer's Cry' (*fáeth fiada*) given to this text may reflect the influence of this legend upon an original title, *fóid fiada*, which is a technical term applied to those charms of druids and *filid* which produced invisibility. See J. F. Kenney,

The Sources for the Early History of Ireland: Ecclesiastical (Dublin, 1979), 273–4.

[18] Michael Silverstein and Greg Urban (eds.), *The Natural History of Discourse* (Chicago, 1996), esp. 1–17.

[19] Paul Ricoeur, *Figuring the Sacred* (Minneapolis, 1995), 68–72.

2

The idea of the Celt

JONATHAN M. WOODING

If, as Oliver Davies claims, it would seem difficult to be a Christian today without encountering the notion of 'Celtic Christianity',[1] it seems equally, if not more, difficult, to be interested in any aspect of Celtic studies without at some point attracting critical comment for use of the term 'Celt'. Since the early 1980s the idea of the 'Celt' has been subjected to a multidisciplinary assault, an assault which would seem to cast doubt upon the use of this name even to describe the ancient peoples to whom it was first attached, let alone to describe the early and medieval 'insular' (that is, British and Irish) Celtic peoples for whom are claimed a Celtic Christianity, Celtic spirituality or a Celtic Church. We might ask 'what's in a name?'; but John Collis, for example, would contend that the term 'Celt' has 'dangerous archaeological and political implications'.[2] If this seems a trifle apocalyptic, Patrick Sims-Williams would reflect a more widely shared concern in seeing in the introductions to some recent books on the Celts, 'disturbing and unsubstantiated claims which seem to undermine their whole purpose', thus identifying a tendency to a now self-conscious use of the term, as *both* a contingent reality and a popular myth.[3] The contingency might be overstated. Simon James has created a minor sensation by revealing the somewhat unsurprising fact that 'Celtic', like all stereotypes, is one to which few persons exactly conform.[4] Barry Cunliffe sees the mythic element as a palliative myth, a 'New Celtomania, which provides a vision of a European past to comfort us at a time when ethnic divisions are becoming a painful and disturbing reality'.[5] The cumulative weight of all this 'Celtoscepticism' is considerable; its engagement with figures singled out by modern cultural studies, in particular Ernest

Renan, has also led to the 'definitions debate' generating its own, self-sustaining, energy.[6] For those whose starting-point in this matter is an interest in the emergence, in late antiquity, of a specifically 'Celtic' Christianity, theology or Church, it may be important to observe that the negative reassessment of the 'Celtic' quantum in these religious conceptions has formed at best a sideshow to a larger epistemological circus.[7] What then are the implications of the epistemological debate for the user of 'Celt' and 'Celtic' in the British or Irish *Christian* context? Ellis Evans has observed that 'perceptions of the Celts ... vary greatly, according to the primary disciplines of the scholars concerned'.[8] This is very much the case and – lest the cumulative weight of such cross-disciplinary scepticism stifle constructive debate – we can establish, by extension, that these discipline-specific critiques impact upon debates in 'Celtic' religious studies in very different ways.

The classical Celt

Celts are found in the earliest historical records of Northern and Western Europe; their seemingly wide distribution and distinct civilization, at least as described in classical sources, form the basis for populist claims that the Celts were the first 'pan-European' civilization.[9]

The term 'Celt' comes to us via the Greeks, to whom the $K\epsilon\lambda\tauοί$ or $\Gamma\alpha\lambda\acute{\alpha}\tauαι$ were people who lived to the north and west.[10] The Greeks spelled the word 'Celt' with an initial /k/ (kappa), but the controversy continues as to whether the modern derivatives of this word, 'Celt' and 'Celtic', should be pronounced with a 'hard' or a 'soft' /c/ – especially over the Scottish border, where more strict observance of the Anglo-Norman pronunciation of /c/ before /e/ is maintained.

The Romans described the $K\epsilon\lambda\tauοί$ as 'Celtae', but more often as 'Galli' or 'Galatae' (cf. Greek $\Gamma\alpha\lambda\acute{\alpha}\tauαι$), names which have left their legacy in such extant regional names as Galatia (Asia Minor), Galicia (Spain and Central Europe), as well as the name of the ancient province, Gallia (Gaul). There is no question that the Romans saw all these terms as synonymous. Pausanias understood $K\epsilon\lambda\tauοί$ to be an indigenous name and Galli a Latin derivation from $K\epsilon\lambda\tauοί$.[11] This is not really susceptible to proof, but it is worth observing that the philological objections to the two words being related in origin are few. Whether or not Celt is a 'native' word will probably remain debated.[12]

As with most proper nouns, the range of reference of Κελτοί expanded across time as the Greek colonies moved further west and as the Greeks speculated more widely upon the origins of the races of the earth.[13] We cannot expect to see any greater consistency in the antique use of the term than we may expect to find between, for example, the medieval and modern uses of terms such as 'French' or 'English'. It goes without saying that this, by itself, is only the most basic of caveats on the use of the term.

The Celts were already a widespread people when first encountered by the Greeks. Hecataeus of Miletus, in his now lost *Peregesis* of the sixth century BC, described the Celts as living in Narbonne and near Marseilles.[14] Herodotus, in the fifth century BC, possibly using the work of Hecataeus, saw them as one of the westernmost of the European peoples, living west of the Pillars of Hercules and stated that the Danube rose in their territory.[15] Over the next two centuries the Celts would be recorded as moving south into northern Italy and through Greece to Asia Minor. The sack of Delphi by the Celts (279 BC), along with that of Rome by the Gauls living in northern Italy (390 BC), would become – in the same way as did the sack of Rome by the Visigoths in AD 411 – symbolic events in the Graeco-Roman psyche.[16]

The Graeco-Roman world saw a natural potential for expansion at the expense of these neighbours. Anthropologists such as Posidonius (*fl. c.* early first century BC), or intelligence officers such as Pytheas (*fl. c.*325 BC), both operating out of bases in the Greek colonies in the south of France, documented the Celts, the latter almost certainly with a direct eye to conquest.[17] From such early Greek writers via the many later writers who used their now no longer extant works, we obtain our cliché of the ancient Celt. The Celts as encountered by the Greeks exhibited a range of 'national' characteristics. Many of these parallel modern clichés of the Irish, the Scots, and even the Welsh as depicted in the 'Blue Books': a fondness for alcohol, for colourful dress, for violent and trivial dispute.[18]

These romantic qualities, as observed in their neighbours by more urbane trading partners and future colonists, though they are quoted fondly in the social gatherings of Celtic studies conferences, have also been subjected to necessary scholarly deconstruction. In this process of ethnographic discovery, the Celts tended to become invested with Graeco-Roman desires to see them as a wild and expressive counterpart to classical civilization. The Celts became fairly typical 'noble savages'; the druids, the intellectual class of the Celts, were at times seen as 'perfect' natural philosophers and cosmologists.[19] Individual details, quoted and requoted often without attribution – even in works by supposed 'eyewitnesses', such as Caesar – created at times a suspiciously seamless garment of Celticity.

In this way the Graeco-Roman world was proactively engaged with its 'Celtic fringe'. The wine which activated much of this romantic Celtic sensibility was fed to these neighbouring peoples by Roman traders. The tacit investment of desired 'noble savagery' in their Celtic neighbours lent itself to propaganda – especially as dictators, such as Sulla and Caesar, used campaigns on the Celtic frontier to enhance their status. Caesar defined ethnic distinctions between Celtic and Germanic groups so as to legitimate their conquest. To Caesar the Germani, living beyond the Celtic Galli and Belgae, were truly different from the Romans, living a martial and healthy existence; the Celts, by contrast, he represented as disempowered by creeping urbanism and ripe to be absorbed into the Roman polity.[20] Colin Wells has argued that Caesar labelled peoples as 'Celtic' or 'Germanic' at will. Caesar's elevation of the druids as a defining element of Celtic culture led later to their propagandistic demonization and subsequent destruction as a stage in the subjugation of Britain.[21]

The homogeneous cultural profile of the Celts as described by ancient writers thus may reflect no more than repeated citation of the same lost sources. At times it may also represent overt propaganda. These facts are caveats on the use of the 'unified' Celtic identity of prehistory to validate hypotheses of a Celtic civilization which would amount, in effect, to a 'Celtic Empire' (a term coined by Peter Berresford Ellis),[22] effectively united by its priesthood. Nevertheless, this possibly false unity does not present a prima-facie case that the concept of the 'Celt' is itself entirely an invention by outsiders. Champion has claimed that 'names such as Celt, Gaul or Gael were given by outsiders . . . never shared by the so-called Celts themselves'.[23] Caesar directly contradicts this statement: 'Gaul is whole, divided into three parts, one inhabited by the Belgae, another by the Aquitani, the third by people called, in their own tongue, *Celtae,* in our own [Latin] named *Galli.*'[24] We might argue over the point that Caesar here limits the self-styled Celtae to a part of Gaul, but he, as well as Pausanias, is unequivocal on the point that the Galli themselves owned the description 'Celt'.

The archaeological Celt

In archaeological terms the Celts are normally identified with the unified cultural impulses named, after the sites at which they were first identified in the modern era, the 'Hallstatt' *(fl. c.*750–600 BC) and 'La Tène' *(fl. c.*500–100 BC) cultures.[25] These cultures are identified through the spread of elite burial fashions and art images, probably arising from bases in the rich settlements of south central Europe; they spread their motifs as far north as Germany and Britain – where some out of their gallery of art motifs would survive into the artistic vocabulary of 'insular' Christian art.

It was in view of this homogeneity of the La Tène culture in particular, and its seeming correspondence with the area which was, on the basis of classical and onomastic sources, defined as speaking Celtic languages, that, in 1958, Terence Powell was moved to claim:

> The term Celts is therefore justifiable in a proper ethnological sense, and should not necessarily be restricted to mean Celtic-speaking which is a concept of academic thought of quite modern times deriving from the pioneer linguistic studies of George Buchanan and Edward Lhuyd.[26]

It has to be said, in the light of subsequent developments, that this now seems to have been a somewhat overly confident statement – if not in terms of its reasonableness, at least in terms of its likely acceptance. Powell's belief was that the sustained use of a distinct vocabulary of art-images over a large area of Celtic-speaking Europe in antiquity allowed us to speak of a relatively distinct culture-group called the Κελτοί or Galli, identifiable in terms both of material culture and language, corresponding to the geographical distribution of the peoples whom the ancient writers called 'Celts'.

There can be little doubt that the La Tène culture flourished early in Celtic-speaking areas and spread to many areas which also spoke Celtic languages. On this basis it has continued to be assumed that use of La Tène motifs is a likely indicator of Celtic identity.[27] This sort of association will inevitably be circumstantial, only arguable on the balance of probabilities. Even if La Tène art was ubiquitous within the area of Celtic speaking and not ubiquitous outside that area, the link will not be universal. A person who drives a Japanese car is not necessarily Japanese; *mutatis mutandis* a user of a La Tène sword is not necessarily always a Celt. Nor is the study of one aspect of elite material culture necessarily to be assumed to be a defining feature of an ethnic identity. The study of wealthy elite groups and their unities may mask actual and possible differences between groups. These are normal caveats in comparisons between material and historical ethnic patterns – these must be argued on the basis of probability, not simply assumed on the basis of association. It is indeed probable that La Tène impulses, like much of modern culture, spread outside the local political unit most easily to other cultures which shared a common language with it. So, while we find that the La Tène imagery is mostly used by ancient peoples whom we regard as 'Celtic', it is also found in areas such as Denmark, which we do not.[28] Champion and Collis would hold that the use by non-Celtic-speaking peoples of La Tène motifs invalidates the hypothesis that the La Tène culture broadly corresponds to the area of Celtic language use. We may admit that the association is at the moment a circumstantial assumption, though not – contra Collis – an 'illogical' one.[29]

The consensus of critique, or at least the most vocal criticism, in archaeology would now appear to be against this assumption. In comprehending this departure from the model of the 'archaeological Celt' we need to consider the critique of Powell's methodology in its place in the evolution of archaeological thought. Powell's method was essentially focused on defining a proto-historic people; archaeology was in this instance brought to 'push back the limits' of early documentary sources. This was typical of pre-war archaeology. Sir Mortimer Wheeler, for example, moved from early work on Roman sites to trying to identify the Celtic centres visited by Caesar and the *oppida* which were built by the Veneti and Belgae, whom Caesar described as recently having migrated to Britain in the first century BC.[30]

Such archaeology was focused on trying to push historic identities back into the nameless mists of prehistory and paralleled what was being done in comparative philology (see below). Models for the slow diffusion of language from a 'proto-Indo-European' singularity in the distant past had led to a theory that the Celts were an offshoot, perhaps in a couple of millennia BC, from the expansion of the Indo-European ancestral language or dialect group from a hypothesized Eastern European homeland. Common words in Indo-European languages were singled out as indicating the likely earliest stratum of the common language and hence in some cases being geographically specific indicators of this 'homeland'.[31]

In this environment of 'backward-looking' prehistory, Powell attempted to take the Celtic identity as far back into prehistory as it could be taken. The Hallstatt art and burial styles were transmitted from a probable origin point in southern Germany or Austria to peoples who lived to the north as far as Britain and west as far as southern Gaul and northern Spain. The initial activity began around 750 BC and continued through to *c.*600 BC. We have no certainty that this transmission involved any actual movement of personnel, as opposed to a cultural idea or impulse. As we can trace little or no population change throughout this region in the transition from the Hallstatt to the La Tène culture we can regard them, in personnel, as more or less co-terminous. Powell was willing to take the Celts back even further. The 'Urnfield' culture, occupying a smaller area than the latter two cultures but giving way to the Hallstatt with no evident change in settlement pattern, suggested to Powell that they must have been an ancestral group, probably also speaking a Celtic language. Though the distinctive 'urn-field' cemeteries of this group were not found over as wide an area as were accessed by the Hallstatt or La Tène impulses, the urn-field idea did spread into southern France and Germany: this Powell took as something of a precursor of the later pattern or diffusion of La Tène and Hallstatt impulses.[32] This was probably pushing the evidence beyond its limits, though it was argued systematically and cannot be lightly dismissed.

We should consider Powell's book – almost a manifesto for the archaeological definition of a Celt – in its context. It was written in the midst of the post-war backlash against diffusionist models which equated language and material culture – acceptable before the war, when even left-leaning archaeologists such as Gordon Childe had written concerning 'Aryan' migrations, now become disreputable through the political use of 'invasion' models of Gustav Kossina.[33] This backlash took the form of a retreat into an environment in which terms such as 'Celtic' and 'Germanic' became held to be defensibly used only to describe language groups. This was overly politically correct. As Ellis Evans, a linguist, has rightly stressed, it is improper to ignore the fact that 'Celt' was coined as an ethnic label;[34] Powell's work was an attempt to define a case-study in which a material criterion could be defensibly used to define an ethnicity.

The failure of Powell's book to carry conviction on this point was perhaps less on account of the specific merits of his case than it was due to the changing of the guard in archaeology in the 1960s. The 'New Archaeologists' explicitly opposed the 'proto-historical' identifications which had characterized the work of dominant figures such as Gordon Childe and Mortimer Wheeler, in favour of a 'text-free' vision of archaeology. It is arguable that this revolution had its roots in different issues to the one under discussion. Archaeology in the 1960s was still a relatively new discipline and its place in knowledge poorly defined. On one level the revolution sought to end a dependent relationship which was seen to hamper the potential of archaeology to explain economic and social questions. A second aim was to disassociate archaeology from disreputable pseudo-historical associations, such as invasion hypotheses and Arthurianism. The positions adopted were often relative and *ad hominem*.[35] There was a tendency to avoid 'historical' terminology, as if it were itself compromising. There was an undoubted benefit to be gained from this jockeying for intellectual position, which led to rapid advances in our understanding of social organization and production in prehistory. The 'baby with the bathwater' character of the model is also, however, self-evident.

It is in this light that we must view statements such as the following by John Collis, the most persistent of critics of the term 'Celtic' amongst the New Archaeology generation:

> 'Die Kelten kommen!' proclaimed the posters on the motorway at Rosenheim Bavaria, 200,000 of them . . . but would they have done so had the exhibition *Die Kelten* been called the 'Iron Age in Southern

Germany'? . . . Ancient Celts have become modern Celts . . . the illogicality of this process and the tacit theories which lie behind the methodology employed, . . . have unfortunate and dangerous archaeological and political implications.[36]

We will not dwell on the irrefutable logic of the claim that 'Die Kelten' would attract more visitors than the 'Iron Age in Southern Germany'; it does not follow that this proves the latter a more 'responsible' title than the former. One cannot help thinking that calling a people 'Iron Age' – essentially defining them by their weapons technology – also has unfortunate implications.

Collis has recently sought to distance himself from the extreme form of Celtoscepticism which would regard the term Celt as entirely invalid for antiquarian studies.[37] He, along with Simon James, continues, however, to debate the congruence of the linguistic definition of 'Celtic' with the ancient distribution of Celtic peoples – arguing that it is invalid to regard any of the early occupants of Britain or Ireland as 'Celts', simply on the basis that they speak languages of what has come to be known as the 'Celtic' family. This is the 'definitions' debate which impacts most directly upon any definition of 'Celtic' Christianity; the question of how 'Celtic' early Christianity in Britain was really comes down to an assessment of the validity of the term Celtic when used to describe the society of Roman Britain, sub-Roman western Britain, Scotland, Ireland and the Isle of Man.

The linguistic Celt

The modern definition of Celtic languages began with George Buchanan in the sixteenth century. Buchanan (1506–82), who included amongst his attainments the status of tutor to Mary, Queen of Scots and later to her son James, late in life wrote a history of his native Scotland, *Rerum Scoticarum historia* (1582), which eschewed the conventional British origin legends in favour of speculation upon the relationship of the Gaelic Scots to the ancient Celts.[38] In particular his theorizing was informed by comparison of personal names as well as place names in ancient sources with ancient and modern Scottish onomastics. He rightly seems to have seen the Gaelic (Irish, Scots Gaelic and Manx) and British (Welsh, Cornish and Breton) branches of Celtic as ultimately, if distantly, related, describing the former as 'Keltic' and the latter as 'British'.[39] The terminology is used slightly differently from the present use, but the distinctions are the same as are now made.

It was Edward Lhuyd (1660–1709), however, in his *Archaeologia Britannica* of 1707, who made thoroughly clear the familial relations between the 'insular' Celtic languages. Lhuyd, Keeper of the Ashmolean Museum and an extraordinary pioneer in scientific studies of both etymology and, originally, botany, brought the principles of fieldwork and ordered classification to the study of the Celtic languages. He travelled extensively in all the nations in which Celtic was spoken, except for Man, for which he appears to have relied on correspondents, and Brittany, from where he was deported on suspicion of being a spy. His records of Cornish, which was soon to become extinct, are of especial importance. Lhuyd virtually invented modern comparative philology – though it remained for Sir William Jones to show the link between Celtic and the other Indo-European languages. It is tempting to speculate that if Lhuyd had not died suddenly at the early age of 49, just prior to writing the second, antiquarian, volume of his projected *Archaeologia*, archaeological method might have progressed by a comparable leap to that undergone by philology.

Celtic was then, in the eighteenth century, one of the most intensely studied of language groups in philological terms. Johann Kasper Zeuss's remarkable *Grammatica Celtica* of 1853 ensured that, in the nineteenth century, it remained in the forefront of comparative research. Zeuss's pioneering research on Old Irish, mostly using the glosses left by Irish *peregrini* on Latin manuscripts in continental libraries, created a wave of interest in Irish studies in Germany, especially by Sanskrit scholars such as Windisch and Zimmer, leading to the teaching of *Celtische Philologie* in several centres and the establishment of a chair of Celtic in Berlin.[40] Whole generations of scholars from insular 'Celtic' countries studied in this external environment in Germany, in which the notion of 'Celtic', philologically established, obtained. This undoubtedly encouraged an influential vision of the 'Celts' as both a general ancient unity and an insular identity. This academic enthusiasm for 'pan-Celticism' also spilled over into more populist displays, such as the Celtic Congresses of the early 1900s and the bardic gatherings *(gorseddau)* which came to be held in various Celtic nations, irrespective of any actual early historic precedent. The Celtic languages in the early 1900s held a central place in the regional nationalism of the United Kingdom and where regions saw common cause this was in part expressed by such reinventions of Celticity. Not all Celtic nations saw value in the exercise – especially those, such as Ireland, who were already in possession of a rich heritage which did not need to be reappropriated from the tradition of its neighbours.[41]

The insular Celt

Celtic speaking evidently outlasted Roman rule on the Continent, but only in Ireland and the remoter parts of Britain did it persist on a sufficient scale to survive beyond the end of the first millennium AD.[42] The more copious records of Celtic languages in Britain and Ireland render the term at its least controversial there in linguistic terms. In Britain and Ireland, on the other hand, the use of the term as an ethnic label is at its most questionable. In antiquity, the people of Britain were always Britanni and never Celtae. Indeed Pytheas and Strabo describe Britain as lying to the north of Celtica. For this reason Collis regards as illogical the tendency to see the early Britons as 'Celts'. Strictly speaking, such use of the term may be inaccurate. Caesar described at least part of the population of Britain – that closer to the coast – as an extension of the population of Gaul. He was in no way ambiguous as to their common language.[43] He noted that druids would travel to Britain for further study.[44] Unless we are to understand the druids as an ethnically neutral priesthood – which they were clearly not – it is evident that Caesar was describing Britain as ethnically related to Gaul. As Caesar regarded the Galli as Celtae it can hardly be, as Collis claims, 'illogical' to regard Britain as 'Celtic' in antiquity – even if it is not literally correct. The central point made by Collis and James – stripped of their preoccupation with the word 'Celt' – is nonetheless a valid one. Britain was no more a central element in the Celtic world in the pre-Roman Iron Age than it was to be in the Roman Empire. The influence of the Hallstatt and La Tène impulses upon Britain, let alone Ireland, are late and comparatively superficial.[45] There is indeed no reason to expect one of the more remote regions touched by the central impulses of Hallstatt and La Tène to reflect a microcosm of Celtic culture; Britain's 'survival' as a Celtic-speaking region out of the general Roman assimilation of the Celts elsewhere carries no implication that it would, as a 'rump' of the ancient Celtic civilization, necessary reassert any characteristics of the Celtic Iron Age.

What we come back to in these debates is a simple problem of the evolution of scholarly method, namely the tendency to concentrate first on that which we can identify and classify. Celtic words and images of an 'international' type lend themselves to comparative study and to dating through wide comparisons. In this sort of process, the local content of a language or a material record will be downplayed and elements highlighted which give a false impression of the whole.

That insular Celts might somehow reflect a larger Celtic paradigm in the sub-Roman period was nonetheless entertained in 1963, when Kenneth Jackson identified parallels between the material and social culture as depicted in the Irish Ulster Cycle tales with the descriptions of the Celts in Posidonius. If the parallels of warriors squabbling over the champion's cut of meat are sometimes striking, Jim Mallory has brought a measure of sobriety to such speculations in observing that the material culture of these tales is more compatible with the archaeology of the later first millennium AD – the period of writing of the tales.[46] To some extent Jackson's speculations flowed naturally from a tendency to cast the study of Celtic linguistic evolution in terms of disseminations from the Continent to Britain. That British Celtic languages, apparently along with what was known of Continental Celtic, pronounced Indo-European $/k^w/$ as $/p/$, in contrast to Irish – hence the well-known tendency to speak of 'P' (British) as opposed to 'Q' (Gaelic) Celtic languages – inspired the thought that British was the legacy of more recent 'waves' of Celtic arrival: this is the so-called 'Gallo-Brittonic' hypothesis.[47] Whatever the likelihood or otherwise of this model there can be no doubt that such thinking downplayed the local characteristics of insular culture in favour of representing it as representative of a larger Celtic civilization.

It is, nonetheless, hard to go entirely past the 'Celtic' symbolism of the sub-Roman era in Britain. Sub-Roman potentates – to borrow a term from Leslie Alcock – in Somerset reoccupied, not simply ancient fortifications, but the giant *oppida* of the Durotriges – one of the more 'internationally Celtic' legacies of Iron Age Britain.[48] The artwork of insular Christianity embraced

La Tène motifs – though in Ireland and parts of northern Britain this would be more or less the first time the La Tène image had achieved any real currency.[49] Undoubtedly this is a 'Celtic revival' of sorts, however unconscious, but how much any users of these central symbols of Celtic antiquity had any sense of their being 'Celtic' remains an unanswerable question. Likely enough the idea would have been no more relevant to them than the 'cultural' distinction between an iron- or bronze-driven technology would have been to the early medieval Irish kings who chose to be inaugurated at Tara.

It is easy to be critical of the vision of culture which seeks to isolate one element and trace it from a remote antiquity to the present, divorcing it from its wider context. For most of the twentieth century Oxford undergraduates were encouraged to believe that they would learn more about 'English' literature from reading the Old English works of King Alfred than they would reading French or Russian novels. Similarly the study of continuities from ancient continental culture through into insular Celtic – at times tacitly downplaying Roman and Latin Christian influences on language and culture – is easily criticized. But the paradigms for study being offered as alternatives are not necessarily themselves without their own blind-spots.

The religious Celt

While speculation on the common distinctiveness of the Irish and British churches goes back to the time of Bede, the term 'Celtic' in relation to this putative commonality of practice only emerged in the 1880s.[50] The term itself derives very much from the philologist's vision of post-Roman nations united by Christianity and two inherited, if mutually unintelligible, dialects. Like the term 'insular art',[51] 'Celtic Church' thus served principally as a term of convenience to describe circumstantial developments which are otherwise difficult to label and often nationally sensitive. Early users of this concept, such as F. E. Warren, were concerned principally to explain regional differences in the practices of the early Church in Britain and Ireland, not any 'native' contribution which would render this Christianity 'Celtic' in a broader geographical sense. Much subsequent academic study of this topic has, likewise, been chiefly concerned with attributing the basis for similarity between some British and Irish Churches to the influence of one over the other, or to entirely external factors.[52] In this context, 'Celtic Church', a term which obviously evokes very different images in Protestant and Catholic audiences, led a fairly inoffensive existence until it was demolished by, first, Kathleen Hughes, then Wendy Davies, on the irrefutable basis that it downplayed dissimilarities and implied the existence of a non-existent ecclesiastical hierarchy.[53]

This 'Celtic' label, as applied to the concept of common liturgical practice, is in some ways only tenuously related to the notion of 'Celtic' spirituality which has emerged in more recent times. This has coincided with the identification, by anthropological and cultural studies, of a shared modern, literary, vision of the Romantic 'Celt'.[54] A desire to seek the distinctiveness of Celtic Christianity in a primarily indigenous context is a dimension of such discourse. Yet the relationship of such a quest for a 'native' dimension to the distinctive elements of Celtic Christianity – whether really distinctive or otherwise[55] – arguably owes as much to the prior adoption of the term 'Celtic Church', and a subsequent proactive influence of the name 'Celtic' in its 'nativist' sense, as it does to a genuinely independent Romantic discourse concerning the Celts.[56] Perhaps one of the paradoxes of popular writing upon Celtic Christianity is the fact that it has moved towards a 'nativist' model at precisely the time that academic investigators have begun more and more to seek explanations for literary motifs and language change in Latin and Christian sources. In this context, some of the strictures against incautious use of the term 'Celtic' might be justified.

Attempts to move the term outside the insular Christian context are not likely to meet with success. It may be fascinating to recall that one of the audiences to whom Paul preached earliest, the Galatians, was no doubt in part by preference a Celtic-speaking one – a fact which Jerome was to record as still true three centuries later;[57] but to attempt to see in Paul's condemnation of the Galatians' failings, such as the tendency to follow variant gospels (Galatians 1: 9) or to 'observe days, and months, and seasons, and years!' (4: 9–10), any distinctive parallels with the controversies of insular Christian practice is fruitless. The Greek cosmological vision and the Celtic as described in classical sources are more or less indivisible. Likewise the condemnation by

Irenaeus of Lyon (early third century) of the manners of his 'Celtic' charges are far too universal and generalized to have the capacity to correlate with insular 'Celtic' religious preferences.[58]

In conclusion, the idea of the Celt is, in antiquity, a complex one. In insular usage it is a term of convenience for circumstantial similarities between different regions around the shores of the Irish Sea which spoke related, often by the early Middle Ages no longer mutually intelligible, languages.[59] If the Celticity of the region is largely a circumstantial matter, so too, however, are most of the objections to the use of the term 'Celtic' to describe it. As Sims-Williams observes, 'at times the term "Celtic" seems to be expected to pass stricter tests of validity than would normally be applied to, say, "Germanic" or "Slavic"'.[60] The Romanticism which at times pervaded classical and early medieval images of Celts presents a 'straw man' for those who wish to pursue a separatist agenda in archaeology; as the most colonized of peoples in this archipelago, the Celts also formed a natural subject for Ardener's revolutionary application of an anthropology, previously targeted at the Third World, to European subjects. If at times this looks disturbingly like the singling out of a minority population, as well as of a minority subject area, the student of Celtic studies should rest assured in the knowledge that Celtic studies continues to be right in the forefront of important intellectual debates.

Notes

[1] See previous chapter.

[2] John Collis, 'The origin and spread of the Celts', *Studia Celtica*, 30 (1996), 17–34, at 17.

[3] Patrick Sims-Williams, 'Celts and Celtoscepticism', *Cambrian Medieval Celtic Studies*, 36 (Winter 1998), 1–35, at 1–2. Sims-Williams's target here is, in particular, the hypersceptical statements by Sara and Timothy Champion in the book *The Celtic World*, ed. Miranda J. Green (London, 1995), esp. p. 88 (Timothy Champion), 'There is no evidence to suggest that anyone in prehistoric or early historic times thought of him or herself as a Celt'; and p. 411 (Sara Champion), 'It is not currently possible to prove that any of the Iron Age peoples who lived in central or western Europe in the first millennium BC definitely spoke a Celtic language'. It need hardly be said that these statements sit uneasily in a book entitled 'The Celtic World'.

[4] Simon James, *The Atlantic Celts: Ancient People or Modern Invention?*

(London, 1998). James's monograph sits in a now well-established genre of works which have managed to achieve surprising notoriety in deconstructing rather obvious artificialities – see, for example: Susan Reynolds, *Fiefs and Vassals: The Medieval Evidence Reinterpreted* (London, 1994), and Christopher Tyerman, *The Invention of the Crusades* (Toronto, 1998).

5   Barry Cunliffe, *The Ancient Celts* (Oxford, 1997), 19.

6   Patrick Sims-Williams, 'The visionary Celt', *Cambridge Medieval Celtic Studies*, 11 (1986), 71–96; Malcolm Chapman, *The Celts: The Construction of a Myth* (Basingstoke and New York, 1992), *passim*. Donald E. Meek, *The Quest for Celtic Christianity* (Edinburgh, 2000), 231, suggests that 'Celtic Christianity' is a construct which can, in some considerable measure, be 'traced to Renan and Arnold'. Also see I. Bradley, *Celtic Christianity: Making Myths and Chasing Dreams* (Edinburgh, 1999), 120–1. Renan's theories in general were singled out for critique by Edward Said, in *Orientalism* (London and Henley, 1978), esp. 130–48, one of the most influential texts in modern 'cultural studies'. A full study of Renan's actual impact upon the development of Celtic Christianity, if any, outside of his use by Matthew Arnold, would be a *desideratum*.

7   See Meek, *Quest for Celtic Christianity*, esp. 5–22; Bradley, *Celtic Christianity*, esp. 226–9; Sims-Williams, 'Celts and Celtoscepticism', 10. For balanced and sustained critique of the notion of a 'Celtic Church' see Wendy Davies, 'The myth of the Celtic Church', in N. Edwards and A. Lane (eds.), *The Early Church in Wales and the West* (Oxford, 1992), 12–21.

8   D. Ellis Evans, 'Linguistics and Celtic ethnogenesis', in R. Black, W. Gillies and R. Ó Maolalaigh (eds.), *Celtic Connections: Proceedings of the Tenth International Congress of Celtic Studies* (East Linton, 1999), 1–18, at 2–3.

9   See Ruth and Vincent Megaw, 'The Celts, the first Europeans?', *Antiquity* 66 (1992), 254–60; Peter Berresford Ellis, *The Celtic Empire* (London, 1993).

10   See most conveniently the texts in translation in: J. Koch and J. Carey (eds.), *The Celtic Heroic Age* (Andover, MA, 1995), 5–40.

11   Caesar, *De bello Gallico* 1. 1 and Pausanias, *Description of Greece* 1. 4. 1.

12   See most recently, Sims-Williams, 'Celts and Celtoscepticism', 22. The combination of velar stop with /l/ /t/ is a notable similarity between the two words, though Sims-Williams notes the expected form in Gaulish should be *kli-* not *kel-* and suggests the not unlikely possibility of reborrowing through Latin into Gaulish. There is no particular reason why the name 'Celt' need have originally been of indigenous origin for it to have been used by the Celts of themselves: there are numerous historic examples of peoples who have used a

general term for themselves from a foreign language, in lieu of the alternative of a collective noun of indigenous origin, which would need to be divorced from its more specific meaning. An example from the early insular world is the kingdom of the 'Picts': from Latin *pictus* (painted), it was originally an epithet used by the Romans of the tribes north of Hadrian's Wall – but by the early Middle Ages it probably would have become, in any event, obscure as to whether it was of Pictish or Roman origin.

[13] P. Freeman, 'The earliest Greek sources on the Celts', *Études celtiques*, 32 (1996), 11–45.

[14] Ibid., 14.

[15] Herodotus, *Historia* 2. 33; 4. 49.

[16] David Rankin, 'The Celts through classical eyes', in Green, *Celtic World*, 21–38; also *idem*, *Celts and the Classical World* (London, 1987).

[17] See J. J. Tierney, 'The Celtic ethnography of Posidonius', *Proceedings of the Royal Irish Academy* 60C (1960), 189–275; C. H. Roseman, *Pytheas of Massalia, On the Ocean* (Chicago, 1994). Also C. F. C. Hawkes, *Pytheas: Europe and the Greek Explorers* (Oxford, 1977).

[18] On Celtic drunkenness: Diodorus Siculus, *Historical Library*, 5.26; Plato, *Laws*, 1. 637; Polybius, *History*, 2. 19. On the tendency to dispute: Diodorus Siculus, *Historical Library*, 5. 31. The costume of the Celts became a consistent image in Graeco-Roman art: T. G. E. Powell, *The Celts* (London, 1955), 65.

[19] Clement of Alexandria, *Miscellanies*, 1. 15; Hippolytus, *Philosophuma*, 1. 25.

[20] Caesar, *De bello Gallico* 6. 11–20.

[21] On the demonization of druids: Tacitus, *Annales*, 3. 30, 14. 29. On Caesar's definition of Germans: C. Wells, *The German Policy of Augustus* (Oxford, 1972); *idem*, 'Celts and Germans in the Rhineland', in Green, *Celtic World*, 603–20.

[22] P. Berresford Ellis, *The Celtic Empire* (London, 1992).

[23] T. Champion, 'Power, politics and status', in Green, *Celtic World*, 85–94, at 88.

[24] 'Gallia est omnis divisa in partes tres, quarum unam incolunt Belgae, aliam Aquitani, tertiam qui ipsorum lingua Celtae, nostra Galli appellantur', *De bello Gallico* 1, ed. and trans. H. J. Edwards, *Caesar, Gallic War* (Cambridge, MA, 1917), 2–3.

[25] Hallstatt in Austria and La Tène in Switzerland are 'type-sites' – not necessarily the earliest or most important centres in their respective cultures.

[26] Powell, *The Celts*, 15.

[27] Ruth and Vincent Megaw, 'Do the ancient Celts still live?', *Studia Celtica*, 31 (1997), 107–123; *eidem*, 'Celtic connections past and present: Celtic ethnicity ancient and modern', in Black et al., *Celtic*

Connections, 19–81 and especially the bibliography to the latter. For a specifically opposed view see T. Champion, 'The Celt in archaeology', in T. Brown (ed.), *Celticism* (=*Studia Imagologica* 8 (1996)), 61–78; T. Taylor, 'Celtic art', *Scottish Archaeological Review*, 8 (1991), 129–32 replies in *Scottish Archaeological Review*, 9–10 (1995), 248–52 (Megaws) and 252–3 (Taylor).

28   This fact has been at times been variously understood as indicating possible Celtic political influence over parts of Germania – a politically 'loaded' notion – or the activities of traders.

29   Javier de Hoz outlines an argument for a spread of the dialect which we identify as 'Gaulish' as an accompaniment to the La Tène into areas which were already Celtic-speaking: see 'Lepontic, Celt-Iberian, Gaulish and the archaeological evidence', *Études celtiques*, 29 (1992), 223–40, at 230–3.

30   See especially R. E. M. Wheeler and K. Richardson, *The Hillforts of Northern France* (London, 1950); general account in Jacquetta Hawkes, *Mortimer Wheeler* (London, 1984). Caesar's own theories as to the northern and western migrations of the Celts arguably contributed to the 'invasion hypothesis' so prevalent in pre-war archaeology.

31   J. P. Mallory, *In Search of the Indo-Europeans* (London, 1989), esp. 9–23, 144–64. For an explicit critique of the entire assumption, which would argue against the diffusion from a singularity, see C. Renfrew, *Archaeology and Language* (Harmondsworth, 1987), *passim*. Renfrew's model, mostly an interpretation on the basis of archaeological evidence, has not really yet found much support from philologists. See also P. Sims-Williams, 'Genetics, linguistics and prehistory', *Antiquity*, 72 (1998), 505–27, at 510. Shippey appositely terms this linguistic search for past homelands 'asterisk reality', after the linguistic symbol used to mark a hypothetical form of a word: T. Shippey, *The Road to Middle Earth* (London, 1982), 17–25.

32   Powell, *The Celts*, 35–45; for a contrary view see de Hoz, 'Lepontic, Celt-Iberian', 224.

33   See B. Arnold, 'The past as propaganda', *Archaeology*, 45 (1992), 30–7; Sims-Williams, 'Genetics, linguistics', 507.

34   D. Ellis Evans, 'The earliest Celts – the evidence of language', in Green, *Celtic World*, 8–20, at 9.

35   Two decades earlier, for example, archaeologists of the 'Wheeler school' had been assaulted by younger colleagues for 'selective excavation' of sites, with neglect of socio-economic evidence obtainable through 'total' excavation of sites. By the 1960s, ironically, selective excavation became politically correct, as it preserved sites rather than destroyed them.

36   Collis, 'The origin and spread of the Celts', 17. *Idem, The European*

Iron Age (London, 1984); *idem*, 'Celtic Myths', *Antiquity*, 71 (1997), 195–200.

[37] John Collis, 'George Buchanan and the Celts in Britain', in Black et al., *Celtic Connections*, 91–107.

[38] Ibid., 91–2.

[39] These groupings are variously named. I will eschew the pseudo-archaic terms 'Goidelic' and 'Brythonic', which principally reflect discomfort with the modern implications of the terms 'Gaelic' and 'British'. The corresponding terms 'Q' and 'P' Celtic are also avoided as they highlight only one point of difference. The 'Gaelic' languages here are Irish and its two early medieval derivatives Scots Gaelic and Manx. The 'British' languages are Welsh and Cornish, along with the overseas offshoot Breton – a product of migration in the sub-Roman period. The Gaelic and British groups have not been mutually intelligible at any time in the historic period.

[40] S. Ó Lúing, 'Celtic scholars of Germany', *Zeitschrift für celtische Philologie*, 46 (1994), 249–71.

[41] See Peter Berresford Ellis, *The Cornish Language and its Literature* (London, 1974), 148–52; for a modern critique of the use of medievalist imagery see Amy Hale and Philip Payton (eds.), *New Directions in Celtic Studies* (Exeter, 2000), 11.

[42] It remains controversial whether we see a previous stratum of Armorican Celtic language as contributing to the speaking of Breton, the language of British migrants, in Brittany.

[43] Caesar, *De bello Gallico*, 4. 20, 5. 12.

[44] Caesar, *De bello Gallico*, 6. 13.

[45] Seamus Caulfield, 'Some Celtic problems in the Irish Iron Age', in D. Ó Corráin (ed.), *Irish Antiquity* (Cork, 1981), 205–15; Barry Raftery, *Pagan Celtic Ireland* (London, 1994).

[46] K. Jackson, *The Oldest Irish Tradition: A Window on the Iron Age* (Edinburgh, 1963); J. P. Mallory, 'Silver in the Ulster Cycle of Tales', in D. Ellis Evans (ed.), *Proceedings of the Seventh International Congress of Celtic Studies* (Oxford, 1987), 33–65.

[47] See J. Koch, '"Gallo-Brittonic" vs "Insular Celtic"', in G. le Menn (ed.), *Bretagne et les pays celtiques* (Rennes, 1992), 471–95.

[48] L. Alcock, 'The activities of potentates in Celtic Britain AD 500–800: a positivist approach', in S. Driscoll and M. Nieke (eds.), *Power and Politics in Early Medieval Britain and Ireland* (Edinburgh, 1988), 22–39.

[49] Ruth and Vincent Megaw, *Celtic Art* (London, 1989), 206–10; 247–56.

[50] The earliest uses of the term include: F. E. Warren, *Liturgy and Ritual of the Celtic Church* (London, 1881); G. T. Stokes, *Ireland and the Celtic Church* (Dublin, 1888).

[51]   See esp. D. Ó Cróinín, 'Rath Melsigi, Willibrord and the earliest Echternach manuscripts', *Peritia*, 3 (1984/5), 17–42.

[52]   Across the century this model has moved generally from one in which the British churches were seen to owe their distinctive character, such as it was, to either direct influence emanating from Ireland, or from an external group such as 'desert fathers' – cf. E. G. Bowen, *Saints, Seaways and Settlements* (Cardiff, 1969), esp. 141 – to being now seen as essentially all part of a subset of the late Roman church in Britain: see e.g. D. N. Dumville, 'Some British aspects of the earliest Irish Christianity', in P. Ní Chatháin and M. Richter (eds.), *Irland und Europa: Die Kirche im Frühmittelatler* (Stuttgart, 1984), 16–24; *idem*, 'British missionary activity in Ireland', in D. Dumville et al., *Saint Patrick, A.D. 493–1993* (Woodbridge, 1993), 133–45; R. Sharpe, 'Gildas as a father of the Church', in Michael Lapidge and David N. Dumville (eds.), *Gildas: New Approaches* (Woodbridge, 1984), 193–205 – though an explicit rebuttal of this model is P. Ó Riain, 'Finnio and Winniau: a return to the subject', in J. Carey, J. T. Koch and P.-Y. Lambert (eds.), *Ildánach Ildírech: A Festschrift for Proinsias Mac Cana* (Andover, MA, and Aberystwyth, 1999), 187–202, esp. 188–9. The similarities between the churches in archaeological terms were clearly overstated by early scholars, such as Radford, who made misidentifications of sites in British zones such as Tintagel and Birsay as 'monasteries' of distinctively Irish type. See I. Burrow, 'Tintagel – some problems', *Scottish Archaeological Forum*, 5 (1973), 88–103; C. Morris, *Church and Monastery in the Far North: An Archaeological Assessment* (Jarrow Lecture, 1989).

[53]   See Davies, 'Myth of the Celtic Church'.

[54]   Particularly under the influence of Edwin Ardener, see Chapman, *The Celts*. Patrick Sims-Williams, however, has also explored a similar discourse in Celtic literature, see 'The visionary Celt'.

[55]   See, most recently, Thomas O'Loughlin, *Celtic Theology* (London, 2000), 1–24.

[56]   For a summary of the polemic see K. McCone, *Pagan Past and Christian Present in Early Irish Literature* (Maynooth, 1990). This is usefully read in conjunction with the comments by Donnchadh Ó Corráin in *Bulletin of the Dublin Institute for Advanced Studies* (1994). On language see T. Charles-Edwards, 'Language and society among the insular Celts', in Green, *Celtic World*, 703–36, esp. 714 and 734–6. The over-emphasis on vernacular sources is a product both of the greater enthusiasm amongst modern Irish and Welsh students for studying the classical form of the language, as well as the tendency of early scholars, such as Stokes and Plummer, not to translate Latin texts, on the assumption of a classical education on the part of the reader.

57 *Commentary on Galatians,* Preface to Book 2. That such an isolated group might have remained Celtic-speaking is not without parallel: for example, a Gothic 'pocket' in the Crimea was still speaking Gothic in the later Middle Ages, having been in isolation for over a millennium.

58 Irenaeus, *Adversus Haerases,* 1. 3. Irenaeus uses the term, probably only as an affectation, in Caesar's specific sense as describing the population of Lugdunensis.

59 One alternative which was mooted in the 1960s was 'Irish Sea Culture-province', a notion which foundered on hostility to its general currency, but which in some ways was a successful enough notion in the early medieval context: L. Alcock, 'Was there an Irish Sea Culture Province in the Dark Ages?', in D. Moore (ed.), *The Irish Sea Province in Archaeology and History* (Cardiff, 1969), 55–64.

60 Sims-Williams, 'Celts and Celtoscepticism', 3.

3

The 'pagan' and 'Christian' identities of the Irish female saint

ELVA JOHNSTON

Introduction

Irish female saints, especially Brigit, are subject to feminist, religious, literary and historical speculations. They have been imagined as avatars of pre-Christian goddesses; they are celebrated as symbols of a lost matriarchal Ireland; they become harbingers of a peculiarly 'Celtic' spirituality. Mary Condron has stated that Brigit was the central figure of pagan Irish cosmology, the Mother Goddess and the divine serpent who was overthrown by the deadening hands of clerical patriarchs and Christian patriarchy.[1] Idiosyncratically, Robert Graves recognized in Brigit the White Goddess, whose many faces purportedly included Athene, Isis, Ishtar, Freya and Ceridwen.[2] A recent starring role has been as a powerful alien in a science fiction series.[3] More seriously, Kim McCone has delved deeply in search of the Indo-European associations of her cult,[4] while Séamas Ó Catháin has identified the folklore surrounding Brigit as being both ancient and essentially pagan.[5] On the other hand, Dorothy Ann Bray has stressed the Christian elements that made up the cults of Brigit and her fellows.[6] This chapter will centre on the perceptions of early Irish authors. Mainly clerics, their texts form our oldest substantial evidence for the cult of the saints in Ireland. These authors were members of the elite, for the ability to read and write was a marker of high status, and they rarely give us insights into the workings of popular devotion.

Nevertheless, the sources, varied in content and form, have much to offer. They include saints' Lives (*vitae*), hymns, genealogies, poems and religious anecdotes. The material, composed in

Latin and Irish, ranges in date from the seventh century to the twelfth century and after.[7] I will concentrate specifically on the Lives and, where necessary, other supporting items from the hagiographical dossiers of four female saints: Brigit of Kildare (d. 524/26/28),[8] Íte of Killeedy (d. 570/79),[9] Mo Ninne of Killeevy (d. 517)[10] and Samthann of Clonbroney (d. 739).[11] I have chosen these saints for two reasons: first, the choice is necessarily limited because there are far fewer Lives of female saints than male saints and, second, these particular women and their respective churches can be identified. Not all holy women and their churches can be pinpointed with any certainty and, obviously enough, secure identification is important for contextualizing the material.[12] Of the four, Brigit presents the greatest difficulty. Her death notices in the annals are clearly artificial and it is doubtful whether early Irish clerics were very sure of her chronology. This has cast a cloud over Brigit's historicity, a point to which I will return. In spite of this problem, the richest and fullest documentation comes from the Brigidine corpus. Brigit's church of Kildare was wealthy and influential and the saint is portrayed as having more power than any other female religious figure. Should Brigit's power be linked to the issue of pagan and Christian identities? Does her importance have a non-Christian root?

Two concepts are particularly important: one is gender, the other the merging of what is arguably native Irish material with early Christian traditions. I will begin with gender. Joan Scott has argued that gender is the social organization of sexual difference, highlighting the potential gendering of all aspects of life from the family to the workplace.[13] This recognizes the social character of sex-based distinctions. However, gender is neither monolithic nor identical with biological sexual difference. It cannot be viewed as immutable throughout time and space and it has been treated and imagined in many ways. The sex/gender distinction played its part in medieval thought. Some of the Church fathers believed that ascetic virgins could transcend the feminine state and be transformed, in a spiritual sense, into men.[14] This transformation rid them of the inherent weaknesses of women and of the female susceptibility to fleshly temptations. Female subordination was reinforced while, simultaneously, the possibility of freedom from a defective femaleness, usually through virginity, was highlighted.[15] Such possibilities are expressed in the Lives of Irish female saints.[16]

These Lives originated in a specific environment. Irish hagiographers were men, and the experiences of the female saint are described and imagined by men. This, with some exceptions, is typical of early medieval Europe.[17] But it must be remembered that these men were individuals. Their perceptions did vary and, although they generally link into a dominant ideology that excluded ordinary women from power, they are not always simple and repay careful, and individual, examination. The ideology in question was strongly influenced, but not completely shaped, by Christianity.[18] Native Irish ideologies played a role as well. Indeed, as the experience of other Western European societies shows, Christianity was not homogeneous. Adaptability was one of its great strengths.[19] In Ireland, the contact between Christianity and native culture created a variegated hybrid that was dominated by clerics and aristocrats.[20] Irish hagiography bears the imprint of an aristocratic, clerical and stratified society that circumscribed the roles of women. They were generally held to be inferior to men and were legally dependants.[21] Motherhood was valued within social structures that empowered men. A woman's honour price, the marker of her social and legal status, was usually half that of her husband, father or male religious superior. This legal inferiority had important consequences. The capacity of women to make contracts was limited; women could not act as witnesses; they had little direct impact on the socio-political level. Does the literary portrayal of Brigit, Íte, Samthann and Mo Ninne reflect this reality? Do their identities mirror the perceived roles of women in Irish society?

Their portrayal was not only rooted in Irish culture. They were saints as well as women and were bound by the conventions of the international genre of hagiography. These very conventions liberated the hagiographers for, within the boundaries of subject and style, the aims of hagiography are flexible, ranging from the theological to the political. Irish hagiography was influenced by the local as well as the international and had a close relationship with the vernacular Irish sagas that celebrate the deeds of pre-Christian and Christian heroes. The saga hero and the saint are closely related – the saint being the ultimate ecclesiastical hero. Brigit is a major figure in the Middle Irish saga *Cath Almaine* (The Battle of Allen).[22] Patrick and the pagan hero Cú Chulainn form an unlikely alliance in the Middle Irish tale *Siaburcharpat Con Culaind* (The Phantom Chariot of Cú Chulainn).[23] The cult of

Brigit benefited from such interactions: she is a saint-hero and this sets her apart from other women.

Ordinary lives?

How far was she set apart? The answer lies in her hagiographical dossier. The two contenders for being the earliest extant saint's Life in Irish hagiography certainly celebrate Brigit. Both texts are in Latin: the Life of Brigit written by the Kildare cleric Cogitosus, at some time around the middle of the seventh century, and the anonymous Life known as *Vita Prima*.[24] The latter, even if it is not as early as Cogitosus (and it may be earlier), contains significant seventh-century material.[25] These two Lives complement each other. Kildare is as much Cogitosus's hero as Brigit and he gives a valuable snapshot of its political ambitions. In contrast, *Vita Prima* was the trendsetter for the later literary development of the cult. It gives us an extended heroic biography of Brigit, one that is even further developed in the ninth-century Old Irish Life of Brigit, *Bethu Brigte*.[26] The term heroic biography has been used by mythologists and anthropologists to describe the life cycle of the hero from birth to death and it is eminently applicable to a saint.[27]

Her status as a hero is clear from the outset of *Vita Prima*. This is announced by a 'resounding' chariot, a fairly popular motif in Irish hagiography whose first appearance is in *Vita Prima*.[28] Here, Brigit's father and her pregnant mother, travelling in a chariot, pass a druid and his servants. The druid remarks that the chariot is resounding *sub rege* 'under a king'. This reflects the future greatness of Brigit; the saint is separated from ordinary women just as the king is from ordinary men. It might be argued that the resounding chariot points up a basic paganism in the cult of Brigit – after all, a druid interprets the event. His presence could equally be the result of the fact that Brigit was supposed to have been born into a pagan Ireland. However, the calling out of the chariot could, and probably should, be linked with the screaming of the Lia Fáil, a stone slab and symbol of sovereignty, under the feet of the rightful king of Tara.[29] A motif of undoubtedly native origin is used to express the power of a Christian saint.

Brigit has other unusual characteristics. According to *Vita Prima* and later Lives, Brigit is conceived out of wedlock. Dubthach, her father, is a nobleman while her mother, Broicsech, is a bondmaid.[30]

This is irregular in Irish legal terms. Cogitosus alone describes her parents as married Christians, presumably of equal social standing.[31] In *Vita Prima* the female slave, as mother of the saint, breaks the norms of Irish society, paradoxically highlighting the saint's sanctity.[32] The violation of a taboo serves only to prove its relevance. The extraordinary, by necessity, cannot be the usual. The man who impregnated a bondmaid had to arrange for the rearing of the child on his own,[33] and the son of a bondmaid could not join the ranks of the noble, whatever his paternity.[34] The bondmaid was a unit of exchange rather than a person with the ability to contract. If anything, *Vita Prima* stresses the servile status of Brigit's mother. We are told how she is sold and undergoes many tribulations before Brigit wins her freedom.[35] In fact, Dubthach thinks of selling his daughter when she displeases him.[36] There is an underlying Christian message: Brigit's mother is an *ancilla* (bondmaid/handmaid). This reminds us of the Virgin Mary who is the *ancilla Domini* (handmaid of the Lord). Brigit, by implication, is a Christ-like figure who can bring freedom to those in bondage.

Brigit frees herself from the possibility of marital bondage. She follows a well-worn literary path in her opposition to marriage, an exceptionally common motif in early Christian writings. The fullest account is in *Bethu Brigte* where, to avoid marriage to an aristocratic suitor, Brigit gouges out one of her eyes. Her brothers are angry because they will lose the lucrative bride-price that formed a central component of the Irish marriage contract.[37] Obviously, the economic loss to a kindred when a female member entered the religious life was considerable and it was probably widely discouraged. One of Brigit's brothers objects and mocks the saint. The result is that his eyes burst apart in his head and his descendants are cursed forever.[38] A very similar incident is described in an anecdote about the Fermoy female saint, Cránait,[39] an incident almost certainly based on Brigit's example. In both cases the mutilation is miraculously temporary. Saints can adopt extraordinary strategies.

Brigit's sanctity is extraordinary. An examination of the careers of other female saints is instructive. Íte was a saint of Dési origin,[40] but patron of the Uí Chonaill Gabra, a dynasty who held lands in what is now Co. Limerick. Her Latin Life, as it stands, is nowhere near as early as the first Brigidine Lives and is dependent on the Brigit traditions.[41] In this *vita*, Íte's parents discourage her celibate vocation. To avoid marriage Íte fasts for three days and three nights against her father.[42] The hunger strike is successful, and reflects a well-known legal redress that the weak could use against the powerful, a redress of native origin.[43] Cleverly, the Life puts it in the context of Íte's battle against the Devil. Thus, an attentive medieval audience would be reminded both of a legal strategy and of Christ's fast for forty days and forty nights in the wilderness. Íte's identity is both local and international.

The legal strategy shows Íte as a suppliant. Íte often adopts what would have been considered appropriate female roles, although as a saint she has more power. One such is that of nurturer and/or mother. The *vita* describes her as *matrona* of the Uí Chonaill Gabra.[44] The term *matrona* carries a different sense from *mater* 'mother'. The Roman *matrona* was a married woman who managed her household and the matronal position was honoured within Roman society. It has been argued by some historians that Christianity revolted against the matronal role.[45] Christian virgins in the late Roman Empire wore the veil of the married woman or even dressed as a *matrona*, simultaneously claiming high status and flouting expectations.[46] It is difficult to be certain how far the Irish made distinctions between the *matrona* and other types of women. However, as has been shown, the term was used for 'mother goddess' in pre-Christian Gaul.[47] The word is not particularly common in Hiberno-Latin and when used most usually refers to a married woman.[48] Íte was not married but she did metaphorically manage the household of her people. Moreover, the Life only uses *matrona* when referring to Íte and, specifically, in reference to her relationship with the Uí Chonaill Gabra. The one exception, where it is prophesied that she will be the *matrona* of many on Doomsday, is an extension of the saint's relationship with the Uí Chonaill.[49]

It seems that Íte's hagiographer viewed the *matrona* as partly fulfilling the role of the *muime* (foster mother). *Matrona* and *muime* do not form an identity. The usual Latin term for foster mother is *nutrix*. However, there is an overlap between *muime* and *matrona* in Íte's case. Foster motherhood did not carry the direct biological weight of motherhood, something appropriate for a virgin saint. Furthermore, although the Uí Chonaill are Íte's clients in a religious sense, the political language of lordship and clientship was generally applied only to men. The term *matrona* covers the grey area and gives Íte the status of an overlord without violating the gendered language of lordship. Íte appears as a foster mother elsewhere and it formed a prominent aspect of her cult. In the Lives of Brendan she is that saint's foster mother,[50] and she fosters other saints as well.[51] Perhaps the best example of Íte as fosterer is in the Old Irish poem *Ísucán*.[52] The poem portrays her as the foster mother of the baby Jesus who nestles at her breast. As E. G. Quin has pointed out, the theme is the commonly attested one of the child Jesus *in sinu sanctorum*.[53] The poem may be the earliest evidence for this perception of Íte. It considerably predates the Latin *vita*. The relevance to Íte is striking and it resonates with her political relationships as the poem contains legal metaphors of lordship which could, perhaps, be read subversively.[54] Yet Íte is portrayed as a client of God in the poem rather than as a lord in her own right. The poem celebrates a religious, not a secular, clientship and Íte's spirituality is imagined in ascetic Christian terms. It would be unwise to view Íte's matronal identity as having its origins in pagan Ireland or in pagan Celtic religion, despite the term *matrona* (as 'goddess') being attested among the Continental Celts. The Irish are unlikely to have been aware of the Continental Celtic practice but would have been knowledgeable about the Roman/early Christian background. Therefore, Íte as *matrona* and *muime* is most easily explained by the realities of Christian Ireland and, possibly, the subversion of those realities.

These realities form the backdrop to the Latin Life of St Samthann. Unlike Brigit, Íte and Mo Ninne, she was not a church founder. Instead she was an eighth-century abbess of Clonbroney, an already existing monastery.[55] Her Life recalls a real historical person in a way that the other Lives of women saints do not. She also figures in near-contemporary documents.[56] Samthann's less spectacular sanctity seems more grounded in the experiences of religious women than Brigit's career. There is an unusual emphasis, for an Irish saint's Life, on the actual running of a monastery. Samthann's Life also intersects with the more common images of female sanctity. Like Íte and Brigit, her guardian – in this case her foster father – tries to force her into marriage. Unlike these two saints, Samthann does not openly object. Only the dramatic intervention of God at the opening of the *vita* saves Samthann. He brings down a fire from heaven that appears to burn the house where Samthann is staying. The household rushes to prevent the blaze. Meanwhile, Samthann flees in the confusion, escaping the consummation of her marriage for a religious vocation.[57]

There is a similar emphasis on the religious life in the Lives of Mo Ninne, the founder of Killeevy, but the slant is different and profoundly idealized. There are two Latin Lives of this saint. The later of the two Lives was written by Conchubranus in the middle of the eleventh century and it was preserved by the English foundation of Burton-on-Trent.[58] The earlier Life can be plausibly dated to the late seventh or early eighth century and forms the basis of the text preserved in *Codex Salmanticensis*.[59] It is linked to the hagiography of Brigit, a major figure in the early Life. Brigit is downgraded and turned into a disciple of Mo Ninne by Conchubranus. The latter makes free use of Scottish and English materials to create a composite saint. Along with Irish churches he credits Mo Ninne with at least four English and seven Scottish foundations, including Edinburgh, Dumbarton and the castle of Sterling.[60] None is remotely credible.

In the *Codex Salmanticensis* Life and in the *vita* by Conchubranus, Mo Ninne's depiction as abbess is central; so is her pastoral role within the religious community. Conchubranus's Life places a great weight on the importance of virginity, indeed unusually so. For Conchubranus, virginity literally frees Mo Ninne from female defects. He describes how she has the soul of a man in the body of a woman, drawing on and extending a passage from the earlier Life.[61] Even this body is hardened by Mo Ninne's asceticism and she is enabled to engage in physically demanding agricultural activity. Virginity is power in this exceptionally gender-conscious text, a text that draws on patristic literature, later Christian commentators, as well as the earlier Life. The main identities of Conchubranus's saint are the Christian ones of church founder and virgin. It would seem then that the identities of Brigit, Íte, Samthann and Mo Ninne are both gendered and Christian. Brigit was very much a heroic saint and her identity overlapped with that of the hero. She stands apart from the other female saints and has the most complex identity. The question remains as to how far these identities empowered the female saints and to what extent this empowerment may be seen as non-Christian.

Female authority

Despite their status as saints, Íte and Samthann, in particular, operate in a female sphere. They spend much of their time supervising their respective monasteries and guiding nuns. The saints do negotiate with kings, and they do have political overtones to their careers, but these pale into insignificance beside the activities of Brigit or even Mo Ninne. Brigit's career resembles that of a male saint such as Patrick; she is on a par with men. In a passage in *Vita Prima* it is Brigit rather than Patrick who is able to save one of Patrick's bishops from an unjustified accusation of paternity.[62] This suggests that Brigit is a figure of authority. Such female authority was more viable in the early Middle Ages when the role of religious women was less defined.[63] The careers of Hild, abbess of Whitby, or of Radegund, Merovingian queen and later abbess, are instructive. Brigit, as a female saint, fits well into an age of powerful abbesses and double-monasteries of monks and nuns.

Kildare appears to have been the only long-term viable Irish double-monastery. Killeedy was an early double-monastery, much like Kildare, but there is little evidence for the survival of the monastery of nuns, as opposed to monks. Killeevy and Clonbroney were communities of nuns from their inception. It is not surprising, then, that Kildare's concern with its female founder spills over into a greater interest in questions involving female authority than might otherwise be the case. No doubt this is one of the reasons that Brigit is given the status of a bishop in *Bethu Brigte*, a status not given to any other Irish woman, as the Life emphasizes.[64] As impressive as this is, the Life goes on to say that Brigit cannot fulfil priestly sacramental duties.

Brigit's authority is underlined by the use of fire imagery – an imagery that is common in Irish literature.[65] Fire is a powerful symbol in any religion and it easily adapted itself to the Christian fire of God.[66] In *Vita Prima*, fire imagery serves to identify Brigit as the hero. We should beware of seeing a solar deity here. The great Charles Plummer even went so far as to find a solar deity in the undoubtedly historical Samthann by fancifully suggesting that the Irish may have etymologized her name as 'summer fire'.[67] This tendency has been reinforced, in the case of Brigit, by Gerald of Wales's famous description of the perpetual fire at Kildare attended by nineteen nuns.[68] This is one of the most commonly quoted features of Brigit's cult, even though it is not attested before the twelfth century. Fire is not necessarily pagan. After all, the apostles were visited by tongues of fire at Pentecost and this did not transform them into sun gods.

Brigit is consistently portrayed in heroic terms. This heroism could be political. Her cult was partly linked to the fortunes of the North Leinster kings,[69] and the saint is portrayed as an active patron of the Leinstermen. In the hymn, 'Brigit bé bithmaith',[70] which is not later than the eighth century, Brigit is called a *nóib di Laignib* (saint of the Leinstermen).[71] Brigit consistently protects and advises her people in time of conflict. In another Old Irish poem, usually called 'Hail Brigit', Brigit's patronage of the Leinster kings is further underlined. She is the *banfhlaith* (sovereign queen) of the Leinstermen, a paradoxical description.[72] Unlike Merovingian Frankia, Ireland did not produce powerful and influential queens. Figures such as Queen Medb are strictly imaginary. Brigit is a type of Christian virago, capable of adopting roles normally associated with men.[73]

The warrior is one such. The participation of women in battle is criticized in other Irish sources as a pre-Christian perversion that conflicts with maternal duties.[74] Brigit, saint and protector of Leinster, transcends the normal female state. *Vita Prima* emphasizes Brigit's warlike abilities. The saint offers the king of Leinster eternal life and kingship for his descendants, but he chooses victory over his arch-enemies in warfare instead.[75] Later, Brigit is described going into battle before the king of Leinster with fire blazing from her head.[76] The saint is a major character in *Cath Almaine*, a saga account of a battle between the Leinstermen and Uí Néill fought in 722.[77] The narrative describes how Brigit appears above the Leinster army. The opposition of her fellow saint, Colum Cille, is brushed aside. Her role is most explicit in the Yellow Book of Lecan recension where the very sight of an actively threatening Brigit is enough to bring a Leinster victory.[78] The transcendent power of Brigit reaches its apogee here. It is just possible that Brigit's identity as a warrior may owe something to late Latin epic as well as to native traditions. In the *Psychomachia* of Prudentius the virtues and vices are pictured as female warriors and, later, the Anglo-Saxon Aldhelm would describe his female heroes as warriors in *De Virginitate*. Both of these, of course, drew on the classical works of Homer and Virgil.

The warlike ardour of Brigit is not often reflected in the dossiers of the other female saints. There are some examples, however. Íte, who is a notable fighter of demons,[79] successfully prays for her adopted the people, the Uí Chonaill, in a battle where they are outnumbered.[80] The battle is recorded for 552 in the Annals of Ulster, perhaps reflecting that this was a well-known legend when the annals were first written down in the sixth and seventh centuries. The entry in the Annals of Ulster is as follows: 'Bellum Cuilne in quo ceciderunt Corcu Oche Muman orationibus Itae Cluano' (the battle of Cuilenn in which the Corco Óche of Munster fell through the prayers of Íte of Cluain [Killeedy]). Here, the Corco Óche, neighbours of the Uí Chonaill, are clearly the losers. Yet, in the account of a battle between the Uí Chonaill and the Corco Óche in the Laud genealogies, the Corco Óche are victorious.[81] The Laud account is not later than the ninth century and probably dates between 700 and 750. The difference between the two accounts may represent the absorption of the saint's cult by the Uí Chonaill, a major dynasty, and the displacement of the weaker Corco Óche. This is completed in the *vita* version of the battle where the Uí Chonaill are the foster people of Íte and she is their *matrona*. Her support for them in battle, however retrospective it might be, is an extension of her matronal duties. The *vita* magnifies the battle. The Uí Chonaill are described as being opposed by a great multitude of enemies from West Munster – a most impressive enemy.

Samthann is far less active. In her Life, the hagiographer refers to a battle between Connacht and the neighbouring kingdom of Tethbae.[82] A devotee of hers goes into battle against the Connachtmen without Samthann's blessing and dies. But Samthann does not totally desert him and, through her prayers, she ensures his soul's salvation. The contrast between armed conflict and prayer is paralleled by the opposition of male and female. While the opposition is gendered, it does not serve as a critique of battle. Samthann's 'femaleness' necessitates the polarity. There is a similar incident in Íte's Life involving the saint's brother-in-law, the artificer Beóán. Like Samthann's follower he goes to battle without his patron's support and dies. Íte has mercy and resurrects him and he goes on to become the father of a saint.

Brigit is not only a warleader. She is also an Irish equivalent of the Virgin Mary. The early archaic Fothairt poem, 'A Eochaid

Airtt Fuath', declares: 'Bid ala Maire már-Choimded mathair' (she will be another Mary, mother of the great Lord).[83] 'Brigit bé bithmaith' describes her as *in máthir Ísu* (the mother of Jesus).[84] Another hymn, 'Ní car Brigit búadach bith', claims that Brigit shares equal status with Mary in heaven.[85] The hagiographers are similarly explicit. Brigit is identified as Mary in *Vita Prima* and *Bethu Brigte*.[86] The late Middle Irish Life in the Book of Lismore drives home the point, stating *Is sí Muire na nGaeidhel* (she is the Mary of the Irish).[87] Such glorification did not reflect on Irish women in general. Like Mary, Brigit was regarded as exceptional rather than representative. The sustained comparison with Mary is not used to anything like the same degree for the other female saints.

Mo Ninne comes closest. The collection of materials relating to the saint at Burton-on-Trent includes two Latin hymns, 'Deum deorum dominum' and 'Audite fratres facta'.[88] These hymns do not seem to contain any internal evidence which might suggest a firm date. There is no reason to push their date back as far as the earliest Life. The sentiments of these compositions are along the same line as the Brigidine hymns, and they probably ultimately originate in the same tradition. In 'Deum deorum dominum' the saint is compared to Mary.[89] There is a similar comparison in 'Audite fratres facta'.[90] Mo Ninne imitates Mary but she is not a second Mary. *Félire Óengusso* describes her as *siur Maire máre* (sister of great Mary).[91] She is a sister of Mary, not a Mary reborn. In a sense Brigit is a Mary reborn, as her designation 'Mary of the Irish' makes clear. Brigit tops the hierarchy of female saints. Thus, Íte's hagiographer is content to declare that Íte is a *secunda Brigida* 'second Brigit'.[92] There could be no more flattering comparison.

Conclusion

Brigit is the most prominent of the female saints and the most powerful. She alone is given an extended heroic birth tale, fights in battle and is imagined gaining episcopal status. These attributes, combined with the confusion concerning her chronology, have led people to see in Brigit the direct descendant of a Celtic goddess, clothed in the disguise of a Christian saint.[93] Most tellingly, the Old Irish glossary *Sanas Cormaic* mentions the three divine sisters named Brigit, daughters of the Dagda. This threefold divinity was so important that, according to *Sanas Cormaic*, the name 'Brigit' could be used as a synonym for goddess.[94] Moreover, the pan-Celtic nature of dedications and geographical sites associated with Brigit are impressive.[95] It seems indisputable that a goddess named Brigit, or the like, was honoured among Celtic communities.

It is another thing, however, to try to match the characteristics of the goddess with the saint. It is often pointed out that Brigit is associated with cattle and agricultural miracles and that her feast-day on 1 February is the same date as the pre-Christian agricultural festival of *imbolc*.[96] Yet, other saints are also associated with cattle miracles and this is hardly surprising in an agricultural society where cattle acted as a major form of wealth and marker of status. Irish saints' Lives have a high proportion of what could be considered folkloristic miracles, magical stories and nature miracles, just the type that we find in the Lives of Brigit. This would seem to be an inheritance from a pre-Christian culture that valued such things, and these inheritances shaped Irish Christianity. It does not turn saints into pagan gods and goddesses.

It is very likely that Brigit's cult represents a successful and complex fusion of Christian and native. Thus, the saint is both the healer of cattle and a second Mary. Her feast-day may have been attracted to that of the pre-Christian festival through this fusion. It might be best to view Brigit's cult as one that grew up around a saint named after a divine figure, gaining many adherents for that reason. The pre-Christian element of the cult was probably particularly important in its early phases and it must have imbued the figure of the Christian saint with extra power. But while the status of Brigit arguably had pre-Christian roots, this is expressed in Christian terms and her essential identity is a Christian one. It is an open question as to how far Irish hagiographers were aware of the origins of their creation. For them Brigit was surely a Christian saint and the goddess no more than a distant memory. Cogitosus believed that the tomb he venerated in Kildare contained her bones.[97]

It might be more useful to look at the identity of the female saints in gendered terms. Sanctity allowed women to escape the straitjacket of gender yet this sanctity could be expressed in ways that mirrored the position of women in Irish society. Íte's role as a *matrona* draws on ideas of the woman managing the household. This does not imply female autonomy. Indeed, as Íte points out to another woman, it is often better to have male support because 'multum demones insidiantur nostro sexui' (demons greatly beguile our sex).[98] However, other aspects of these saints – their ability to perform miracles and interact successfully with the secular world – did not generally reflect on perceptions of 'ordinary' women. While the political role of women in the shifting marriage alliances of early Ireland was undoubtedly important, women were not seen as the agents in this relationship. Their influence was covert. The overt influence of the female saints was unusual. Thus, the image of the 'ordinary' woman and the image of the female saint do not constitute a two-way street. The female saints did things which women did not do. The female saint, and above all, Brigit, is a woman liberated by sanctity. Through sanctity these saints transcended the perceived limitations of their gender and gained the identity of Christian heroes.

Notes

I would like to thank Professor Joseph Nagy for helpful comments on earlier drafts of this paper.

1   Mary Condron, *The Serpent and the Goddess* (New York, 1989).
2   Robert Graves, *The White Goddess: A Historical Grammar of Poetic Myth* (London, 1961).
3   Julian May, *The Saga of the Exiles*, 4 vols. (London, 1981–4).
4   Kim McCone, *Pagan Past and Christian Present in Early Irish Literature* (Maynooth, 1990), ch. 7.
5   Séamas Ó Catháin, *The Festival of Brigit: Celtic Goddess and Holy Woman* (Blackrock, 1995).
6   Dorothy Ann Bray, 'Saint Brigit and the fire from heaven', *Études celtiques*, 29 (1992), 105–13; *eadem*, 'The manly spirit of St Monenna', in R. Black et al. (eds.), *Celtic Connections: Proceedings of the Tenth International Congress of Celtic studies*, i (East Linto, 1999), 171–81.
7   For some idea of the range of extant materials: Charles Plummer (ed.), *Miscellanea Hagiographica Hibernica* (Brussels, 1925); James F. Kenney (ed.), *The Sources for the Early History of Ireland: Ecclesiastical. An Introduction and Guide* (New York, 1929); Pádraig Ó Riain (ed.), *Corpus genealogiarum sanctorum Hiberniae* (Dublin, 1985); J. H. Bernard and R. Atkinson (eds.), *Liber Hymnorum*, Henry Bradshaw Society 13–14, 2 vols. (London, 1897–8).

8   These three Annals of Ulster dates are suspect: Séan Mac Airt and
    Gearóid Mac Niocaill (eds.), *The Annals of Ulster (to A.D. 1131)*
    (Dublin, 1983).

9   The first date is from the Annals of Ulster; the second comes from the
    Annals of Inisfallen: Seán Mac Airt (ed,), *The Annals of Inisfallen*
    (Dublin, 1951).

10 The date is from the Annals of Ulster; a second obit is interpolated
    for 519.

11 Samthann has a trustworthy obit in the Annals of Ulster.

12 Two other saints might have been considered: Lasair and Attracta.
    The Life of Lasair of Achad Beithe is late; that of Attracta of Cell
    Sáile cannot properly be studied until the site of Cell Sáile and the
    chronology of the saint's life is determined.

13 Joan Wallach Scott, *Gender and the Politics of History* (New York,
    1988), esp. 15–27.

14 Joyce Salisbury, 'The Latin doctors of the church on sexuality',
    Journal of Medieval History, 12 (1986), 279–89; *eadem*, *Church
    Fathers: Independent Virgins* (London, 1991), 4–58; Peter Brown, *The
    Body and Society: Men, Women and Sexual Renunciation in Early
    Christianity* (New York, 1988); John Anson, 'The female transvestite
    in early monasticism: the origin and development of a motif', *Viator*,
    5 (1969), 1–32; Vern L. Bullough, 'Transvestites in the Middle Ages',
    American Journal of Sociology, 79 (1974), 1391–4.

15 Noticeable in Paul, Gal. 3: 28 in contrast with Col. 3: 18; discussion
    by William Walker, '1 Corinthians 11: 12–16 and Paul's views regard-
    ing women', *Journal of Biblical Literature*, 94 (1975), 94–110. See also
    Jerome, letter 22 to Eustochium, in *Patrologia Latina*, xxii, col.
    325–1197; Ambrose, *De Virginitate*, in *Patrologia Latina*, xvi, col.
    187–232.

16 Elva Johnston, 'Transforming women in Irish hagiography', *Peritia*, 9
    (1995), 198–220; Bray, 'Manly spirit', 171–81.

17 An exception is the Life of St Radegund by Baudonivia. For a study
    of Radegund, Etienne Delaruelle, 'Sainte Radegonde, son type de
    sainteté et la chrétienté de son temps', *Études Mérovingiennes: Actes des
    journées de Poitiers* (Paris, 1953), 67–74.

18 The relationship between the two has been subject to controversy.
    The dominant position is summed up in Donnchadh Ó Corráin,
    'Nationality and kingship in pre-Norman Ireland', in T. W. Moody
    (ed.), *Nationality and the Pursuit of National Independence* (Belfast,
    1978), 1–35.

19 Judith Herrin, *The Formation of Christendom* (London, 1987), 90.

20 Ó Corráin, 'Nationality and kingship', 1–35.

21 For an overview, Fergus Kelly, *A Guide to Early Irish Law* (Dublin,
    1988), 68–79. Recent studies include: Donnchadh Ó Corráin

'Women and the law in early Ireland', in Mary O'Dowd and Sabine Wichert (eds.), *Chattel, Servant or Citizen: Women's Status in Church, State and Society* (Belfast, 1995), 45–57; Lisa M. Bitel, *Land of Women: Tales of Sex and Gender from Early Ireland* (Ithaca, NY, and London, 1996); Bart Jaski, 'Marriage laws in Ireland and on the Continent in the Early Middle Ages', in C. E. Meek and M. K. Simms (eds.), *'The Fragility of her Sex'? Medieval Irish Women in their European Context* (Dublin, 1996), 16–42.

22   Pádraig Ó Riain (ed.), *Cath Almaine*, Mediaeval and Modern Irish Series, 25 (Dublin, 1978).

23   Diplomatic edn. in R. I. Best and Osborn Bergin (eds.), *Lebor na hUidre: Book of the Dun Cow* (Dublin, 1929), 278–87.

24   For Cogitosus, *Acta Sanctorum*, 1 February (Brussels, 1658), 135–41 (henceforth Cogitosus); translated by Seán Connolly and Jean-Michel Picard, 'Cogitosus: Life of St Brigit', *Journal of the Royal Society of Antiquaries*, 117 (1987), 5–27. *Vita Prima* is edited by John Colgan, *Triadis thaumaturgae acta* (Louvain, 1647), 517–45 (henceforth *Vita Prima*); trans. S. Connolly, '*Vita Prima Sanctae Brigitae*', *Journal of the Royal Society of Antiquaries*, 119 (1989), 14–49. I will use Colgan's section numbers for *Vita Prima*. For Cogitosus, I will give the pagination from the *Acta Sanctorum*, followed by Connolly and Picard's section number.

25   Richard Sharpe, 'Vitae S. Brigitae: the oldest texts', *Peritia*, 1 (1982), 81–106, argues that the *Vita Prima* is the oldest Life; Kim McCone, 'Brigit in the seventh century: a saint with three lives?', *Peritia*, 1 (1982), 107–45, gives the priority to Cogitosus; David Howlett, 'Vita I Sanctae Brigitae', *Peritia*, 12 (1998), 1–23, has argued for the seventh-century date and priority of *Vita Prima*.

26   Donncha Ó hAodha (ed.), *Bethu Brigte* (Dublin, 1978). The later Middle Irish Lives come from the same tradition: for the first Irish Life see Whitley Stokes (ed.), *Three Middle Irish Homilies on the Lives of Saints Patrick, Brigit and Columba*, (Calcutta, 1877), 50–82; idem (ed.), *Lives of the Saints from the Book of Lismore*, 2 vols. (Oxford, 1890), i. 34–51.

27   Jan de Vries, *Heroic Song and Heroic Legend*, trans. B. J. Timmer (London, 1963).

28   *Vita Prima*, §2; for other examples, Charles Plummer (ed.), *Vitae Sanctorum Hiberniae*, 2 vols. (Oxford, 1910), II. 4, §v (Comgall); 141, §ii (Máedóc); 166, §v (Mo Chóemóc) (henceforth *VSH*); another example concerns Ciarán of Clonmacnoise, Stokes (ed.), *Lives from the Book of Lismore*, vol. 1, p. 120, ll. 4013–17.

29   Tomás Ó Broin, 'Lia Fáil: fact and fiction in the tradition', *Celtica*, 21 (1990), 393–401; Johnston, 'Transforming women', 206–7.

30   *Vita Prima*, §1.

31 Cogitosus, 129 (*recte* 135), §1.

32 Similar tales are related of Ailbe, *VSH*, I. 46, §i; Finbarr, in Charles Plummer (ed), *Bethada Náem nÉrenn: Lives of Irish Saints*, 2 vols. (Oxford, 1922), I, 11–12 §i. It is, of course, common in many mythologies.

33 Kathleen Mulchrone, 'The rights and duties of women with regard to the education of their children', in Rudolf Thurneysen et al. (eds.), *Studies in Early Irish Law* (Dublin, 1936), 191–2.

34 Kelly, *Guide*, 95–6.

35 *Vita Prima*, §15.

36 Ibid., §16.

37 *Bethu Brigte*, §§14–15.

38 Ibid., §15. See also *Vita Prima*, §19.

39 Edited by Plummer in *Miscellanea*, 160–3.

40 The Dési dominated what is now Co. Waterford.

41 Edited in *VSH*, II. 116–30.

42 Ibid., 117, §v.

43 D. A. Binchy, 'A pre-Christian survival in medieval Irish hagiography', in Dorothy Whitelock et al. (eds.), *Ireland in Early Medieval Europe* (Cambridge, 1982), 165–78.

44 *VSH*, II. 118, §vii (twice), §viii, 119, §ix, 128, §xxxiii (twice), 129, §xxxiii, 130, §xxxvi (twice). For a fuller discussion, see Elva Johnston, 'Íte: patron of her people?', *Peritia*, 14 (2000), 421–8.

45 Jo Ann McNamara, '*Matres Patriae/Matres ecclesiae*: women of the Roman Empire', in Renate Bridenthal and Claudia Koonz (eds.), *Becoming Visible: Women in European History* (Boston, 2nd edn 1987), 118. For a discussion of veiling in an Irish context, see Máirín Ní Dhonnchadha, '*Caillech* and other terms for veiled women in medieval Irish texts', *Éigse*, 28 (1994–5), 71–96.

46 Aline Rousselle, 'Body politics in ancient Rome', in Pauline Schmitt Pantel (ed.), *From Ancient Goddesses to Christian Saints*, trans. Arthur Goldhammer, *A History of Women in the West*, i (Cambridge, MA, 1992), 315, has pointed out that Christian women in general adopted the matronal role.

47 For the Continental Celtic belief, Proinsias Mac Cana, *Celtic Mythology* (London, 1970), 49–50.

48 Examples in Antony Harvey, Kieran Devine and Francis J. Smith (compilers), *Royal Irish Academy Archive of Celtic-Latin Literature*, first (preliminary) CD-Rom edn. (Turnhout, 1994).

49 *VSH*, II. 118 §vi.

50 There are several recensions of the *Vitae*: see *VSH*, I. 98–151; also W. W. Heist, *Vitae Sanctorum Hiberniae ex codice olim Salmanticensi nunc Bruxellensi* (Brussels, 1965), 56–78.

51 Íte is described as St Mo Chóemóg's foster mother in *VSH*, II. 167, §viii, 170, §xiv.
52 The poem is contained in the notes to *Félire Óengusso* but is edited separately by Gerard Murphy, *Early Irish Lyrics: Eighth to Twelfth Century* (Oxford, 1956), 26–9; by E. G. Quin, 'The early Irish poem Isucán', *Cambridge Medieval Celtic Studies*, 1 (1981), 39–52.
53 Ibid., 51.
54 Ibid., 40–1.
55 Her Life is edited in *VSH*, II. 253–61.
56 She appears as Samdan in E. J. Gwynn and W. J. Purton (eds.), 'The monastery of Tallaght', *Proceedings of the Royal Irish Academy*, (C) 29 (1911–12), 149–51, §61.
57 *VSH*, II. 253–4, §ii.
58 Ed. Mario Esposito, '*Conchubrani Vita Sanctae Monennae*', *Proceedings of the Royal Irish Academy*, (C) 28 (1910), 202–38; reprinted in Mario Esposito, '*Conchubrani Vita Sanctae Monennae*', in M. Lapidge (ed.), *Irish Books and Learning in Mediaeval Europe* (London, 1990), 202–38; ed. with a trans. by the Ulster Society for Medieval Latin Studies, 'The Life of St Monenna by Conchubranus: part 1', *Seanchas Ard Mhacha*, 9 (1979), 250–73, part 2, 10/1 (1980–1), 117–41, part 3, 10/2 (1982), 426–54.
59 Ed. Heist, *Vitae Sanctorum Hiberniae ex Codice . . .*, 83–95. Mario Esposito, 'The sources for Conchubranus' Life of St Monenna', in *Irish Books and Learning*, 73–8, dates the text to 600 × 624; Johnston, 'Transforming women', suggests 665 × 690 or sometime soon after.
60 *Conchubrani Vita*, 209, 210, 230, 233–4.
61 *Vitae Sanctorum ex Codice*, 89, §19; *Conchubrani Vita*, 228, §1; discussed by Johnston, 'Transforming women', 210–13; Bray, 'Manly spirit', 171–81.
62 *Vita Prima*, §39.
63 Jane Tibbetts Schulenburg, 'Women's monastic communities 500–1100: patterns of expansion and decline', in Judith M. Bennett et al. (eds.), *Sisters and Workers in the Middle Ages* (Chicago, 1989), 208–39.
64 *Bethu Brigte*, §19; discussed by Johnston, 'Transforming women', 214–15.
65 McCone, *Pagan Past*, 161–78.
66 Bray, 'Saint Brigit and the fire from heaven', 105–13.
67 Plummer, 'Introduction', in *VSH*, I, lxxxviii.
68 John J. O'Meara (ed.), *The History and Topography of Ireland* (Atlantic Highlands, NJ, 1982), §§67–9.
69 Felim Ó Briain, 'The hagiography of Leinster', in John Ryan (ed.), *Féilsgríbhinn Eoin Mhic Néill* (Dublin, 1940), 33–42.
70 John Strachan and Whitley Stokes (eds.), *Thesaurus Palaeohibernicus*, 2

vols. (Cambridge and Halle a.S, 1901–3, repr. Dublin 1975), ii. 323–36.

[71]   Ibid., 326, l. 8.

[72]   Kuno Meyer (ed.), *Hail Brigit: An Old Irish Poem on the Hill of Alenn* (Dublin and Halle, 1911), 12, l. 2.

[73]   Isidore, *Etymologiae*, xi, ch. 2, §§21–2; Joan Cadden, *Meanings of Sex Difference in the Middle Ages: Medicine, Science and Culture* (Cambridge, 1993), 205–6.

[74]   A classic statement is Kuno Meyer, *Cáin Adamnáin: An Old Irish Treatise of the Law of Adamnán* (Oxford, 1905), §3.

[75]   *Vita Prima*, §90.

[76]   Ibid.

[77]   Ó Riain, 'Introduction', in *Cath Almaine*, xxiii–xxvii.

[78]   *Cath Almaine*, 21.

[79]   *VSH*, II. 117, §v, 119, §xi.

[80]   Ibid., 128–9, §xxxiii.

[81]   Kuno Meyer (ed.), 'The Laud [610] genealogies and tribal histories', *ZCP*, 8 (1911), 307-9.

[82]   VSH, II. 256–7, §xiii.

[83]   M. A. O'Brien (ed.), *Corpus genealogiarum Hiberniae*, i (Dublin, 1962), 80.

[84]   *Thesaurus palaeohibernicus*, ii. 325, l. 6.

[85]   Ibid., 349, ll. 105–6.

[86]   *Vita Prima*, §14; *Bethu Brigte*, §11.

[87]   *Lives of the Saints from the Book of Lismore*, i. 51, l. 1705.

[88]   Ed. Esposito, *Conchubrani Vita*, 239–42 (Deum deorum dominum), 242–4 (Audite fratres facta).

[89]   Stanza 15, 22.

[90]   Stanza 12.

[91]   *Martyrology of Oengus*, 161.

[92]   *VSH*, II. 130, §xxxvi.

[93]   Mac Cana, *Celtic Mythology*, 34–5.

[94]   Kuno Meyer (ed.), *Sanas Cormaic: An Old Irish Glossary Compiled by Cormac Úa Cuilennáin King-Bishop of Cashel in the Tenth-Century Edited from the Copy in the Yellow Book of Lecan*, Anecdota from Irish Manuscripts, 5 (Halle and Dublin, 1913, repr. Felinfach, 1994), §150.

[95]   E. G. Bowen, 'The cult of St Brigid', *Studia Celtica*, 8 (1973), 33–47.

[96]   Mac Cana, *Celtic Mythology*, 34–5.

[97]   Cogitosus, 141, §32.

[98]   *VSH*, II. 124, §xxiv.

4

Saxon or Celt? Cædmon, 'The Seafarer' and the Irish tradition

MARK ATHERTON

'Saxon or Celt?' she continued, laughing in the darkness.[1]

In E. M. Forster's novel *Howard's End*, Margaret Schlegel stands one dark evening on an old castle mound in the Welsh border country and shouts out the challenge of a medieval border guard: 'Saxon or Celt?' She is heard, of course, by the disapproving Charles Wilcox, who half recognizes the irony of her repartee, since the connotations of 'prosaic Saxon' and 'visionary Celt' were commonplace by the late Victorian and Edwardian periods.[2] With his Saxon name, Charles Wilcox is the pragmatist, the philistine and the businessman, the one who favours 'things as they are', whereas Margaret Schlegel represents the Romantic;[3] she is the artist and idealist striving for 'things as they ought to be'. In his playful irony, Forster the novelist thus aligns the associations of 'Saxon' and 'Celt' with other pairs of opposites which he sees as characterizing the spiritual state of England in his own time. His use of the term 'Celt' raises questions not only of identity but also of mentality, personal expression and spiritual attitude.

But what of the 'Saxon' element? According to the historian Bede, writing in the early eighth century, the island of Britain consisted of four national groups: English, Irish, British and Picts; each had their own language, but all were linked by Latin, the language of the Church. Throughout this period, Latin, or 'Book-Latin' as it was called, remained the main medium by which both texts and ideas were transmitted from one culture to the next. Given the geographical proximity to Brittany, Cornwall, Wales, Scotland and Ireland and connections with Irish centres of Hiberno-Latin on the continent of Europe, it seems likely that

Celtic ideas and ways of thinking could have passed into the religious literature of England.

Let us try a test. Look now at two passages of Anglo-Saxon literature. Both were very popular at the time; both were probably composed in Latin, but existed in English. The one has never fallen out of circulation, for it was copied widely by scribes throughout the Middle Ages and printed in editions in the early modern period, the other was widely read from the tenth century until at least a hundred years after the Norman Conquest.

The first passage, from Bede's *Ecclesiastical History* (written in 734), is the account of how Paulinus and the Roman mission from Canterbury converted the Anglo-Saxon Edwin, king of Northumbria, to Christianity in the year 627. As Bede tells it, Edwin summons a council of his principal advisers to discuss the acceptance of the new religion. While Coifi the pagan priest speaks first and gives a materialist reason for accepting the new teachings as a way of gaining greater favour and success, one of the other counsellors is more philosophical; for him Christianity is a way of gaining greater certainty and knowledge:

> Another of the king's men signified his agreement with this prudent argument, and went on to say: 'Your Majesty, when we compare the present life of man on earth with that time of which we have no knowledge, it seems to me like the swift flight of a single sparrow through the banqueting-hall where you are sitting at dinner with your thanes and counsellors. In the midst there is a comforting fire to warm the hall; outside, the storms of winter rain or snow are raging. This sparrow flies swiftly in through one door of the hall, and out through another. While he is inside he is safe from the winter storms; but after a few moments of comfort, he vanishes from sight into the wintry world from which he came. Even so, man appears on earth for a little while; but of what went before this life or of what follows, we know nothing. Therefore, if this new teaching has brought any more certain knowledge, it seems only right that we should follow it.'[4]

The image of the hall is the epitome of Anglo-Saxon society, the symbol of government, patronage and social stability; it appears often in Old English poetry.[5] Though the flight of the bird is evocative, almost poetic – as we shall see, the image was adapted to good effect by William Wordsworth and D. H. Lawrence – the message of the king's counsellor is practical and down to earth. In Forster's terms, it is 'Saxon'.

Contrast the second passage. Less well-known today, and not part of the accepted canon of Old English literature as reflected in the standard anthologies, it comes from a lively religious prose tradition that may originate in Mercia. First preserved in a manuscript from the south-east of England, the celebrated late tenth-century Vercelli Book,[6] the piece is a striking sermon illustration that was copied, recopied and adapted by later scribes.[7] Employing colourful rhetorical devices based on somewhat bizarre apocryphal sources, the story tells of an anchorite or hermit in the desert who traps a kind of minor devil and forces him to describe the cosmos, hell and finally heaven. In each case lengthy similes are used as a method of description. Here is the passage for heaven, the essential rhetorical device being to paint an elaborate picture of an earthly paradise and then to clinch the description with the simple statement that all this is as nothing compared with one night in heaven:

> Thus that devil said to the anchorite: 'Though there be a mountain all of pure gold at the rising of the sun in Paradise, and it towers over all the earth, and that man were to sit as magnificently as a royal prince above the golden mountain and have the beauty and wisdom of Solomon, and though all the earth were to be given into his power along with the treasures which are throughout all the earth, and though every night a new bride were to be brought to his bed, and she had the beauty of Juno, daughter of Saturn, and though each stone be golden and all the streams flow with honey, and then over the earth there were no enemy, and though in him all special arts and glorious songs were gathered, and though all comforted him and all sweetnesses were brought to him with the fairest of treasures, and though for him then there be continuous summer without any change and he may always live without sorrow; yet if he had been one night in the glory of heaven's kingdom, then he would relinquish what he had earlier experienced in this glory that I described before in favour of the heavenly kingdom in which he had been for one single night . . .[8]

The picture here is one of the Otherworld as found in Irish or Welsh legend. In addition, the enumeration and gradual intensification of the delights of the Otherworld all have parallels in Irish sources,[9] while the rhetoric of the fantastic or the inexpressible and the repetition of the syntax are reminiscent of such Irish texts as the tenth-century *The Evernew Tongue*, discussed elsewhere in this volume. This, it is argued, is the Celtic side of Old English literature.

As in the rest of this book, this chapter will continue to look at the literary texts of the insular world and how they may reflect a distinct type of Christianity, which we may from our perspective term 'Celtic'. But the focus here is on the Anglo-Saxons and their literature. For various literary-historical reasons, I divide the literature into three time periods: (1) the Age of Bede (Northumbria, seventh and eighth centuries) (2) the Reign of Alfred (Wessex and Mercia in the eighth and ninth centuries) (3) the Age of Ælfric (the kingdom of England in the tenth and eleventh centuries). We will look at a selection of texts: first, 'Cædmon's Hymn' and its influence from Bede to Ælfric, then the Vercelli Homilies, and finally the poem 'The Seafarer' from the Exeter Book. We can date 'Cædmon's Hymn' to the first period, but the other two texts are undated; they occur in manuscripts written down in the Age of Ælfric, but they may be quite a bit older. Because much of the literature in Old English survives in manuscripts of the later period, that will be the main orientation point for looking back at the earlier literature.

Cædmon

With its many international connections Northumbria in the age of Bede was an ideal situation for religious, cultural and literary contacts. Within the pages of Bede's *Ecclesiastical History* itself, there is a huge range of cultural influences, mirrored for instance in its diverse collection of Latin poems: hymns, psalms, prayers, epitaphs and lyrics – as well as the Latin version of the interesting Old English poem 'Cædmon's Hymn'. The Cædmon episode related in book IV of Bede's *History* takes place in 680 at the monastery of Whitby under Abbess Hilda (614–80). The daughter of Hereric, the nephew of King Edwin, Hilda had been influenced by the Roman mission of Paulinus from Canterbury but later, when the alternative dynasty of King Oswald and Oswiu came to power, she was also on friendly terms with the Irishman Bishop Aidan from the Ionan mission (IV. 23). In other words, she was in a position to be influenced by both Irish and southern English ecclesiastical centres, which may have some bearing on the interpretation of events.

At IV. 24, Bede tells the full story. The incident of the feast and the guests passing round the harp so that each in turn could perform and entertain the company places the story firmly in a context of courtly poetry improvised in performance. There is a similar incident in the epic *Beowulf*, where the bard (or scop as they were called in Old English) sings a song of creation during a feast in the great hall of Heorot.[10] In Bede's story, Cædmon is a shirker: he misses his turn at the harp, slips away from the feast early and falls asleep in the stable, where suddenly in a dream he sees a man standing there who calls him by name: 'Cædmon,' he said, 'sing me a song.' Here there are faint echoes of biblical stories, the calling of Moses or Samuel (Exodus 3: 5; 1 Samuel 3), and just as Moses questions 'But who am I?', Cædmon protests to his visitor: '"I don't know how to sing," he replied. "It is because I cannot sing that I left the feast and came here." The man who addressed him then said; "But you shall sing to me." "What should I sing about?" he replied.' In reply he is told to 'sing the creation of all things', and in the later Old English version of this Latin tale, we hear 'immediately he began to sing'.[11] In the subsequent lines, Bede gives his Latin paraphrase of the verses that Cædmon composed.

The actual Old English text is not in the oldest manuscript, the Moore Bede; however, a slightly later manuscript, the St Petersburg Bede, also of the eighth century, has the same Latin text, written out as prose but, at the bottom of the page in the margin, a scribe has added the verses in the Old Northumbrian literary dialect. Here is an edited version of the Old Northumbrian text, perhaps the oldest poem in the English language; the text should be read aloud with a strong emphasis on the repeated initial consonants, since the alliteration acts like a rhyme scheme in this kind of verse:[12]

> Nu scylun hergan   hefenricæs Uard,
> Metudes mæcti   end his modgidanc,
> uerc Uuldurfadur,   sue he uundra gihuæs,
> eci Dryctin,   or astlidæ.
> He ærist scop   ælda barnum
> heben til hrofe,   haleg Scepen.
> Tha middungeard moncynnes Uard,
> eci Dryctin   æfter tiadæ
> firum foldu,   Frea allmectig.[13]

The following is a modern English paraphrase (based on Hamer):

> Now we should praise heaven's Guardian
> the Measurer's power and his thought,
> the works of the Father-of-Glory, as He, eternal Lord,
> started every wonder.
> First he created heaven as a roof,
> The holy Maker, for the sons of men.
> Then mankind's Keeper furnished the earth below, the land for men,
> Eternal Master and Lord almighty.

We should note the imagery, diction and metre of the ancient oral-formulaic verse tradition that lies behind the story. The basic line is made up of two half-lines (or 'verses'), linked by fixed patterns of alliteration.[14] The special poetic vocabulary occurs in set formulas, often of one verse in duration. Variations occur, for instance, on the parallel expressions for God: (l. 1) *hefenrices uard* (heaven kingdom's guardian), (l. 7) *moncynnes uard* (mankind's guardian), (ll. 4, 8) *eci Dryhten* (eternal Master), (l. 9) *Frea allmectig* (Lord almighty). The words *Dryhten* and *Frea* are particularly ancient, with parallels in other Germanic languages. Note also the words for divine power (ll. 2, 3).

If we compare passages from 'The Seafarer', composed at an unknown date but copied in the tenth century, we find the same patterns, with similar fixed phrases and traditional ideas, occurring in a passage on creation (ll. 103–5):

> Micel biþ se Meotudes egsa,   for þon hi seo molde oncyrreð;
> se gestaþelade   stiþe grundas,
> eorþan sceattas   ond uprodor.

> Great is the fear of the Lord, before which the earth will turn,
> he established the solid foundations,
> the earth's corners and the sky above.

and a passage on God's power (115–16):

> Wyrd biþ swiþre,
> Meotud meahtigra, þonne ænges monnes gehygd.

> Fate is stronger,
> the Lord mightier, than any mind of man.[15]

Note here *Meotud* (the Measurer) or *uprodor* (heaven above) and the act of creation of the cosmos as sky, earth and abyss. The closing lines of 'The Seafarer' (122b–124) with the phrases *wuldres Ealdor* (prince of glory) and *ece Dryhten* (eternal Lord) also echo the phraseology of 'Cædmon's Hymn':

> þæs sy þam Halgan þonc
> þæt he usic geweorþade, wuldres Ealdor
> ece Dryhten, in ealle tid.

> Therefore thanks be to the Holy One,
> that he has honoured us, the Prince of Glory,
> the eternal Lord, for ever and ever.

Like many traditional poets, Cædmon is portrayed as receiving a divine gift – the ability to compose moving poetry; it is unique, for, as Bede says, 'others after him tried to compose religious poems in English, but none could compare with him'. Cædmon is also 'singularly gifted by God's grace', like a prophet commissioned by God. There are Celtic parallels to the poem, and it has been argued that 'Cædmon' is a British Celtic name; some influence from Irish or British sources is not inconceivable. However, it should also be noted that Hilda, abbess of Whitby, was an Englishwoman, and Bede specifically says that Cædmon composed in English. As I have said, the metre and diction belong to an ancient form of poetry which the Anglo-Saxons appear to have brought with them when they arrived in Britain in the fifth century. In the case of 'Cædmon's Hymn' – along with its parallels in many languages – we have to see an early medieval emphasis on creation, on the divine inspiration of poetry and the suggested parallels between the creativity of the divine artisan and the creativity of the human poet or artist. Perhaps surprisingly, given the cultural situation in Northumbria, its mode of expression is Anglo-Saxon and Old English.

Cædmon and his influence: from Bede to Ælfric

According to Bede, Cædmon is a monastic and didactic poet who practised meditation on the Bible as the source of his poetry and who followed a theological programme, a specific curriculum which covered all the events of Christian history from creation to last judgement:

He sang of the creation of the world, the origin of the human race, and
the whole story of Genesis. He sang of Israel's exodus from Egypt, the
entry into the Promised Land, and many other events of scriptural
history. He sang of the Lord's Incarnation, Passion, Resurrection, and
Ascension into heaven, the coming of the Holy Spirit, and the teaching
of the Apostles. He also made many poems on the terrors of the Last
Judgement, the horrible pains of Hell, and the joys of the Kingdom of
Heaven. In addition to these, he composed several others on the bless-
ings and judgements of God, by which he sought to turn his hearers
from delight in wickedness and to inspire them to love and do good.

This programme is clearly based on the style of catechism recommended by St Augustine of Hippo, just as Bede's many writings
on the Bible were also strongly rooted in that widely influential
father of the Church. The scheme laid out here can be seen as
programmatic for later medieval religious literature.[16] Generally
speaking, we could say that this is the kind of Christianity that was
taught and practised in the early medieval West. In Bede's presen-
tation it is all very clear-cut, a summary of a theology and a
scheme for teaching it. And though some scholars have been
tempted to apply this scheme too closely to the interpretation of
Old English literature, nevertheless a large proportion of the Old
English religious literature that survives is based upon it.[17]

But not all. The scheme did not always work according to plan.
There were problems for those who wanted to create such a teaching programme based on Bede's Augustinian scheme. Books were
expensive and scarce. They could be – and often were – lost,
damaged, destroyed by fire and warfare, especially in the period
from the late eighth century onwards when England came increas-
ingly under attack from Viking raiders. There were other problems.
Many people could not read, or could not read Latin (most books
were composed in Latin), and much teaching was done by dicta-
tion and memorization of any reading matter available. The
problem was whether the right books were available. And what of
the content of the text books? How could a suitable subject matter
be guaranteed?

Such were the questions faced by King Alfred at the end of the
ninth century, troubled as he was by wars against the Danish
Vikings (who had overrun most of the north of England) but
anxious to reform the education of the country. His solution was
to choose a selection of books 'most necessary for all men to

know'.[18] These included the theology of Augustine and Gregory the Great, as well as the historical works of Orosius, Bede's *Ecclesiastical History* and the *Consolation of Philosophy* of Boethius. These were the kinds of books that an Anglo-Saxon king thought important. But Alfred was an innovator. The new idea was to have full-scale books actually written in English. So Augustine and Bede were translated into English for the first time ever. This policy of using the vernacular was fairly unique, and it was pursued much more intensively than in countries such as France, or Germany, where there was only occasional use of the vernacular.

To see the result of Alfred's policy, we need to move on another century until the time of the monk Ælfric, later the abbot of Eynsham, and a prolific writer of English religious prose in the tradition begun by Alfred on the models of Augustine and Bede. As is obvious from the many prefaces to his works, Ælfric was not happy with the situation of literature and theology in England.[19] There were too many 'unlearned priests' around, who did not know Latin and could not adequately explain the difficulties and profundities of scripture. There was also – Ælfric complained – 'too much error' in the English books available (this is important to note and I will return to it shortly). Error could be one of transmission: in an age of scribal copying and editorial selection, there was a consequent adaptation and instability of texts.[20] But the main objection appears to have been to the authors and texts chosen.[21] So Ælfric set himself the task of putting the Augustinian educational programme into effect by three series of sermons and homilies which cover the basics of the Christian story and the need for moral exhortation, just as in the Cædmonian scheme. Unlike the books of 'great error' which he attacked, Ælfric's writings are noted for their clarity and structure, and for their use of reliable sources like Augustine, Gregory the Great and Bede himself.

Politics was on the side of Ælfric. The tenth century saw a powerful movement for monastic reform in England, of which important figures were King Edgar (Alfred's great-grandson) and Archbishop Dunstan, along with his supporter Bishop Æthelwold.[22] This Benedictine revival was implemented with some degree of force. A symbolic moment during the Reform is the ejection of the secular clerics from the cathedral at Winchester in the year 964, and their replacement with Benedictine monks.

The political changes were accompanied by a flourishing of arts and written literature. As in the Northumbrian Age, many luxurious illuminated gospels and prayerbooks were produced, as well as later the homilies of Ælfric and his contemporaries.[23] But one wonders whether the lay clerics who were in charge of the unreformed monasteries and cathedrals were owners and users of books and, if so, what these were like. St Dunstan himself was educated at Glastonbury by Irish monks. This kind of contact, as we shall see, is significant. Ælfric never says he disapproves of Irish teaching, but he never uses it himself, and he clearly disapproves of the apocryphal themes which turn up so often in Insular Latin texts. It is conceivable that part of what Ælfric was objecting to was the Irish tradition in Old English literature.

Insular and Irish influences on Old English literature

Research now shows that some of the anonymous religious prose (especially from the Vercelli Book) and some of the surviving Old English poems belong to a recognizably Irish tradition.[24] This tradition, perhaps more appropriately called 'insular' (as it may have reached England by various routes, including Hiberno-Latin texts from the Continent) is recognizable by its own specific themes, sometimes apocryphal, and by its idiosyncratic use of language and colourful rhetoric.

Like much of Old English literature, the majority of the Irish-influenced texts appear in manuscripts from around the time of Ælfric or later. But they could reflect an earlier tradition of Irish-influenced teaching. The Irish, of course, had been the great teachers of Bede's Northumbria and they had maintained this teaching reputation ever since. As we shall see, King Alfred himself had many Irish contacts. The Mercian and West Saxon private prayerbooks that have survived often contain Irish, English and Continental material side-by-side.[25] A survey of the books owned by King Alfred's grandson, the powerful King Æthelstan (924–39), shows that he obtained many of them through his contacts with important figures in the early tenth-century Irish Church. As I have noted, Archbishop Dunstan was educated originally by Irish *peregrini* (wandering clerics).

The classic example of an Irish apocryphal theme in Old English is the second text with which I began, the description of the Celtic Otherworld in Vercelli IX, a country of sensual delights evoked in colourful language as a means of describing heaven using the rhetoric of the inexpressible that was so typical of many Irish texts. There are many more examples of such themes and rhetoric. The lurid descriptions of hell in the rest of this sermon have their origins in an Irish rescension of the Vision of Paul (of which Ælfric complained). Passages from Vercelli Homily IX were also taken over – either by copying or hearsay – in another Irish-influenced Old English prose text: the legend of the Irish deacon Niall and the so-called 'Sunday Letter'. This apocryphal and apocalyptic story relates how a certain Irish deacon Niall died and was resurrected, after which he never ate again for the rest of his life, giving out dire warnings through a letter supposedly written by Christ and transported to earth by an angel: fire would descend on the earth and destroy everything, and many other plagues and dire punishments would occur if people did not observe the rules of Sunday observance.[26] If Ælfric disapproved of that, we can hardly blame him. It is typical of a severely apocalyptic and also coercive approach which we find in much of this prose. This is its negative side: the writers of the genre seem to operate by evoking extremes of fear and attractiveness as a way of influencing people's behaviour.

A gentler tone in the anonymous prose is found in its attempts to encourage people to change their lives by engaging in flights of litanic prose: lists of parallel qualities build up an emotional response in the reader's or listener's mind. Vercelli Homilies III and XX, for example, evoke in the form of enumeration some rather surprising benefits of almsgiving as a personifed virtue: 'she traverses the heaven, and she precedes givers in the glory of the kingdom of heaven, and she knocks on the door of the kingdom of heaven, and she rouses the angels towards her'.[27] Similarly, Vercelli Homily V, a Christmas homily which appears to draw its material directly from Hiberno-Latin texts, sounds the following note of praise: 'But let us praise and glorify our Lord in pure thoughts and in holy words and in faithful actions and in true beliefs, since his power is higher than heaven, wider than earth, deeper than the sea, brighter than the star in heaven.'[28] It seems that laudatory passages of this type were common in insular sermons, whether written in Irish, Hiberno-Latin or Old English.[29]

In a poem from a similar milieu, the poetic *Dialogues of Solomon and Saturn*, we are given the promises of protection provided by the Lord's Prayer, again expressed in interestingly exaggerated rhetoric in which the prayer is described as 'the wisdom of the heart and the honey of the soul, milk of the mind, most blessed of glories'. The powers of the prayer are extensive:

> He is bolder than the foundation of the earth,
> he is stronger than the grip of all stones.
> He is the physician of the lame, light of the blinking,
> also he is the door of the deaf, the tongue of the dumb,
> the shield of the guilty, the hall of the Creator,
> bearer of the flood, saviour of the people,
> guardian of the waves and poor fishes,
> glory of serpents, forest of wild beasts,
> guardian of the desert, court of honours.[30]

Though it is written in the traditional Old English verse, the theme is reminiscent of Old Irish prayers, particularly the famous *loricae* or 'breastplate' prayers of St Patrick and of Gildas. In St Patrick's Breastplate, we find comparable lists of qualities, as in the following two extracts:

> I bind myself today with the power of heaven, the light of the sun, the lustre of the moon, the splendour of fire, the swiftness of lightning, the speed of the wind, the depth of the sea, the steadiness of the earth, the stability of rock.
>
> I bind myself today with the power of God to steer me, the might of God to uphold me, the wisdom of God to guide me, the eye of God to look ahead for me, the ear of God to hear for me, the word of God to speak before me, the path of God to go before me, the shield of God to shelter me . . .[31]

The insular panegyric element is well illustrated by the soul's praise of God in the otherwise severe eschatology of Vercelli Homily IV:

> Lord, before all worlds existed you were,
> You reign for ever over all worlds,
> And you are ever in all eternity.
> Lord your beginning was never,
> Your end will never come,

Your power will never fail
For those who keep your commandments.
You are the maker of life,
And you are the hymn of praise of all the saints;
You are the hope for the mournful,
You are the saviour of the world,
You are rest for the afflicted;
And you are the light of the blind, the speech of the dumb, the
    hearing of the deaf, the balm of the sick, and the footsteps of the
    lame.
And of all bitterness you are the sweet fragrance,
And all the unhappy will find their bliss in you.
You are the doer of all deeds, the maker of all abundance, and the
    light of all darkness.
You are the source of all nobility.[32]

As well as the repetitive syntax of this litanic style, there is a
sensual quality to this prose as the homilist (like the author of St
Patrick's Breastplate) evokes sight, speech, hearing, walking, taste
and smell as he builds towards the conclusion.

Though very different, such a passage compares favourably with
Ælfric in the first of his Catholic Homilies:

> There is one origin of all things, that is God Almighty.
> He is beginning and end.
> He is beginning because he was ever;
> He is end without ending, because he is ever unending;
> He is king of all kings, and Lord of all lords.
> He holds with his power heaven and earth.
> He measures all the hills with his hand;
> No thing can withstand his will, and no creature can perfectly
>   ponder or understand about God.[33]

Though there are similarities, both passages have different qualities. Ælfric is predominantly visual, and more biblical in his
reminiscence of the psalms. His style is also more rational and
considered, balancing positives and negatives. The contrast between Ælfric on the one hand and the Irish-influenced texts on
the other is important, and much more could be discussed. Not
only in the themes but also at the level of language, style and rhetoric, there is recognizably a 'Celtic' or 'insular' style in Old English
literature.

'The Seafarer'

An often quoted passage in the Old English poem 'The Seafarer'[34] gives a catalogue of names of sea birds encountered on a sea-voyage along the coast: the swan, the gannet, the kittiwake, the sea-eagle. In this poetic conceit, the cries of the birds somehow echo the poet's own sense of isolation from kin (ll. 25b–26). The poet then remembers the comfort of life in hall or town, before the powerful image of the storm continues (ll. 31–3):

> Night shadow darkened, snow from the north
> Frost bound the land and hail fell on earth,
> Coldest of corns.

'The Seafarer' is almost unique. Look at the strange passage where the man's mind takes on the form of a bird ranging far from him and returning greedy with longing; the cry of this 'solitary flier' impels him to start out on his pilgrimage and follow the path of the whale. This seems to have moved beyond pathetic fallacy to a visionary, shamanic or mystical experience (ll. 58–64):

> Now, therefore, my thought roams beyond the confines of my heart; my mind roams widely with the ocean tide over the whale's home, over earth's expanses, and comes back to me avid and covetous; the lone flier calls and urges the spirit irresistibly along the whale-path over the waters of oceans.[35]

The Christian motivation of this experience is given in the lines immediately following (64b–66a): 'the joys of the Lord are warmer to me than this dead life on the land'.

A poem about seafaring and pilgrimage, 'The Seafarer' is in many ways steeped in the vocabulary and diction of the traditional Germanic epic, with its themes of the hall, the generous patron, the bestowal of gifts, exile and loss of kinsmen. But there are some similarities of theme and genre in a Welsh poem on pilgrimage of roughly the same period.[36] Other features – the elegiac mood and the images of nature in transience – suggest that the poets of the elegies were working with the same formulas, motifs, themes and ideas as the composers of some of the insular-style Vercelli Homilies.

The theme of penance linked to the harshness of the winter sea has analogues in Muirchú's Life of Patrick, where the saint imposes a penance on Macc Cuill that he should bind his feet with an iron fetter and throw its key into the sea, 'then get into a one-hide boat and put to sea without a rudder or an oar'.[37] The extreme aceticism of the Northumbrian saints might also be compared, a good instance being the various Lives of St Cuthbert, where the saint is depicted as standing up to his neck at prayer in the icy sea-water.[38] Above all, the dominant idea in 'The Seafarer' is one of a sea-pilgrimage, an exile on the sea as an equivalent to the traditional hermit's desert; all this has roots in the Irish idea of *peregrinatio pro amore dei* (pilgrimage for the love of God).[39] The most famous example of such *peregrini* is the annal from the Anglo-Saxon Chronicle for 891, which tells how three Irish holy men arrived at the court of King Alfred having set themselves adrift in a boat without oars or rudder. In the original texts, the key term is *elþeodig*, which means 'stranger, exile, pilgrim'. In the Chronicle, the motivation of the Irishmen 'for þon hi woldon for Godes lufon on elþeodignesse beon and hi ne rohton hwær' (because they wanted, for the love of God, to be on pilgrimage; and they did not care where) echoes the similar urge of the lyrical speaker in the poem:

> monað modes lust mæla gehwylce
> ferð to feran, þæt ic feor heonan
> elþeodigra eard gesece
>
> my mind's desire time and time again
> urges the soul to set out, so that I may seek out
> the land of pilgrims far away from here[40]

It would be tempting to locate the poem in the court of King Alfred; or perhaps earlier in the lost and relatively unknowable world of Mercian culture. Some find that the elegiac mode of the poetry, especially the scene with the mind as a bird, has affinities with the story of the sparrow in the hall at the conversion of King Edwin. This is attractive. But the attempt to locate the poem in the Northumbria of Bede seems to me to be simply too conjectural. The passage giving names of sea birds has been cited as evidence for an origin of the poem on Lindisfarne. Surely this is going too far. We cannot know how much a poem could accrue further material by oral or written transmission.[41] In fact the composite structure of these poems may have encouraged scribes or performers to add or adapt the themes and motifs. Perhaps 'The Seafarer' began as a lyric a few lines long like 'Cædmon's Hymn', and was added to gradually by other poets and compilers over the centuries.

Bede and 'The Seafarer' in modern English

The process of adding to and adapting these images did not stop with the writing of the Exeter Book. There have been various paraphrases of 'The Seafarer', each giving its own slant on the poem and its interpretation. The most famous perhaps, is the one by the poet Ezra Pound, which attempted a 'pagan' interpretation.[42] Images from Bede have also received re-presentations, sometimes fruitful, at the hands of later writers and poets. It is time to take one final look at the image of the bird in the hall with which we began.

The first person to translate Bede's Latin added his own touch in the reign of King Alfred. In the modern period the poets William Wordsworth, D. H. Lawrence and Seamus Heaney have continued this tradition. In the ninth-century Old English translation of Bede, an elegiac note is added with the touch about the duration of the flight through the hall as a mere 'twinkling of an eye'.[43] The transformations recur and are taken further in Wordsworth's version in the 'Ecclesiastical Sonnets' (1822), no. 16, entitled 'Persuasion', and beginning with the line 'Man's life is like a Sparrow, mighty King!'[44] In Bede's original, the flight of the bird signifies the duration and transience of human life. In Wordsworth, the bird represents the human soul itself. In a similar vein, D. H. Lawrence uses the image of the bird as the soul to capture the feel of Ursula Brangwen's seething emotional life in *The Rainbow*. Like the lyrical speaker of 'The Seafarer', she almost becomes the bird itself:

> Making on toward the wood, she saw the pale gleam of Willey Water through the cloud below, she walked the open space where hawthorn trees streamed like hair on the wind and round bushes were presences showing through the atmosphere. It was very splendid, free and chaotic.
>
> Yet she hurried to the wood, for shelter . . . She glided between the tree-trunks, afraid of them. They might turn and shut her in as she went through their marshalled silence.
>
> So she flitted along, keeping an illusion that she was unnoticed. She

felt like a bird that has flown in through the window of a hall where vast warriors sit at the board. Between their grave, booming ranks she was hastening, assuming she was unnoticed, till she emerged, with beating heart, through the far window and out into the open, upon the vivid green, marshy meadow.

She turned under the shelter of the common, seeing the great veils of rain swinging with slow, floating waves across the landscape. She was very wet and a long way from home, far enveloped in the rain and the waving landscape. She must beat her way back through all this fluctuation, back to stability and security.[45]

Finally, I turn to Seamus Heaney, the recent translator of *Beowulf*, who studied English at Queen's, Belfast, and now lives in Dublin, a poet fascinated like his Protestant counterpart John Hewitt with the roots of his culture and literature, the 'archaeology' of his language. In the poem 'Bone Dreams', the poet pushes back through 'the tongue's old dungeons' – the historical layers of the English language – till he finds at last the ancient consonantal language of the Old English poet and 'in the coffered riches of grammar and declensions' the image of the head or the body as a hall or 'bone-house' (an Old English compound), a hall with its expected fire, benches and rafters, 'where the soul fluttered a while in the roofspace'. At the centre of the hall swings the 'cauldron of generation', a symbol of feeling, inspiration and imagination.[46] Here Heaney creates a new synthesis: he takes 'The Seafarer' and its bird/soul symbolism, combines it with the theme of the hall of King Edwin from Bede and supplements it with imagery from *Beowulf* and Irish myth.

'Saxon or Celt?' was my opening question. They suggest oppositions, irreconcilable attitudes. Forster's theme was 'only connect'. Perhaps Ælfric would have agreed, for he was a master of the balanced statement; but his solution was apparently to ignore the 'insular' themes and try for a new expression. As we have seen, the anonymous Old English homilists felt freer to adapt images and themes from the insular and Hiberno-Latin texts they knew and admired: in contrast to Ælfric they used sensually extravagant images to convey the inexpressibility of the things of heaven. Clearly, the oppositions between a Celtic/insular or Saxon/Roman expression of Christian literature definitely existed in the prose of Anglo-Saxon literature. There is a world of difference between the homilist Ælfric and the author of the anchorite legend. But what of the poetry? Can we look to 'The Seafarer' for a synthesis of 'Saxon' images of hall and transience and 'Celtic' images of soul and pilgrimage? In this respect, the modern reinterpretations of Bede's image of the bird in the hall provide a valuable service, indicating as they do that, in some unknowable and undatable milieu of the Anglo-Saxon world, where the poet of 'The Seafarer' lived and worked, the two opposing attitudes were, after all, reconcilable.

Notes

1   E. M. Forster, *Howard's End* (1910), ch. 25. For a recent edn. see E. M. Forster, *Howard's End*, ed. Oliver Stallybrass (Harmondsworth, 1985), 216.
2   The stereotypes of the Celt and the Saxon are found in the opening pages of George Eliot's *Adam Bede* (1859) and are discussed in Matthew Arnold, *The Study of Celtic Literature* (1867).
3   Compare her German philosopher namesakes Friedrich Schlegel and August Wilhelm Schlegel, both of whom were interested, like many Romantics, in the literature of the ancient and medieval world.
4   Bede, *Historia Ecclesiastica*, II. 13: trans. R. E. Latham in Bede, *Ecclesiastical History of the English People*, ed. D. H. Farmer (Harmondsworth, 1999), 129–30.
5   Barbara Raw, *The Art and Background of Old English Poetry* (London, 1978).
6   The Vercelli Book manuscript (Vercelli, Biblioteca Capitolare CXVII) is a late tenth-century compilation of Old English poems and prose that was left in Vercelli in the eleventh century, perhaps by an English pilgrim to Rome. D. G. Scragg, 'The compilation of the Vercelli Book', *Anglo-Saxon England*, 2 (1973), 189–207. Its poems, which famously include *The Dream of the Rood*, are translated by S. A. J. Bradley, *Anglo-Saxon Poetry* (London, 1982), 107–97.
7   D. G. Scragg (ed.), *The Vercelli Homilies and Related Texts* (Oxford, 1992), 153–7. For discussions of this text and its background, see Charles Wright, *The Irish Tradition in Old English Literature* (Cambridge, 1993), esp. 215–91; Fred C. Robinson, 'The devil's account of the next world: an anecdote from Old English homiletic literature', *Neuphilologische Mitteilungen*, 73 (1972), 362–71, and D. G. Scragg, '"The devil's account of the next world" revisited', *American Notes and Queries*, 24 (1986), 107–10.
8   Vercelli Homily IX, ll. 184–98. For the full text see Scragg, *The Vercelli Homilies*, 158–84; there is a text with facing translation in Wright, *Irish Tradition*, 276–91.

9   Wright, *Irish Tradition*, 206–14.

10 *Beowulf*, trans. Seamus Heaney (London, 1999).

11 The Old English Bede is a product of the reign of Alfred. For the text see Dorothy Whitelock (ed.), *Sweet's Anglo-Saxon Reader* (Oxford, 1967), 45–50.

12 For the pronunciation of Old English, see Norman Davis (ed.), *Sweet's Anglo-Saxon Primer* (Oxford, 1953), 1–4.

13 Richard Hamer, *A Choice of Anglo-Saxon Verse* (London, 1972), 122.

14 See D. G. Scragg, 'The nature of Old English verse', in Malcolm Godden and Michael Lapidge (eds.), *The Cambridge Companion to Old English Literature* (Cambridge, 1991), 55–70.

15 Compare the trans. by S. A. J. Bradley, *Anglo-Saxon Poetry* (London, 1982), 334.

16 Virginia Day, 'The influence of the catechetical "narratio" on Old English and some other medieval literature', *Anglo-Saxon England*, 3 (1974), 51–61.

17 Judith N. Garde, *Old English Poetry in Medieval Christian Perspective* (Cambridge, 1991).

18 Simon Keynes and Michael Lapidge (trans.), *Alfred the Great: Asser's Life of King Alfred and Other Contemporary Sources* (Harmondsworth, 1983).

19 Jonathan Wilcox (ed.), *Ælfric's Prefaces* (Durham, 1994).

20 Paul Szarmach, 'The recovery of texts', in Katherine O'Brien O'Keeffe (ed.), *Reading Old English Texts* (Cambridge, 1997), 124–45. Even the text of a well-known poem like 'Cædmon's Hymn' underwent changes as it was copied by later scribes; see Katherine O'Brien O'Keeffe, *Visible Song: Transitional Literacy in Old English Verse* (Cambridge, 1990).

21 Malcolm Godden, 'Ælfric and the vernacular prose tradition', in Paul E. Szarmach and Bernard F. Huppé, *The Old English Homily and its Backgrounds* (Albany, NY, 1978), 99–117.

22 David Knowles, *The Monastic Order in England, 940–1216*, 2nd edn. (Cambridge, 1966). Michael Lapidge and Michael Winterbottom (eds.), *Wulfstan of Winchester: Life of St Æthelwold* (Oxford, 1991).

23 Milton McC. Gatch, 'The achievement of Ælfric and his colleagues in European perspective', in Szarmach and Huppé, *Old English Homily*, 43–73.

24 Wright, *Irish Tradition*, 215–71. Charles Wright's research has been very fruitful in revealing the many connections between Old English and early Irish literature; most of my argument here is based on his work.

25 Kathleen Hughes, 'Some aspects of Irish influence on early English private prayer', in *Church and Society in Ireland: AD 400–1200* (London, 1987), ch. 17, repr. from *Studia Celtica*, 5 (1970), 48–61.

26   Clare Lees, 'The "Sunday Letter" and "Sunday Lists"', *Anglo-Saxon England*, 14 (1985), 129–51.

27   Vercelli Homily XX, ll. 49–51. The Latin source which the English homilist translates is a Continental sermon collection with some Hiberno-Latin connections; see James E. Cross (ed.), *Cambridge Pembroke College MS 25: A Carolingian Sermonary Used by Anglo-Saxon Preachers*, King's College London Medieval Studies, 1 (London, 1987).

28   Vercelli V, ll. 194–7. The source is Hiberno-Latin; a similar passage occurs in the commonplace book of Sedulius Scottus: 'For our Father remains in the heights, higher than heaven, firmer than the earth, deeper than the sea, purer than the air, brighter than the sun.' See Sedulius Scottus, *Collectaneum miscellaneum*, ed. D. Simpson, CCCM 67 (Turnhout, 1988), 135.

29   On the stylistic characteristics of insular homilies, see H. L. C. Tristram, *Early Insular Preaching: Verbal Artistry and Method of Composition*, Sitzungsberichte der österreichischen Akademie der Wissenschaften, 623 (Vienna, 1995), 29–38.

30   Wright, *Irish Tradition*, 242.

31   D. G. Calder et al., *Sources and Analogues of Old English Poetry*, ii. *The Major Germanic and Celtic Texts in Translation* (Cambridge and Totowa, NJ, 1983), 186. For another trans., see Oliver Davies and Fiona Bowie (eds.), *Celtic Christian Spirituality: An Anthology of Modern and Medieval Sources* (London, 1995), no. 18. The text is discussed by Oliver Davies in Chapter 1 of this volume.

32   Vercelli Homily IV, ll. 173–83.

33   See also Peter Clemoes (ed.) *Ælfric's Catholic Homilies: The First Series. Text* (Oxford, 1997), 178.

34   Richard Hamer (ed.), *A Choice of Anglo-Saxon Verse* (London, 1970), 184–95; Ida Gordon (ed.), *The Seafarer*, 2nd edn. with bibliography by Mary Clayton (Exeter, 1996).

35   S. A. J. Bradley (trans.), *Anglo-Saxon Poetry* (London, 1982), 333.

36   'Maytime is the Fairest Season', from the Black Book of Carmarthen, in Oliver Davies, *Celtic Christianity in Early Medieval Wales* (Cardiff, 1996), 39–40.

37   Thomas O'Loughlin (trans.), 'The Life of Patrick by Muirchú', ch. 26, in Oliver Davies (ed.), *Celtic Spirituality* (New York and Mahwah, NJ, 1999), 108. For further quotations and discussions of this incident, see the Introduction and Chapter 6 of this volume.

38   Bede, *Life of Cuthbert*, ch. 10. In D. H. Farmer (ed.) and J. F. Webb (trans.), *The Age of Bede* (Harmondsworth, 1983), 56.

39   Dorothy Whitelock, 'The interpretation of *The Seafarer*', in *The Early Cultures of North-West Europe* (Cambridge, 1950), 259–72; repr. in

J. B. Kessinger and S. J. Kahrl (eds.), *Essential Articles for the Study of Old English Poetry* (Hamden, 1968), 442–57.

40 Ll. 36–8. The modern English is adapted from S. A. J. Bradley, *Anglo-Saxon Poetry*, 333, who translates the key phrase as 'land of strangers'.

41 Carol Braun Pasternack, *The Textuality of Old English Verse*, Cambridge Studies in Anglo-Saxon England, 13 (Cambridge, 1995).

42 Ezra Pound, 'The Seafarer from the Anglo-Saxon', in M. J. King (ed.) *The Collected Early Poems of Ezra Pound* (London, 1977). F. C. Robinson, ' "The Might of the North": Pound's Anglo-Saxon studies and *The Seafarer*', *Yale Review*, 71 (1982), 199–224. Pound's version paraphrases the poem omitting most of the Christian references and the final homiletic passage; in so doing he follows some nineteenth-century 'pagan' interpretations which regarded the text as a very early, pre-Christian poem into which Christian material had been interpolated at a later date.

43 The passage is discussed by Janet Bately, 'The nature of Old English prose', in Malcolm Godden and Michael Lapidge (eds.), *The Cambridge Companion to Old English Literature* (Cambridge, 1991), 71–87, at 82.

44 John O. Hayden (ed.), *William Wordworth, The Poems*, 2 vols. (Harmondsworth, 1977), ii. 453.

45 D. H. Lawrence, *The Rainbow* (1915). The definitive text is D. H. Lawrence, *The Rainbow*, ed. Mark Kinkead-Weekes (Cambridge, 1989), p. 450, ll. 30–5 and p. 451, ll. 3–13.

46 Seamus Heaney, *North* (London, 1975), 28–9.

II
Theologies

5

'There is no resurrection where there is no earth'[1]: creation and resurrection as seen in early Welsh poetry

A. M. ALLCHIN

I want in this chapter to explore the subject of creation and resurrection in some of the vernacular religious writing of Wales and Ireland in the period from the ninth to the twelfth century, that is to say in the later part of what we may call the classical period of Celtic Christianity. I assume, perhaps too confidently, that there is such an entity as Celtic Christianity,[2] that the lands of Celtic language and culture in the west of Britain, in Ireland and in Brittany, despite their manifest differences from one another, share a generally common culture and common approach to the central points of Christian life and doctrine, which allows us to consider them together as one of the major regions of first millennium Christianity in the West. I also assume that we can speak of a classical period of Celtic Christianity, a long period of six or seven centuries which runs from the fifth to the twelfth century, until c.1150, at which time in a variety of ways all the Celtic countries found themselves becoming more closely integrated into the main body of Western Christendom than they had been before.

It will be my aim to show that there is, in the theological vision of this period in the Celtic world, a great unanimity with the theological vision of Christian East and West and, needless to say, also close resemblances to that of Anglo-Saxon Christianity. What is specific, and what I believe justifies us in speaking of a Celtic spirituality or a Celtic Christianity, is a particular way of relating creation to redemption and resurrection, and a certain sharpness and vigour of imaginative expression, the striking clarity and beauty of the way in which the world is seen and experienced as full of the clarity and beauty which comes from God. The texts which I use come, in the case of Maximus the Confessor, from the seventh century, in the case of the Irish from the ninth and tenth centuries, and in the case of the Welsh from the ninth to the twelfth. They cover a wide period of time but they are all, I would maintain, characteristic expressions of the late development of first-millennium Christianity, a Christianity which is formed before the schism between East and West and before the development of the Western Middle Ages.

In thinking of creation and resurrection together in this way, we shall find ourselves thinking in terms of a cosmic Christology, a way of understanding both creation and redemption which centres in the person and work of Christ, and focuses particularly on his death and resurrection. Christ the Word by whom all things are made in the beginning, in whom all things hold together, is Christ the crucified who descends into the place of death and there destroys the power of death, not only for humanity but for all creation. This is a way of seeing things which sees that central point of death and resurrection as an eternal as well as a temporal reality, the moment of the paschal mystery, Christ's passover from death into life through dying. It can thus see this mystery as present and at work throughout the whole world of nature and in the whole course of human history. It also sees it in an explicitly Trinitarian way, for the Son of God who dies on the cross is raised from the dead by the Father, and in his rising the transforming power of the Spirit is released into the world in a way which is radically new, thus fulfilling the original design of God from the first moment of creation until now.

The Juvencus Englynion

I intend to approach this subject by looking first at a group of verses found in a Cambridge University manuscript, the Juvencus Englynion, which we may confidently affirm constitute the earliest religious, or perhaps better, theological poem which we have in Welsh. I shall then compare this with an Irish vernacular prose text of the same period and, in the light of what we may gather from these two very different but in some ways complementary texts, we shall look back briefly at aspects of this theme as seen in classical Byzantine theology as well as in other vernacular poems from the early Welsh tradition.

The group of verses known as the Juvencus Englynion is found in a manuscript in the Fitzwilliam Library in Cambridge, a manuscript which contains a Latin paraphrase of the four gospels by the fourth-century poet Juvencus and which is generally ascribed to the ninth century. In its margins there are a number of verses and notes written by different hands, dating perhaps from the tenth century, some of them in Old Irish, some of them in Old Welsh. One set, the nine three-line verses at which we shall be looking, are written in the margin at the top of the first page of the manuscript. Thus they are evidently an afterthought, but they can scarcely be considered a casual one.[3]

I accept what seems to be the general consensus both about the ninth-century date of the manuscript, with tenth-century notes and additions, and about its place of origin, a monastic community in Wales, whether in the north or south, or in mid Wales, perhaps at Llanbadarn, in which Welsh and Irish monks are living side by side and collaborating in the work of the scriptorium. The details of this consensus are not in themselves vital to my argument, but taken together they are certainly suggestive and they enable us to situate the poem more confidently than is usually the case with these early Welsh texts. Here we have a poem which comes from the century when under two outstanding rulers in Gwynedd, Merfyn Frych (d. 844) and Rhodri Mawr (844–77), Wales rallied in the face of the first Viking invasions, and achieved a greater degree of unity than was usual in this early period. This is a time in which we know that the court of Gwynedd provided a stopping place for Irish travellers, especially monks and scholars, on their way from Ireland to the court of Charles the Bald, king of the West Franks, a journey which may well have been made, amongst others, by the greatest speculative theologian of the period between Augustine and Anselm, John Scottus Eriugena.

It seems important to situate the poem in this way in its possible, even perhaps probable, intellectual and historical context, in order not to underestimate the quality and complexity of its theological content. Unfortunately it seems to me that this is something which has not been done frequently. Even Jenny Rowland, when she discusses this poem in her masterly study of the saga poetry of this period, contrasts the sophistication and skill of the poem's literary technique with the 'fairly stereotyped' nature of its subject-matter.[4] I shall argue that form and content go closely together here, and suggest not only a sophisticated literary craftsman but also a subtle and careful theological thinker.

The work is first of all a striking early example of a praise poem to God. We need to see it as the product of a monastic milieu which is shaped by the daily use of the psalter, and in particular of the praise psalms (145–50) used every day at the end of the morning office in first-millennium monasteries both of East and West. The poem is also nourished by a knowledge of the Latin patristic tradition of biblical interpretation. It is a vernacular poem, but it begins with two words of Latin, *Omnipotens Auctor*, and as we shall see key terms within it reflect the meeting between the Welsh and Latin languages that had taken place much earlier – in the centuries of the conversion of western Britain to the Christian faith.[5] We see here an example of a remarkably fruitful interaction of two languages and two cultures, Roman and Celtic.

Already in the second stanza the poet affirms that, though all creation praises God, God is always beyond the praise of his creatures.

> The world cannot comprehend in song bright and melodious,
> Even though the grass and the trees should sing,
> All your wonders, O true Lord!

Thus at the outset of a poem which itself stands at the beginning of a long historical development, it is made clear that if God is present within the life of his creation, he is in no way limited or entrapped by it. The God who is praised is both utterly immanent and utterly transcendent, at one with the God of the Old Testament scriptures.

As I have said, there can be, in Jenny Rowland's judgement, no doubting the poet's capacity as a poet:

> Despite some gaps in the text and linguistic difficulties, it is clear that this is praise poetry to the Trinity of a high order . . . the chief glory of the poem is its metrical structure with verbal repetitions found in overlapping and cyclical patterns, as in some of the most sophisticated poems in the *Canu Heledd*.[6]

Twice in the poem, once at the end of stanza five, once at the end of stanza nine, at the end of the whole poem, the poet declares 'it is not too great toil' (*ni guor gnim*) to praise God, in the first case specifying the praise of God as Trinity and in the second specifying the praise of God as the son of Mary. Therefore, the poem is to be seen as explicitly Trinitarian and incarnational.

In his book on medieval Welsh religious literature, Simon Evans draws attention to the use of the word *gnim* in the *Llywarch Hen* Cycle in a line which says that human life is 'a long toil with no escape from fatigue' (*hir gnim heb escor lludet*). He contrasts this use of the word with its use in the Juvencus Englynion.

> The author exults in the opportunity offered to praise Jesus, the son of Mary . . . Here we find a new medium expressing new hope and vigour, a new faith and vision which is in sharp contrast with the use of *gnim* in a famous stanza of *Llywarch Hen*, where the poet thinks of his life as being dominated by a stern unyielding fate . . .[7]

In the saga poetry the theme of fate, *tynged,* is a recurring one. Fate is seen to have an inexorable quality about it, which the hero's courage and good judgement may for a time be able to turn aside, but which in the end is not to be escaped. But in the Juvencus verses the sense that life must come to a dead end, with no way through, has been overcome through the promise of the resurrection, in which Christ's death is seen as the destruction of death and the opening of the way into an eternal kingdom. This reversal of the old fear of fate is celebrated in striking lines in other poems of this period: 'In God there is no fate/death' (*en nuw nid oes dynghedven*). Or again in words which point us directly to the paradoxes of the cross and the empty tomb, 'When it is most restricted for man, it is most expansive with God' (*pan vo ygaf gan dyn ehangaf vyd gan duw*).[8] One might indeed say that the early religious praise poetry of Wales grows out of the discovery that human life is rooted in God's creative and eternal will, and finds its fulfilment in the promise of resurrection to eternal life, which goes beyond the dimensions of time. Certainly the poem of the Juvencus manuscript seems to be built up around this basic understanding of creation and resurrection.

Presen, Bedydd, Elfydd

To substantiate that assertion I intend to look more closely at three crucial words which occur in stanzas three, four and five of the poem. Jenny Rowland points to their highly significant role in the composition of the poem, commenting on 'the unique use in the early *Englynion* of three consecutive synonyms as the *gair cyrch* . . . in stanzas three to five'.[9] The *gair cyrch* is the word which in each stanza is placed in what is metrically a particularly prominent place, and in each case here it is a word which signifies universe, creation, inhabited world. The three terms which the poet employs each bring out some particular aspect of God's relationship with the world seen as his creation. Each one of these three terms has a Latin word lying behind it, and must therefore be a fairly new coinage in the Welsh of the time, the product of a fusion of languages and cultures made, one supposes, in the context of sustained theological study and reflection.[10]

The first word for world which is used in these verses is *presen*, and it derives from the Latin *presentia* or *presens*. In this word it is suggested that the world is that which is present to us, now in this moment of time, poised between past and future here in this particular point in space. But perhaps we may see it as implying more than that; this precariously poised point in time and space is rooted and made sure in the God who is its creator. There is a deeper meaning here. The world is the place of God's presence, and it is God's presence which makes the world at every moment. This means that God as creator does not leave his world to its own devices. He sustains it by his constant creative act.

The second word used is *bedydd*, a word which has a specifically sacramental reference. Its first meaning is baptism, and it can be linked with a related word *bydysawd* which is still, in modern Welsh, the word for universe. This is a word which is derived from the late Latin word *baptizatio*, baptism, or *baptizati*, those who are baptized, or perhaps *baptizandi*, those who are apt for baptism, 'ready and desirous to be baptized'. The primary meaning both of *bedydd* and *bydysawd* in medieval Welsh is Christendom, that is to say the world in which Christ is acknowledged, that part of the human race which has received baptism and been received into the Church of Christ.

Both words, however, have other and wider meanings, for both speak of creation as well as redemption. Baptism, like the eucharist, is seen in a cosmic context, as a universal sacrament, a mystery, of dying and rising; in it men and women are plunged into the death and resurrection of Christ and in that action it is not only their own purpose and destiny which is revealed but also the purpose and destiny of all creation. In Christ's resurrection all creation is raised to new life. The word *bydysawd* implies that the movement from death to life is hidden at the very heart of the universe, a universe which in some sense is apt for baptism. Christ is the word by whom all things were made. In his death and resurrection, all things are changed because he is the one in whom all things hold together from the beginning. By the resurrection of Christ the whole destiny of the world is made manifest.

This brings us to our third word, *elfydd*, which is related to the Latin *elementa*.[11] It refers to the common belief of the classical and early Christian world that the world and human beings within it are made up of a number of elements, or basic building blocks. When we remember this ancient way of viewing things, still very much alive in the time of Shakespeare, and still active in eighteenth-century Wales, in the verses of Twm o'r Nant, we usually think of four elements, earth, air, fire and water, as the components of the world and the components of the human person. But often in the early Celtic centuries people thought of seven elements; air would be double, calm air on the one side, cloud and tempest on the other; water would be double, salt water in the sea as opposed to fresh water in the streams and rivers. In some texts, the seventh element out of which the world and human beings were made was flowers; flowers, as it was said, for the variety and beauty of the eyes of men and women.[12]

This third term, *elfydd*, seems particularly appropriate to the third person of the Trinity even though the Spirit is not specifically mentioned in these lines. Out of these varied elements in the universe and in humankind, the Spirit of God creates a living world, an organic unity. As at the beginning, so still today, the Spirit broods over the waters of chaos, making of them *elfydd*, a universe, a world. The Spirit is not only giver of light but creator of life, creating at once the diversity and variety of the world and of human life, and at the same time producing its coherence and unity.

There is a great deal more that might be said about this poem. But I intend to leave it, and to pass across the Irish Sea and come to a vernacular prose text which itself has been ascribed to the second half of the ninth or the first quarter of the tenth century. This text, which is called *In Tenga Bithnua* (The Evernew Tongue), is in a very different style and a very different mood from that of the verses in the Juvencus manuscript. But in its underlying vision and purpose there are unexpected similarities.[13]

The Evernew Tongue

In a recent study of this text John Carey has traced the various
strands which have gone into its making, some biblical, some
Egyptian gnostic, some coming from pre-Christian Irish story and
myth. But the whole is held together by being given the form of a
homily for the Easter Vigil, which takes as its starting-point the
creation story in Genesis 1, read as the first in the long series of
Old Testament readings which mark the vigil; the text sees it in
direct relation to the story of Christ's death and resurrection and
the expectation of the day of judgement. It is a remarkable and in
some ways excessive text, as John Carey remarks of it,

> On the most obvious level, *In Tenga Bithnua* is held together by the very
> grandiosity of its aims: it sets out to provide us with a supernaturally
> revealed knowledge of *everything* – of God and all that he made, of the
> beginning and end of the world, of heaven and hell. I would like to
> suggest however, . . . that its author seeks to do more than this: the
> overwhelming totality of things is *unified*, brought together and
> harmonised in the figure of Christ and the resurrection.[14]

The homily begins with a brief but remarkable evocation of the
situation of the human race before the coming of Christ. 'For the
situation of the race of Adam was "a head in a bag" or "being in a
dark house"'. But it goes on:

> The tale tells us of the making of heaven and earth and likewise of the
> creation of the world which has been accomplished by Christ's resur-
> rection from the dead on this eve of Easter. Every material and every
> element and every nature which is seen in the world, they are all
> brought together in the body in which Christ rose again – that is, in the
> body of every human.

The text then continues:

> There is in it, first of all, material from wind and air; from it proceeds
> the respiration of breath in people's bodies. And there is in it material
> from fire; that is what makes the red heat of blood in bodies. And there
> is in it material from the sun and the stars of heaven also; so that that is
> what makes the brightness and the light in people's eyes. And there is
> in it material of bitterness and saltiness; so that that is what makes the
> bitterness of tears and the gall of the liver, and abundance of anger in
> people's hearts. And there is in it material from the stones and clay of

the earth; so that that is what makes the mingling of flesh and bones in people. And there is in it material from the flowers and bright colours of the earth; so that that is what makes the freckling and pallor of faces and the colour in cheeks.

We have here an unexpected comment both on the word *elfydd*, elements, and on the word *bedydd*, baptism, into Christ's death and resurrection. The homily goes on:

> With him the whole world rose again; for the nature of all creation was in the body which Jesus had put on. For if the Lord had not contrived that, if he had not suffered for the sake of the race of Adam, and if he had not risen again after death, the whole world would have been destroyed together with the race of Adam at the coming of the Judgement, and no creature of sea or land would be redeemed, but the heavens would burn up; save for the three heavens of the lofty sky alone, nothing would survive unburned. There would be no earth, nor any race of the living or the dead in the world, but only hell as far as heaven, unless the Lord had come for their redemption: all things would perish thus, without renewal.[15]

I have already said that there seems at least an element of the extreme, the excessive, in this remarkable work. It does nothing by halves. It speaks of a great gathering of the peoples of the East at Jerusalem, a gathering marked by the presence of 3,485 bishops, 54,969 kings, a festival which lasts for a year and four months with processions of clergy and lay people each night throughout the time. But in its basic message, in particular in its linking together of the themes of creation and resurrection, its purpose seems clear and entirely sober. John Carey sums up his impressions of the work, speaking of it as 'one of the most remarkable examples known to me of that inspired fusion of learning and creativity that distinguishes so much of early Irish literature'.[16]

If one turns back to an earlier Irish text, this time in Latin, entitled *De mirabilibus sacrae scripturae* (On the Wonders of Holy Scripture), one can see how deeply embedded in this tradition of faith and understanding is the thought of a constant interaction between the two levels which in later theology have often become separated out and become in the end not only distinct but opposed to one another, the levels of creation and redemption, nature and grace, human and divine. This work on the interpretation of the

miracles of scripture proceeds by arguing that when rightly understood they should all be seen as natural, not because the miraculous
has been reduced or explained away but because the latent quality
of miracle which is present in all things from the beginning has been
fully realized and displayed. There is a miraculous element in all
things waiting to be revealed.[17]

If we return for a moment to the Juvencus Englynion from
which we set out, bearing in mind the various ideas associated
with the idea of the created world, we can now read verses two and
three with new understanding.

> The world cannot comprehend in song bright and melodious,
> Even though the grass and the trees should sing,
> All your wonders, O true Lord!

> The Father created the world by a miracle;
> it is difficult to express its measure.
> Letters cannot contain it, letters cannot comprehend it.[18]

God is in all things and all things are in God; yet God is altogether
beyond his creation, wholly transcendent, never confined or
comprehended by it. This is panentheism not pantheism. All
things are full of the presence and of the energies of God. The
miraculous waits to be revealed in the natural, the resurrection of
Christ comes to show us the true purpose and destiny of creation.
Creation itself is a work of miracle.

Maximus and Dionysius

I turn now from this world of the Irish and Welsh monastic
communities, towards the end of the first millennium, and I pass
to a very different part of the Christendom of that period, and to a
very different kind of language and discourse, metaphysical and
contemplative rather than imaginative and poetic. Here it seems to
me we find a similar way of seeing things, of discovering Christ at
the heart of his creation and seeing all things in Christ, a way of
discovering the inner meaning of the world through the incarnation, the death and the resurrection of God the Word.

I quote from Maximus the Confessor, one of the greatest
theologians of the Byzantine world, some would judge one of the
greatest Christian thinkers of all time, a passage which speaks of

the interconnectedness of creation, incarnation and fulfilment in Christ:

> The mystery of the incarnation of the Word bears the power of all the hidden meanings and figures of scripture as well as the knowledge of visible and intelligible creatures. The one who knows the mystery of the cross and the tomb knows the principles of these creatures. And the one who has been initiated into the ineffable power of the resurrection, knows the purpose for which God originally made all things.

Commenting on this passage in a recent study of the place of mystical theology in the Christian tradition, the American scholar Mark McIntosh remarks:

> an important epistemological principle is at work here: the mystery of the incarnation is the hermeneutical key that discloses the mystical presence of God in the theophany of cosmos and ecclesia. But one can also sense an ontological grounding: the very same divine ekstasis at work in creation comes to full concrete expression in the incarnation, and in the ongoing assumption of creation into the divine life which the incarnation inaugurated: 'for the word of God who is God wills always and in all things to work the mystery of his embodiment'.[19]

In quoting such a passage from a Byzantine theologian of the seventh century, a thinker and saint who himself stood between the Christian East and West, I am not of course suggesting that the monks and scholars of Wales and Ireland in the eighth and ninth centuries were acquainted with Greek in such a way as to be able to read him, or indeed any other Byzantine theologian, with any ease. The formulation of Clare Stancliffe is one which has long struck me with its wisdom: 'The scholars of the Celtic world did not know Greek, they knew about Greek.'[20] In other words, they knew the letters of the alphabet and could at a pinch make out particular words and sentences. But in quoting this passage of Maximus in conjunction with the very different texts which I have quoted before, I think we can see why a linguistic and intellectual genius of the calibre of Iohannes Scottus Eriugena, once he had reached the court of Charles the Bald, should have turned to mastering the Greek language and to mastering it in such a way as to allow him to translate the writings of the pseudo-Dionysius and the commentaries on them of Maximus the Confessor.[21]

In this other language and this very different idiom, Eriugena would have found a theology which could both stimulate and respond to the powers of his own deeply penetrating and speculative mind. Certainly his translations and his later writings take him into a different world from that of the Celtic West, with its strongly imaginative use of material provided by scripture and pre-Christian tradition, into the world of Graeco-Roman philosophical contemplative reflection. But this world which was, culturally and in terms of its intellectual articulation, so different from his own, was in terms of its inner vision, its depth of hunger for the divine presence and the divine beauty revealed alike in creation and resurrection, not distant at all. In fact we may say that the two worlds were at one.

In this connection I would quote a passage of Andrew Louth from his study of Dionysius, a passage also used by Mark McIntosh in the work cited, in which he speaks of the world as a theophany, a manifestation of God:

> The world is God's glory made manifest, it exists to display his glory and draw everything into contemplation of his beauty. The doctrine of creation is necessary to such an understanding of the world as theophany; God is immediately present in his whole creation as its creator; created reality is not, as created, an obstacle to his glory, neither because it owes its being to something other than (or even alien to) God, nor because it is an increasingly remote echo of God's original creative urge. But if God is to manifest himself outside himself, that implies multiplicity, which in turn implies difference, which must be either ordered or disordered: and for Dionysius, only an ordered hierarchical creation could manifest the glory of the One.

So in a world which is ordered yet infinitely diversified, the one glory of the creator shines out. McIntosh comments:

> it is precisely because the yearning triune love gives existence immediately to each creature that the whole of creation is not opaque to God but is luminous with divine glory; and it is because this creative love is the effulgence of God's triune relationality and order that the cosmos itself has a sacred mutuality and order – it is not, in other words, a monochromatic indistinctness but the reciprocal play of unique creatures that together reflect the infinite play of the divine persons.[22]

Adwyneu Taliesin – The Loves of Taliesin

There are words here which might be used directly to illuminate and to expound some of the most characteristic early Christian theological praise poetry in Welsh. For instance, 'the whole of creation is not opaque to God, but is luminous with divine glory; . . . not . . . a monochromatic indistinctness but the reciprocal play of unique creatures that together reflect the infinite play of the divine persons.' Such words as these ask to be applied to some of the outstanding poems of this early period in Welsh.

I quote as an example the poem in praise of God as creator, which starts with the image of Christ as coming into the world as a great broad-breasted wave:

> Heaven's blessing to creation's fair kingdom
> Is the one who comes like a broad-breasted mighty wave.
> In every land his name is God,
> Mighty flood – Mary reared him,
> Well it was you came in flesh.

There follow verses which praise God as the creator of all the elements of the universe, verses which especially celebrate the element of water in its two qualities of salt and fresh and which praise above all its constantly mobile quality. 'Water never remains where it was.' The poet ends with a personal plea to the creator who on Easter night descended into hell.

> We beseech the one who created, mighty God, Son of Mary
> When on Easter night you harrowed hell
> All who were there were freed –
> Oh Lord of heaven may we purchase the kinship of your kindly
>   pardon.[23]

But in particular I want to apply this understanding of the relationship of creation to resurrection to the interpretation of one of the finest of all these poems, a work which is, I believe, one of the great religious poems of the Western Middle Ages, *Adwyneu Taliesin* (*The Loves of Taliesin*).[24] It is a poem which may surprise us by starting and ending with the thought of penance; but this is because we have been used to thinking of penance and repentance primarily in moralistic terms. For the early Christians, however, repentance was, before all else, a matter of life and death, of new life emerging out of death through the miracle of the resurrection. The categories of evil and forgiveness, of release from the power of sin and guilt, were of course always present in their thinking, but they were seen as contained within this greater and more all-inclusive dialectic of life and death itself. So, when the poem speaks of the beauty of doing penance, it sees that action as a new affirmation of our share in Christ's death and resurrection, through the reactivation of the original gift of our baptismal dying and rising with Christ.

It is the fact that it is in penance that we renew the gifts and grace which were made ours in baptism which gives to all the Celtic Christian peoples their immense seriousness, we might say their rigorism, about penance. It is the one way through death into life for sinful mortals, day by day. This is made very clear in one of the earliest monastic texts in Irish, the *Apgitir Chrabaid* (*The Alphabet of Devotion*). In the three waves which go over us in baptism (triple immersion was greatly insisted upon), we renounce:

> the world with its vanities . . . the devil with his snares . . . the passions of the flesh. It is this which changes a person from being a son of Death to being a son of Life, from being a son of Darkness to being a son of Light. When he breaks these three renunciations . . . unless he shall go again through these waters he cannot go into the Kingdom of God; a pool of tears of repentance, a pool wrung out of blood in penance, a pool of sweat in labour.[25]

But through this way, a way of dying, there is a new way opened into the kingdom of God, into the resurrection life, now and not just in the future. When the monks of the Celtic lands went on pilgrimage, in search of the place where they would find their stability, they went seeking 'the place of their resurrection'.

This very rich expression certainly refers to the place where they would die and be buried. It also refers to the place where, day by day, they would be entering, through penance, into what is sometimes called the first resurrection, and sometimes the little resurrection. There is implicit in these texts, both in prose and in verse, a very Johannine view of eschatology in which eternal life, resurrection life, is not only something of the future, but a gift and possession of now.

This gift of new life to each one is nothing less than the gift of resurrection. One of the prayers of the Nunnaminster Book, in Winchester, a collection made at the end of the ninth century, puts this very clearly:

> O life of the one who is dying, health of the one who is sick, and last remaining hope of the deserted. You are the resurrection of the dead, who on the third day rose again for the lost who dwell below, the chains of death smashed about you, free and full of joy. I thank you most high God and ask you for this in my wretched state; a share in the first resurrection through the forgiveness of my sins, and a place in the second resurrection with all the saints without an end . . .[26]

The life of constant penitence is thus a way of coming to life day by day, repeatedly making our own the life which is given to us in principle in the beginning. It involves not only the overcoming of death but also the gifts of the Spirit. For, in the early Christian centuries, the one to be baptized, whether adult or infant, was plunged first into the waters of baptism, going down into death and rising to new life, and was then anointed with oil, the sacrament of the Holy Spirit. This anointing touched all the senses, ears, eyes, nostrils, mouth, hands and feet, as a sign that all the senses were renewed and transformed in this coming into life, the new and eternal life of the resurrection. This was done not only for humankind but for all of creation, for as we have seen it is in baptism that not we alone, but all creation, are united with the dying and rising of Christ. So here all creation is enlivened, made transparent in the coming of the Spirit. To see this involves both an inner and an outer transformation, the cleansing both of our hearts and minds and the opening of our senses, so that we may perceive God's world in its original beauty. Thus it is that the poem *Adwyneu Taliesin* (*The Loves of Taliesin*) runs:

> The beauty of the virtue in doing penance for excess,
> Beautiful too that God shall save me.
> The beauty of a companion who does not deny me his company,
> Beautiful too the drinking horn's society.
> The beauty of a master like Nudd the wolf of God,
> Beautiful too a man who is noble, kind and generous.
> The beauty of berries at harvest time,
> Beautiful too the grain on the stalk.
> The beauty of the sun, clear in the sky,
> Beautiful too they who pay Adam's debt.

The beauty of the herd's thick-maned stallion,
Beautiful too the pattern of his plaits.
The beauty of desire and a silver ring,
Beautiful too a ring for a virgin.
The beauty of an eagle on the shore when the tide is full,
Beautiful too the seagulls playing.
The beauty of a horse and gold-trimmed shield,
Beautiful too a bold man in the breach.
The beauty of Einion, healer of many,
Beautiful too a generous and obliging minstrel.
The beauty of May with its cuckoo and nightingale,
Beautiful too when good weather comes.
The beauty of a proper and perfect wedding-feast,
Beautiful too a gift which is loved.
The beauty of desire for penance from a priest,
Beautiful too bearing the elements to the altar.
The beauty for a minstrel of mead at the head of the hall,
Beautiful too a lively crowd surrounding a hero.
The beauty of a faithful priest in his church,
Beautiful too a chieftain in his hall.
The beauty of a strong parish led by God,
Beautiful too being in the season of Paradise.
The beauty of the moon shining on the earth,
Beautiful too when your luck is good.
The beauty of summer, its days long and slow,
Beautiful too visiting the ones we love.
The beauty of the flowers on the tops of fruit-trees,
Beautiful too covenant with the Creator.
The beauty in the wilderness of doe and fawn,
Beautiful too the foam-mouthed and slender steed.
The beauty of the garden when the leeks grow well,
Beautiful too the charlock in bloom.
The beauty of a horse in its leather halter,
Beautiful too keeping company with a king.
The beauty of a hero who does not shun injury,
Beautiful too is elegant Welsh.
The beauty of the heather when it turns purple,
Beautiful too moorland for cattle.
The beauty of the season when calves suckle,
Beautiful too riding a foam-mouthed horse.
And for me there is no less beauty
In the father of the horn in a feast of mead.
The beauty of the fish in his bright lake,

Beautiful too its surface shimmering.
The beauty of the word which the Trinity speaks,
Beautiful too doing penance for sin.
But the loveliest of all is covenant
With God on the Day of Judgement.[27]

Thus the poem, having spoken at the outset of the beauty of penance, goes on to show us the world of nature and of grace, the world of human life and society, the world of animals and plants, in all its particularity and difference, in all its clarity and variety, as a world full of beauty. 'The world is God's glory made manifest, it exists to display his glory, and to draw everything into the contemplation of this beauty.' All this is seen encompassed in the love and wisdom of God and in the supreme beauty of his design, revealed in the death and resurrection of the Lord. 'And yet', as Oliver Davies comments,

> the recognition of the unsurpassable quality of this beauty does not demand that we should deny other forms of God given beauty, rather it invites us to savour them, for the good things of life communicate to us the goodness of God the creator. And indeed, it is creation which is the deepest thematic centre of this poem: creation of the world in all its magnificent diversity together with the new creation through the divine Word 'which the Trinity speaks' through the Redemption.[28]

The role of the Holy Spirit in this third and culminating stage in the work of redemption is memorably brought out in the writing of a twentieth-century Orthodox theologian, Father Sergey Bulgakov, a contemporary witness to the tradition so powerfully presented by Maximus the Confessor. Speaking of 'the self-revelation of the Trinity in the creation of the world', he affirms that 'the world is created by God in his being as Trinity and each of the hypostases is revealed in the world's creation in a way appropriate to its own mode of being'. Thus the act of creation proceeding from the Father's originating act of will, taking shape in the self-giving love of the Son from all eternity, reaches its fulfilment in the coming of the Holy Spirit:

> The participation of the third hypostasis in the creation of the world is the decisive or determinative factor. It gives being to the Father's fiat, it 'finishes' the making of 'the heavens and the earth and all the host of

them' (Genesis 2: 1). With his divine thought realised, his Word having become reality God the Father sees what he has made in its finished beauty and 'sees that it is good . . .' The object of God's creativity, the world, is not only the universe but an artistic work, the *cosmos* in which the artist rejoices. The Holy Spirit, the crown of creation, is the joy of the creator over his creation: for the Father it is the joy of the Word's being made manifest; for the Son it is the joy of the Father's self-revelation in the world. The Holy Spirit is what inspires the creative activity of God in his making of the world.'[29]

It is difficult not to see such a theology of creation and resurrection as realized, indeed almost embodied in the praise poems of early medieval Wales, and in a particular way in *The Loves of Taliesin*. There is the perception as with cleansed and transfigured senses of the whole world as good, of the whole world as beautiful. There is the abundant joy of the singer in the vision of this goodness and beauty and in his own responsive act of creativity in shaping the act of praise. The gift of the Spirit is at the heart of the poet's inspiration and effort. There is a human response which at the creaturely level is wholly appropriate to the divine gift received. Of relevance here is another Welsh poem, *Praise to the Trinity*, in the manuscript known as the Black Book of Carmarthen.[30] The poet writes:

> I praise the threefold
> Trinity as God,
> Who is one and three,
> A single power in unity,
> His attributes a single mystery,
> One God to praise
> Great King I praise you,
> Great your glory.
> Your praise is true;
> I am the one who praises you.

And then to confirm his understanding of the poet's gift he adds: 'Poetry's welfare is in Elohim's care.'[31]

We started from a vernacular poem from the ninth century in Wales. We have come back to other such poems which are more difficult to date, but which I myself would feel confident in placing in the period before the mid-twelfth century. We have passed by way of texts from Wales and Ireland and we have looked briefly by way of parallel at some of the central insights and articulations of Eastern theology, seeing it at its most mature in the work of Maximus the Confessor. That there is great diversity here no one could deny. But I should like to suggest that there is also an underlying unity of vision, a vision of the interaction of creation and resurrection in a cosmic Christology which is characteristic of the Christian world of the first millennium. We find this vision in the poems and writings of the Celtic West, we find it also in the great central body of Graeco-Roman theology, the more familiar works of the Greek and Latin fathers of the universal Church; in all the variety of that world we see the divine wisdom shining out in its 'manifold and yet harmonious dissimilitude'.[32]

Notes

[1] 'Nid oes atgyfodiad, lle nad oes pridd.' From a poem of Euros Bowen in *Amrywion* (Llandysul, 1980), 87. English trans. in Cynthia and Saunders Davies (eds.), *Euros Bowen: Priest Poet – Bardd Offeiriad* (Cardiff, 1993), 133.

[2] See the discussion of this issue by Oliver Davies in Chapter 1 above.

[3] For an English trans. of the poem and discussion of its contents see Oliver Davies, *Celtic Christianity in Early Medieval Wales: The Origins of the Welsh Spiritual Tradition* (Cardiff, 1996), 50–2.

[4] Jenny Rowland, *Early Welsh Saga Poetry: A Study and Edition of the Englynion* (Cambridge, 1990), 289.

[5] The period of conversion is surveyed in J. Fletcher, *The Conversion of Europe* (London, 1997).

[6] Ibid.

[7] D. Simon Evans, *Medieval Religious Literature* (Cardiff, 1986), 5.

[8] Rowland, *Early Welsh Saga Poetry*, 29. See the whole discussion of the meaning of fate in this early poetry, ibid., 23–38.

[9] Ibid., 289.

[10] In the interpretation of these words and of the poem as a whole I am greatly indebted to my friend Paul Bryant-Quinn.

[11] It must be recognized that the derivation of *elfydd* from *elementa* is by no means universally accepted.

[12] As Oliver Davies writes: 'The relatively frequent occurrence in Irish and Welsh literature of the theme of the constitution of the human body (whether as the body of Adam or of Christ) from four, six, seven, or eight components is an indication of the extent to which this motif engaged the imagination of early Celtic authors'; see his discussion with references to other texts, see Oliver Davies, *Celtic Spirituality* (New York and Mahwah, NJ, 1999), 50, nn. 162–5.

13   The English trans. of the work is to be found in John Carey's invaluable collection, *King of Mysteries: Early Irish Religious Writings* (Dublin, 1998), 77–96.

14   John Carey, 'In Tenga Bithnua: from apocalypse to homily?', in Thomas O'Loughlin (ed.), *The Scriptures and Early Medieval Ireland* (Turnhout, 1999), 67.

15   Carey, *King of Mysteries*, 79.

16   Ibid., 75.

17   Ibid., 51–74.

18   Oliver Davies, *Celtic Christianity*, 50.

19   From Maximus' *Chapters on Knowledge*, II. 4, quoted in Mark A. McIntosh, *Mystical Theology: The Integrity of Spirituality and Theology* (Oxford, 1998), 58–9.

20   A remark made in discussion.

21   Michael McCormick's article 'Diplomacy and the Carolingian encounter with Byzantium down to the accession of Charles the Bald', in *Eriugena: East and West* (Notre Dame, IN, 1994), 15–50, throws light on the nature of cultural and social exchanges between Constantinople and the Carolingian court.

22   McIntosh, *Mystical Theology*, 50.

23   A. M. Allchin, *God's Presence Makes the World*, (London, 1997), 29.

24   The manuscript was compiled in the first half of the fourteenth century; some of its poems are considerably earlier, although *The Loves of Taliesin* may have been composed in the thirteenth century. Oliver Davies, *Celtic Christianity*, 76, 84–5.

25   I have used the trans. of *Apgitir Chrabaid* to be found in T. O. Clancy and G. Markus (eds.), *Iona: The Earliest Poetry of a Celtic Monastery* (Edinburgh, 1995), 205–6. Another trans. of this text is to be found in John Carey's book, *King of Mysteries*, 233–45.

26   David Scott, *An Anglo-Saxon Passion* (London, 1999), 72.

27   Oliver Davies, *Celtic Christianity in Early Medieval Wales*, 84–5.

28   Ibid., 88.

29   *Sergii Bulgakov: Towards a Russian Political Theology*, ed. Rowan Williams (Edinburgh, 1999), 194–5.

30   The Black Book of Carmarthen was compiled in the second half of the thirteenth century either in a Cistercian monastery such as Hendy-Gwyn or in the Augustinian Priory of St John the Evangelist at Carmarthen. Many of its poems could be considerably earlier than the date of the manuscript itself: Oliver Davies, *Celtic Christianity*, 28–9.

31   Ibid., 57.

32   Words of Richard Hooker in his *Ecclesiastical Polity* (III. xi. 8) quoted by C. S. Lewis in *English Literature in the Sixteenth Century, Excluding*

Drama (Oxford, 1954), 461. Compare the same writer's phrase 'the beautiful variety of all things'.

I had finished and corrected this article before I received John Carey's remarkable study *A Single Ray of the Sun: Religious Speculation in Early Ireland* (Andover, MA, and Aberystwyth, 1999). In this book John Carey has worked out, in much greater detail and with a much greater knowledge of the Celtic world, some of the basic intuitions I have tried to express in this article. Starting from rather different vantage points and approaching the matter in rather different ways, there is a significant convergence between his treatment of the subject and my own. This is particularly the case in what relates to the inter-action of creation and resurrection in the theological vision of this period both in Wales and Ireland, and in a growing and shared convic-tion that 'behind the unfamiliar imagery and arcane diction of the early texts may lie broad learning, subtle reasoning and spiritual profundity' (*Single Ray*, 81).

6

Muirchú's theology of conversion in his Vita Patricii

THOMAS O'LOUGHLIN

Hagiography: pitfalls and opportunities

Muirchú moccu Machthéni[1] wrote his *Vita Patricii*[2] some time in the closing decades of the seventh century. At first sight it seems little different from many other early medieval *vitae*, whether from the insular region or elsewhere in the Latin West, in that within a broad biographical framework it strings together a chain of wonders linked to its subject. Muirchú portrays Patrick as the great, indeed sole, missionary to Ireland who is now, in the author's time, that country's great heavenly patron. And it is this top layer of meaning that has been the central concern of most studies of the *vita*. Until a generation ago[3] the work was read as part of the evidence for the historical Patrick and historians often went to great lengths to relate the events mentioned in the *vita* to the life of the earlier Romano-British bishop. More recently, having recognized that hagiography is a genre of literature distinct from historical narrative or biography, historians have concentrated on what the *vita* tells us of the time of its composition – a sound instinct with every hagiographical item – and the focus has shifted to it as a witness to a political power-play, partly ecclesiastical and partly secular, relating to the growth of Armagh as a centre of Uí Néill power. This latter tendency among historians, while noting that hagiography is not biography, has failed to notice that, even if there is a political dimension within a *vita* – and there is certainly such a bias in favour of Armagh in the case of Muirchú[4] – these compositions were not commissioned as

political propaganda but within a Christian tradition of hagiography reaching back to the fourth century.[5] Moreover, unless
this formal religious motive is acknowledged and examined, we
abuse these texts just as much as happened when they were used
as factual accounts of Patrick's work in Ireland.[6]

When we view a *vita* as a document composed within a religious textual tradition,[7] we note, especially when it is written by
someone such as Muirchú, who was competently conversant with
the tradition, that it contains many other levels of meaning which
relate to aspects of the theological world of its author and the religious assumptions which he shared as preacher/teacher with his
congregation/audience. Moreover, any attempt to understand a
vita must begin with such questions as the view it assumes and
fosters of the Christian community,[8] its view of the condition of
human nature,[9] its ideal of holiness[10] and its perspective of how
the holy interacts with the world around us.[11] These questions
relate to the imaginary universe of the author and his audience
which embraces the past of the saint, the present of the intended
readers and their futures as Christians, both in terms of their ideal
of society while alive and their view of their destiny *post mortem*.
That world built within the imagination of the hagiographer
embraces the creation relative to the creator, and assumes a view
of the intervention in the creation by Christ which somehow
brings about the mysterious purposes of God, whether it is viewed
as deification, sanctification or salvation. It is within that world
that we must locate the tales of miracles, wonders and signs which
the *vitae* relate – for the saint's *potestas* and *signa* are witness to the
divine at work in the creation. When we have produced a plausible
reconstruction of that world, we can begin to appreciate the text;
and within our understanding of that world we can locate particular topics which the hagiographer touches upon, whether they
are religious (such as his view of the place of liturgy within
Christianity[12]), historical (such as his image of his people[13]) or
relate to the politics of his time. The process involved can be seen
by comparison with the way New Testament scholars study the
gospels, their underlying theology, their authors' various attitudes
to issues in their communities and societies, along with their
historical worth, but do not lose sight of the distinctiveness of
the gospel-genre nor of the fundamental religious motivations of
their authors.[14] In this sense both the gospels and the *vitae* are

propaganda in the strict sense of the word: texts which are intended to help the growth into reality of the imaginary world they describe. If we accept this notion that a *vita* provides us with an access to the imaginary world of an early medieval Christian, then the study of these *vitae* for the Celtic lands is only beginning.

Our first step is to note the main elements that Muirchú drew upon in setting out to compose his text. Muirchú's knowledge of Patrick is built upon three pillars. The first is what he could glean from Patrick's own explanation of his work in Ireland, the *Confessio*.[15] From this he was able to derive about as much information as we can today. For instance, he knew from the *Confessio* that Patrick's home was at Bannavem Taburniae, but knew that the location of this place was already obscure and a matter of conjecture[16] – and the situation has not altered despite the fact that every few years someone comes up with yet another way to find out its position. Second, Muirchú had other scraps of information about Patrick or the distant past in Ireland. An example of this kind of information is the care he takes to integrate the story of Patrick with the information available in the Chronicle of Prosper of Aquitaine about Palladius.[17] About Patrick he knew that 17 March was his date of death (the date of death is usually one of the most secure facts we have in a saint's dossier[18]) as it was part of the liturgy throughout Ireland.[19] Perhaps most importantly, he considered Patrick to be the central force in the conversion of Ireland to Christianity. The third pillar of Muirchú's knowledge was his theological understanding of what was involved in the conversion of a people and of an individual. This understanding was not derived from historical knowledge of what had happened in Ireland or elsewhere, but from his theoretical perception of what was essentially involved in each of these conversions, and so *must* have underpinned the arrival of Christianity among the Irish – simply because it must underpin any actual historical occurrence of conversion. It was this a priori structure of what the conversion of Ireland must have involved that allowed him to spin his few fragments of factual, a posteriori, information together and weave a tale which, while it might provoke scorn from the modern historian interested in Patrick, would convey, from its author's viewpoint, the essence of Patrick's work far more accurately than a catalogue of dates, places or observations on reactions to Patrick.[20] It is this third segment of the information which

Muirchú brought to his study of Patrick that is my concern here, and in particular how he imagined the two termini of conversion: the state of the people (*gens*) or the individual prior to the encounter with Christ, and their state after that encounter. It is the process of change from one terminus to the other that I refer to as conversion.[21]

The drama of baptism

The aim of Muirchú in the *vita* was to develop the understanding of his audience as the people who have been brought to Christianity by Patrick and, as he is their father in faith on earth, so he is still their intercessor in heaven.[22] As such, to understand themselves as Patrick's people, they must understand who they are as baptized people. Thus the primary imagery running through the whole *vita* is that of baptism.[23] Muirchú presents the audience with a drama of twenty-four hours duration which encapsulates the whole history of the work of the conversion of Ireland.[24] This single night and its following day[25] is the first Easter on Irish soil, and its focus and structure is that central event of the whole Christian year: the Easter Vigil. That vigil celebrated many memories within the Christian Church, all of which were perceived as profoundly interconnected. First, it was the re-enactment of the deliverance of the people of Israel from slavery and their salvation by being led through the Red Sea,[26] an event which in itself was interpreted as foreshadowing baptism.[27] Second, it was the night re-enacting the first Easter, and so each year it was, from their perspective on the liturgy, the very night when Christ broke the slavery of death, liberated those held captive in the depths,[28] rose from the dead and brought light into the darkened world.[29] Thirdly, it was the great night of baptism whereby the individual was plunged into the mystery of Christ's dying to rise with him on this night,[30] and the community rejoiced in being God's people,[31] the new Israel brought through the new Red Sea of baptism.[32] Patrick, as Muirchú portrayed him, set about the great sacramental event of the vigil and lit the great vigil fire for the king and his whole court to see,[33] and the candidate for baptism at that first Easter 'on our island'[34] was the Irish people. The vigil then became the scene of a trial between two faiths, two priesthoods and two ages, and the faith of Patrick is presented as superior, for the age of Christ replaces the age of preparation and waiting. And just as the setting and time structure were not derived from any memory of earlier events in Ireland but from Muirchú's own experience and understanding of the liturgy he celebrated each year at the Easter Vigil,[35] so his tales of a trial of divinities is based on his reading of similar events in scripture – and on Daniel 3 in particular.[36]

However, Muirchú was aware that, while the people (*gens*) was 'baptized' in the events of that first Easter and so became one of 'the number of the gentile nations' (Rom. 11: 25) to whom the full revelation of God was disclosed (cf. Rom. 11: 26), he also had to present a model of the conversion of an individual who moves out of darkness and wickedness to begin the new life of the Christian, and the need for repentance in anyone who would call him or herself a Christian. This is presented in a further drama where Patrick encounters the wicked Irish 'Cyclops': Macc Cuill.[37] As with the events at the Easter Vigil at Tara, so here too there is a trial of the righteous Patrick versus the wicked Macc Cuill. But Patrick the missionary is under the divine protection[38] as he was at Tara, and so Macc Cuill's evil rebounds on himself and eventually, brought to his senses, 'he became a convert that very hour, believing in the eternal God and being baptized'.[39] Muirchú presents him as the *exemplum* of what conversion means, for Macc Cuill is transformed through his encounter with the gospel from the extreme of evil to the extreme of holiness: a monastic bishop.[40] For Muirchú the movement from pagan to Christian is, in the case of the individual, intrinsically linked to the conversion of one's life from one moral path to another. In this he reflects one of the themes of conversion that was central to hagiography, where the great conversions were those of the sinners who became monks – as presented in the monastic *vitae* which were his prototypes. In this instance Muirchú followed John Cassian's image of conversion both for the theology involved in setting out the basis for the conversion, the structure of penitence and the desired end of conversion, as well as for the basic storyline of the encounter with Macc Cuill. The whole incident is based on what Cassian tells us of Abba Moses of Calamus in his third book of *Conlationes*:[41] Moses was a murderer who repented, went into a deserted place called Calamus and there grew to 'the highest level of perfection',

to become a teacher of others and model of repentance/conver-
sion.[42]

Muirchú relates both the conversion of the people and the
conversion of individual men and women[43] to baptism, but his
theoretical framework stops at that point. Patrick is commanded
to preach to the nations and baptize them[44] and he must also
convert individuals and baptize them, but Muirchú does not present us with a single integrated and coherent theology which
integrates these two aspects of Christian mission, but rather with
two well-crafted tales: one encapsulates a theology dealing with
the baptism of 'nations' and another deals with the baptism of
individuals.[45] Hence we must now look at Muirchú's view of the
termini of conversion in each story/situation separately.

Becoming a 'chosen people'

As Muirchú read the scriptures he was in no doubt that Christ
had commanded the apostles to go out to the ends of the earth
and baptize *nations* – groups with ethnic identities. The saying of
Jesus – which he interpreted as a command (*praeceptum*) – in
Matthew 28: 19, along with what he perceived as its parallel in
Mark 16: 20, was for Muirchú at the heart of Patrick's mission
and the key to his work with the Irish *gens* and its ruler:

Gospels

[Matt. 28: 18] *et accedens Iesus
locutus est eis dicens . . .*

[Matt. 28: 19] *euntes ergo docete
omnes gentes baptizantes eos in
nomine Patris et Filii et Spiritus
Sancti*

[Mark 16: 20] *illi [apostoli]
autem profecti
praedicauerunt ubique Domino
cooperante et sermonem confir-
mante sequentibus signis.*

Vita Patricii, I. 22

*Sanctus autem Patricius secun-
dum praeceptum Domini Iesu
iens et docens
omnes gentes baptizantesque eos[46]
in nomine Patris et Filii et
Spiritus Sancti*

profectus a Temoria

*praedicauit ubique Domino
cooperante et sermonem confir-
mante sequentibus signis.*

Muirchú could have found many other places in the New Testament where descriptions of the new Christian community are formulated in terms of a *gens* which has been baptized or where baptism is understood as forming a people.[47] In his tale about Patrick being prepared for his mission Muirchú notes that Patrick's task is to take Christianity to the nations (*in nationibus exteris*) beyond the Roman Empire,[48] and here he picks up on Patrick's own interest, expressed in the *Confessio*, in working 'at the ends of the earth'.[49] Some other scriptural texts may have been especially important as they stress the contrast between a people before and after baptism:

> But you are a chosen race, a royal priesthood, a holy nation, God's own people, that you may declare the wonderful deeds of him who called you out of darkness into his marvellous light. Once you were no people but now you are God's people; once you had not received mercy but now you have received mercy. (1 Peter 2: 9–10)

Ideas such as these seem to lie just beneath the surface in Muirchú: his people have now received divine mercy with Patrick's arrival, have moved from darkness into the light through Patrick's liturgy and with Patrick they can now declare the wonderful deeds of Christ. So how great a change had to come about and how did the people's past relate to their present?

While Christianity was from its first decades a missionary religion, Christian attitudes to the religious value of the cultures it encountered varied enormously.[50] At one extreme there were some who saw all to do with the former religions as darkness and evil which had to be rooted out as the work of the Devil and the effect of Adam's sin: this usually took the form of wishing to put as much distance between themselves and the literary culture of Greece and Rome as possible. Jerome exhibits this position in his dream where Christ accuses him of being a 'Ciceronian and not a Christian'.[51] Closer to Muirchú's time we find a not dissimilar attitude in Caesarius of Arles.[52] On the other hand, we have those who saw in those cultures 'a natural law'[53] which was acting as a preparation for the gospel, perhaps by analogy with the Law given to Israel, and so the new religion did not have to tear down the existing structures but rather to build upon, purify or complete them. No two adherents of this approach expressed the relationship between Christianity and what it encountered in the same way, but they can be characterized as those who saw a providence at work in every human society which was somehow pointing to the gospel.[54] Between these positions were many who wanted to take elements from the surrounding culture and reuse them within Christianity.[55] Again, there was a wide diversity of approaches but this 'middle position' can be characterized by Augustine's phrase of 'taking over the Egyptian gold'.[56] On this spectrum we find that Muirchú falls very close to the extreme providential view of God secretly working to bring a people to the position that they are not only ready for the gospel, but are even aware of their need for it.

Muirchú seeks to present history as the unfolding of a divine providence which plans to bring about the conversion of the Irish people at 'the appropriate time':[57] just as God prepared Patrick to be sent to Ireland;[58] so for a long time he had been preparing Irish society to receive Patrick.[59] The resulting picture of the religion and society of early Ireland which Muirchú imagines as that awaiting Patrick is probably his most elaborate literary creation, for it is not an illiterate tribal society that he presents as Patrick's destination, but an elaborate urban empire, the equal to any other earthly kingdom. His purpose in creating this image is unclear but probably reflects a complex of desires. First, if it is a rustic illiterate group to which Patrick comes, then his task seems far less significant than if he has to convert a great nation. Second, unless there is a single ruler who can be converted, then the liturgical drama lacks a subject for baptism in Ireland's Easter Vigil. Third, a kingdom being replaced by the kingdom of God allows him to bring many scriptural images into play. Fourth, it may be an expression of his pride in his own people and their past expressed in the most noble register he knows: that of the scriptures. And fifth, it may be because he knows that, in order to make his point about the superiority of the kingdom of Christ, a superior human kingdom is needed to establish the base of comparison. In this case we could say that Muirchú most truly got inside the message of his scriptural sources, for his story has the exact same ratio between theological tale and historical report that is to be found in the Book of Daniel (with Daniel meeting King Nebuchadnezzar) and 1 Kings (with Elijah challenging the Prophets of Baal). The Irish are ruled by an 'emperor' with a full court and a full body of religious specialists – Muirchú's lists are all drawn from the Old

Testament, for example, 2 Chronicles 33: 6, so we should avoid the word 'druid' when translating him – and, just as Herod's experts had books when they awaited the coming of Christ to their kingdom,[60] the Irish religious experts have books which record their prophecy.[61] Although they are experts in evil arts, they are not cut off from the truth and can know what will happen in the future: a more powerful kingdom and revelation will replace their own. Moreover, they know it is approaching soon for they speak much of this prophecy in the years just before Patrick's arrival and have directions on how they should recognize the bearer of this new kingdom. Then when it arrives and they see Patrick's fire they are in no doubt as to the visitor's power or that their actions that night will affect their nation's destiny forever. The content of the prediction is significant for our understanding of Muirchú, for it shows us how he as a Christian imagined how his pagan ancestors would have imagined Christianity:

> It is a foreign way of life, a foreign kingdom that comes from far
>   beyond the seas,
> with an unknown and gentle teaching (*doctrina modesta*),[62]
> taught by a few,
> received by many,
> honoured by all.
> It will overturn kingdoms,
> kill the kings who resist it,
> seduce the crowds,
> destroy all their gods casting out their cult,[63]
> and it will reign forever. (*Vita*, I. 10. 4)

Christianity is presented as the definitive religious force, and one beside which they recognize their own inferiority in power and permanence: they worship gods which will pass away, but Muirchú worships 'the eternal God'.[64] So as Patrick sets out for Ireland and Tara by divine command, laden with spiritual treasure and intent on smashing the head of idolatry,[65] so the Irish prepare for their own great liturgy, and providence brings them to the same place at the very same hour. Muirchú assumes his audience will see the significance: an unknown providence is leading the Irish towards the night of their baptism while they think they are merely following their own rituals. And then, in the clash of divinities, the unknown becomes known, and the eternal religion replaces transient cults.[66] Patrick's fire is the final fire, and the others have been merely anticipations.[67]

Muirchú has an ambivalent attitude to his own pre-Christian identity: his *gens* was engaged in idolatry and this had to be crushed, for it could not stand as equal with the faith of Christ; but it was also a nation which existed within God's plan and which was being prepared by providence to recognize its need to change. There was no corresponding ambivalence about Patrick: his greatness lies in destroying what is rotten in the kingdom, perfecting it and taking it into the creation's final age. For Muirchú this was the key role of Patrick within the whole plan of God. This is signalled in the *vita* by a major break in the text: the principal story ends with a coda made by conflating the endings of Matthew and Mark's gospels.[68] What remains in the *vita* is declared to be simply a collection of miracles and other stories about Patrick the bishop and eminent teacher,[69] and they are followed by tales relating to Patrick's death.

Repenting and believing

The Irish may now be one of the *gentes* to whom the gospel has been preached and who are now a new people, but what of those to whom the bishop had to preach as he went around the country? Here the key texts for baptism were sayings by Jesus such as 'The time is fulfilled, and the kingdom of God is at hand; repent, and believe in the gospel' (Mark 1: 15). Exactly how *metanoeite*, here and elsewhere in the New Testament, should be translated has been a matter of dispute since the later Middle Ages, but for Muirchú it was linked to being penitent and doing penance.[70] He imagined the act of conversion as having three aspects: repenting, believing and then being baptized. This understanding made no distinction between a conversion of life (*conuersio morum*) and a conversion of beliefs, or between charity as an active principle and faith, for the two were inextricably united. This unity between believing and a change of moral behaviour was reinforced within his pastoral environment where the penitential system for obtaining forgiveness for sins committed after baptism played on the notion that penance was a continuation of a process begun in baptism,[71] and so portrayed baptism as the beginning of a life-long process of conversion of life, of which penitential discipline

was an intrinsic component.[72] So, for Muirchú, the ideal
baptismal candidate – most actual baptisms in late seventh-
century Ireland would have been of infants – must recognize that
he/she is a sinner, declare his/her sorrow, declare belief, receive
baptism and then grow in holiness through doing penitential acts.

Part of the rationale of hagiography was that doctrine be
communicated by means of well-formed stories, and that of Macc
Cuill is a model example of this.[73] Muirchú first tells us how evil
he is: depraved in thought, sinful in body, bitter, angry, cruel,
without conscience or piety and living (though we should expect
nothing more since he has not yet met Patrick) 'a gentile life'. He
leads a wicked bunch of bandits who, for fun and occupation,
descend from their mountain lair to kill travellers. The sign of his
wickedness is that when he sees Patrick he exclaims that the saint
seduces and tricks people into belief, and so he will trap Patrick
and put his god's power to the test. There follows a small-scale
trial of divinities that shows Patrick's power, after which the
bandits recognize that Patrick is 'truly a man of God and' that
they 'have done evil in testing him'. Patrick now questions Macc
Cuill as to why he did it and is told: 'I now repent of it, I shall do
what you command for I am now in the power of the God you
preach.' He is ordered to believe, confess his sins and be baptized.
This happens, and Macc Cuill declares that he is now ready to
embark on the task of the Christian life. He must leave his lair, go
to the seashore and, without weapons, food, drink, spare clothing,
and with his feet shackled, set himself adrift in a small boat without rudder or oar for providence to decide his destiny. Patrick
then says that whatever shore he lands upon, there he must live
and follow the divine commands (*diuina mandata*). All this he did,
and he landed on the Isle of Man where he found two 'spiritual
fathers' who trained him 'in body and soul according to their rule'
and he eventually succeeded them as a bishop in that place. The
conversion of Mac Cuill is the transformation through seeing the
power of God from being a sinner and leader of bandits to being a
penitent and leader of Christians: baptism is perceived as the
divine gift, belief and repentance as the human response. In short,
baptism and penance were the twin keys to the Christian life.

We should also note a major shift in Muirchú's perception of
the relationship of baptism to sin from that of the great Latin
fathers of the fifth century. The key indication of this shift is that,

for the sins which Macc Cuill committed before baptism, and for which he is repentant before baptism, there is still the need for penitence after his baptism. The patristic position[74] had been that baptism marked a complete break with the past, after which the soul was cleansed of sin, and then the problem was what happened if another major sin was committed: in that case there was the one-off opportunity of a very difficult penance. In this patristic perspective the notion of the decisive nature of baptism determined the praxis of penance as a means of forgiveness for sin to such an extent that the fear of 'sins after baptism' became destructive of the ritual of penance and many aspects of actual Christian life. The route around this impasse was through the penitentials which, by viewing penance as medicine, allowed for repeated penance and the integration of regulated penance for the forgiveness of specific sins within the larger Christian agenda of a penitential lifestyle. The effect of this was to see the overcoming of sinfulness, the repair of the damage done by specific sins, and the growth in holiness through Christian discipline as a single process – and we see this in Muirchú's description of Macc Cuill's post-baptismal career. However, this process model has so embedded itself within Muirchú's understanding in this part of the *vita* that baptism is no longer presented as the great clean break such that life can be reckoned in two parts: before baptism and after baptism.[75] When Macc Cuill continues his penitence after baptism for the sins he committed before it, penitence is seen as the great continuous process in human life on its journey towards God, and baptism is just one moment in that process. This shift in the way that baptism and its effects were viewed can be accounted for by two factors. First, Muirchú lives in a community where the penitentials were part of the normal life of the Church, and the theology of penance was a far more obvious element than the theology of baptism. In the patristic period the theological perception of baptism drove the praxis of penance; now we have the reverse situation: the praxis and theology[76] of penance drive the understanding of, and approach to, baptism. In effect, forgiveness of specific sins without repentance and penance – perceived as a unity, inseparable aspects of the command *paenitemini / paenitentiam agite* – was inconceivable. Secondly, within Muirchú's community, baptism was not, in perception, the great moment separating two parts of a life, but something that happened at the very outset of life. And it is possible that Muirchú's operative theology was that baptism marks the beginning of Christian life, and the removal of Original Sin, but that this is the extent to which baptism's forgiving power entered his consciousness as a preacher, and that all actual sins had to be overcome by penitence. In this case Macc Cuill is joining the Christians when he is repentant, believing and baptized; but he is also a man who has committed many sins prior to that day, and these still have to be dealt with by accepting the penance Patrick lays upon him. In short, the notion that baptism remits all prior actual sins is now so far from Muirchú's pastoral situation – since normally all baptisms were those of infants – that he has forgotten this aspect of baptism in creating this tale. The *vita* is a valuable monitor of the shifts that were taking place, almost invisibly, in Latin theology at that time and which would later become hotly debated issues for the university theologians. Often the histories of these theological changes are well documented for the later patristic and early scholastic periods, but are blank for the period between Augustine (354–430) and Abailard (1079–1142) when the actual change in understanding was taking place.[77] This is an aspect of the value of these *vitae* as historical evidence that, to date, has been barely exploited by historians.

This leaves us with a question: was Muirchú's distinction between the baptism of the *gens* and the baptism of individuals a failure to see the inherent connection between these events (that is, a failure of theological understanding or imagination) or has it some other origin? Muirchú shows himself too well acquainted with the Latin tradition for this distinction to be explained in terms of ignorance or some theological blind-spot. A far more cogent reason for the distinction is that he wished to convey two different lessons to his audience. There was the need to create a sense of Christian identity as the Church, the community of Christ who rejoice in the liberation that Christ has brought them. They must see themselves as a chosen people. Alongside this there was the preacher's need to preach repentance and moral renewal: a task that was an intrinsic part of the work of every pastor. And, given his perception of penance as a continuous activity within the Christian life, so there was a continual need to offer teaching and examples which focused upon it. Each discrete story conveyed its own message and was to be read as an individual tale, not as a section from a systematic theology. As such, the differing emphases and different theologies do not show Muirchú as an inconsistent theologian, but a good communicator. Moreover, it is inappropriate for us to take his latent theology and oppose one part to another with the implication that he had left issues unresolved: the hagiographer preaches (and so is no more inconsistent than any other communicator who must find stories now for this message, now for another message), while the text-book writer seeks consistency at the theoretical level.

Continuities and discontinuities

The significance of Muirchú's text is that through it we can see both how an early Irish Christian imagined his own religious history and how he understood a central element within Christian theology. Thus Muirchú is a source for the cultural history of the British Isles, as well as a source for the history of Latin theology. The world conjured for readers in the *vita* is a world of the imagination – and we distort it if we seek to question it as to its 'historical accuracy' or seek to isolate its 'verifiable elements'. It is a theologian's tale that should be judged alongside other expert pieces of story-telling both before (the Elijah-cycle in 1 Kings or the Daniel stories or *The Pastor* of 'Hermas') and since (the *Nauigatio sancti Brendani* or John Bunyan or C. S. Lewis's 'Screwtape' books).

That said, we find some aspects of his theology surprising. His distinction between the nation and the individual is one to which many of us can hardly relate: the *gens* is, for us, merely the collective noun for the assembly of individuals. Theologically, the idea of the 'nation being baptized' does not recall scriptural echoes but seems to be an extreme example of 'Constantinian Christianity', and references to 'Christian nations' recall missionary propaganda from the nineteenth century. On the positive side, we could note that he sees Christianity in terms of a community, a new people, and the need to see salvation in communal rather than individualistic terms – themes many theologians still stress when presenting baptism in ecclesial terms. When we look on his theology of individual conversion we may be surprised by his emphasis on Christian life as penitential or his assumption that monasticism represents the Christian ideal, but many contemporary Christians place emphasis on baptism as the beginning of 'costly disciple-ship'. There are other aspects of his theology which remind us that he lived in another world to ours: his notion of providence seems to reduce human freedom to that of compliance or rebellion, while he and his readers shared a view of the world which allowed for divine interventions and wonders in a way we can no longer imagine without laughter. But such theological comparisons and contrasts aside, reading Muirchú reminds us just how difficult is the task of the historian of ideas: we cannot simply follow threads from the past to his present or from his present to our own. Rather we must see his short work as a fragment with which we can try to reconstruct an intellectual universe. However, once we embark on that task, we have one comfort: the *Vita Patricii* is a very rich frag-ment.

Notes

1   For a summary of what we know of the author's life, see T. O'Loughlin, *Celtic Theology: Humanity, World, and God in Early Irish Writings* (London, 2000), 87–9.

2   The edn. being used here is that of L. Bieler (ed.), *The Patrician Documents in the Book of Armagh* (Dublin, 1979), 62–125, which provides a facing English translation; however, all translations used in this paper, unless otherwise noted, are my own. The *Vita* is item no. 303 in M. Lapidge and R. Sharpe, *A Bibliography of Celtic-Latin Literature 400–1200* (Dublin, 1985).

3   The turning-point in the study of material relating to Patrick was the 1962 study by D. A. Binchy, 'Patrick and his biographers, ancient and modern', *Studia Hibernica*, 2 (1962), 7–173, which pointed out that these works were historically worthless for the time of Patrick and rather should be read, according to the principles laid down by H. Delehaye, *The Legends of the Saints* (Brussels, 1905; trans. London, 1962; repr. Dublin, 1998); see the introduction by T. O'Loughlin to the 1998 repr. for Binchy's debt to Delehaye and the principle that a *vita* tells us more about its time of composition than about the time of its subject.

4   See II. 4 and II. 13 for examples of his interest in Armagh and the Uí Néill.

5   See L. Bieler, 'The Celtic hagiographer', *Studia Patristica*, 5 (1962), 241–65; 'Muirchú's Life of Patrick as a work of literature', *Medium Aevum*, 43 (1974), 219–33; 'Hagiography and romance in medieval Ireland', *Mediaevalia et Humanistica*, 6 (1975), 13–24; and on the

origins of the genre, see T. O'Loughlin, 'Hagiography: Christian perspectives', in W. M. Johnston (ed.), *Encyclopedia of Monasticism* (Chicago and London, 2000), 564–6.

6   For a case where a contemporary historian recognizes the limitations of seeking to understand *vitae* as variants of political posturing, see E. Bhreathnach, 'Temoria: caput Scotorum?', *Ériu*, 47 (1996), 67–88, at 73.

7   For how I understand such a tradition in Muirchú's period, see my *Teachers and Code-Breakers: The Latin Genesis Tradition 430–800* (Turnhout, 1999), 24–71.

8   What in contemporary theology would be referred to as its 'ecclesiology'.

9   For some modern theologians this would be referred to as its 'theological anthropology', while for others it would be the author's 'theology of grace'.

10   Its 'spirituality'.

11   Its 'sacramentology' in contemporary terms, or its image of the place of sacraments in the Christian life in an older theology.

12   For this topic in an insular text from slightly later than Muirchú, see my 'Distant islands: the topography of holiness in the *Nauigatio Sancti Brendani*', in M. Glasscoe (ed.), *The Medieval Mystical Tradition: England, Ireland, Wales (Exeter Symposium VI)* (Woodbridge, 1999), 1–20.

13   For a study of how Bede in his *Historia ecclesiastica gentis anglorum* wishes to present his people as a *gens electa*, see C. W. Jones, 'Some introductory remarks on Bede's Commentary on Genesis', *Sacris Erudiri*, 19 (1969), 115–98.

14   It is worth recalling that many of the methods which were hailed, or condemned, as revolutionary in studies of early Christian literature, such as the gospels, and linked with writers such as Rudolf Bultmann, were already commonplace with investigators of hagiographical texts such as Hippolyte Delehaye. This is explored further in my introduction to the reprint of *The Legends of the Saints*.

15   See T. O'Loughlin, *St Patrick: The Man and his Works* (London, 1999).

16   *Vita*, I. 1. Muirchú gets over his difficulty with a rhetorical display: 'we have ascertained, with certainty and beyond any doubt, that Ventre is that place'.

17   *Vita*, I. 9. On this material see T. Charles-Edwards, 'Palladius, Prosper, and Leo the Great: mission and primatial authority', in D. N. Dumville et al. (eds.), *Saint Patrick, A.D. 493–1993* (Woodbridge, 1993), 1–12; and O'Loughlin, *Celtic Theology*, 25–6.

18   See Delehaye, *Legends of the Saints,* where it is repeatedly pointed out that the name and a 'date of birth into paradise' are the kernel of every cult. In the calendar of St Willibrord (658–739) we find this

entry for 17 March: '[The feast] of Saint Patrick, Bishop in Ireland' (Paris, BN Lat. 10837, fol. 35ᵛ; there is a facsimile and edition by H. A. Wilson, *The Calendar of St. Willibrord from MS. Paris. Lat. 10837*, Henry Bradshaw Society 55 (London, 1918; repr. Woodbridge, 1998).

[19] See what Muirchú says about 17 March at *Vita*, II. 7; and this is confirmed by the evidence of Willibrord's calendar (see n. 18).

[20] Indeed, over the years many details in Muirchú have been used as evidence for 'druids' (see below) and the like, in early Ireland, but in fact the *vita* tells us more about Muirchú's perception of Babylon as found in the Book of Daniel than about early Irish society.

[21] It is important for the study of any early medieval text that we attempt to use words which are familiar to us from Christian discourse, such as 'conversion', as neutrally as possible until we have established a possible range of meaning for them through an analysis of our texts. Using words with a subsequent semiotic loading, for instance, using 'conversion' with a value similar to that which it has among contemporary Evangelicals – see, for example, J. Finney, *Recovering the Past: Celtic and Roman Mission* (London, 1996) – reduces rather than enhances our understanding of Christianity as an historical phenomenon. It could be objected that it would be better to avoid words such as 'conversion' which have particular meanings within various segments of modern Christianity (and where we have no assurance that any of these meanings is identical with a past value), but such linguistic caution would render a history of ideas impossible.

[22] This Abrahamic image of the patriarch would have been familiar to Muirchú from the eucharistic liturgy (*patriarchae nostri Abrahae*) in conjunction with Rom. 4; and can be seen in use by him in *Vita*, I. 27.

[23] It is central in the first part of the *vita* (up to I. 22) and then recurs in the remainder of the work.

[24] I have developed this point in greater detail in the chapter on Muirchú in *Celtic Theology*.

[25] Easter Day, both in the Latin liturgy and in the structure of Muirchú's narrative, is merely the remainder of the day which begins with the lighting of the new fire at the opening of the vigil: this is liturgically the moment of the resurrection and the subsequent morning is the sequel, just as all the events narrated for Easter Day are, collectively, the sequel to Christ leaving the tomb.

[26] This is recalled in the *Vita* at I. 13.

[27] For an account of how theologians in the seventh century understood Old Covenant events (that is, events recorded in the Old Testament) as an anticipation through antetypes of what would become perfect with the New Covenant (and recorded in the New Testament), see T.

O'Loughlin, 'Christ as the focus of Genesis exegesis in Isidore of Seville', in T. Finan and V. Twomey (eds.), *Studies in Patristic Christology* (Dublin, 1998), 144–62.

[28] For the significance of this theme in Ireland at the time of Muirchú, see T. O'Loughlin, 'Adam's burial at Hebron: some aspects of its significance in the Latin tradition', *Proceedings of the Irish Biblical Association*, 15 (1992), 66–88.

[29] These images were canonized for the Easter Vigil liturgy through their use in one of its major texts: the *Exultet*.

[30] Cf. Rom. 6: 3–5.

[31] The basis of this imagery is to be found in Jude 5, 1 Pet. 2: 9–10.

[32] See 1 Cor. 10: 1–2, Acts 7: 36, and Heb. 11: 29 for the beginnings of this imagery which was fundamental to Muirchú's understanding of baptism/the Easter Vigil.

[33] *Vita*, I. 15.

[34] *Vita*, I. 13.

[35] It might be objected that this notion that it is the Easter liturgy which forms the structure of Muirchú's image of Ireland's conversion puts far too great an emphasis on a single piece of ritual. This is compounded by the fact that there is a major discontinuity in Christians' perceptions since Muirchú's time: that is, most Christians imagine that their ritual experience is very ancient and so they feel that should understand how earlier Christians celebrated their liturgy; yet many Christians today have never even heard of, much less taken part in, an Easter Vigil, and even those Christians whose traditions still include that vigil do not see it as the high-point of their ritual year. However, if you want to glimpse some of the significance of Easter night in the seventh-century British Isles just note that this is the period of the 'Easter-Dating Controversy' and that this was a live issue on Iona (see Bede, *Historia ecclesiastica gentis anglorum*, V. 15) at the time when Muirchú was writing. While a great deal of attention is devoted to the Easter-dating question, few studies recognize precisely why it was of such importance to all concerned. It is with that controversy in mind that we should read what Muirchú himself says (*Vita*, I. 13. 2) about the Vigil as 'the chief Christian solemnity' (*caput omnium sollempnitatem*).

[36] This theme has been explored in my 'Reading Muirchú's Tara-event within its background as a biblical "trial of divinities"', in J. Cartwright (ed.), *Celtic Hagiography and Saints' Cults* (forthcoming).

[37] *Vita*, I. 23.

[38] Muirchú's notion that missionaries receive special divine protection is based on his interpretation of Mark 16: 18.

[39] *Vita*, I. 23. 11.

40 This result says a great deal about how Muirchú saw holiness and the structures of the Church as indivisible, but this topic cannot be pursued here.

41 *Conlationes*, III. 5. 2. M. Petschenig (ed.), *Corpus Scriptorum Ecclesiasticorum Latinorum* 13 (Vienna, 1886), 72. However, to understand its full theological value to Muirchú, what Cassian says of Abba Moses must be seen as exemplary of the topic already discussed in *Conlatio*, III, and especially of III. 3 and 4 on 'the three vocations and three renunciations'.

42 For an introduction to Cassian's theology see C. Stewart, *Cassian the Monk* (Oxford and New York, 1998), 40–61; and for information on Abba Moses, see ibid., 138–40.

43 See *Vita*, I. 27 which recounts the baptism of the British woman Monesan where Muirchú says that following her profession of faith, Patrick 'washed her with the Holy Spirit and the washing of water (*aquae lauacro*)', which is a deliberate allusion to Church as wife/woman to Christ in Eph. 5: 25: 'Christus . . . ea . . . mundans lauacro aquae in uerbo' (and cf. Tit. 3: 5) and which is intended to echo John 3: 5 for the reader.

44 *Vita*, I. 22.

45 The terminology for each – if we wish to separate them – can be found in scripture.

46 Here I depart from Bieler's text (supported by two witnesses) in favour of the variant cited in his apparatus (also supported by two witnesses) and which, Bieler notes, agrees with the Vulgate.

47 Apart from the nations mentioned in Paul, there are references in the Old Testament about the nations being gathered together to the Lord in the final age (e.g. Ezek. 5: 5) and there are references in the New Testament to the spread of the Christian message to the ends of the earth (e.g. Acts 1: 8); and we know from the writings of Adomnán (his contemporary whom Muirchú met) and Bede (a generation later) that these were important themes in theology at the time.

48 *Vita*, I. 5. Bieler's emendation of *exteris* to *externis* is redundant.

49 See my *Celtic Theology*, 36–8.

50 R. P. C. Hanson, 'The Christian attitude to pagan religions up to the time of Constantine the Great', *Aufstieg und Niedergang der Römischen Welt*, 23/2 (1980), 910–73.

51 The source of the image is *Epistola*, 22, but it became a stock item of knowledge.

52 See A. Ferreiro, '*Frequenter legere:* the propaganda of literacy, education, and divine wisdom in Caesarius of Arles', *Journal of Ecclesiastical History*, 43 (1992), 5–15.

53 Built on a particular reading of Rom. 1–2.

54 Eusebius of Caesarea's historical works are perhaps the most famous expression of this approach, but he had predecessors such as Clement of Alexandria: see W. Telfer, ' "Bees" in Clement of Alexandria', *Journal of Theological Studies*, 28 (1927), 167–178; and E. F. Osborn, 'Teaching and writing in the first chapter of the *Stromateis* of Clement of Alexandria', *Journal of Theological Studies*, NS 10 (1959), 335–43. For an overview of this approach, see C. Saldanha, *Divine Pedagogy: A Patristic View of Non-Christian Religions* (Rome, 1984).

55 This has become the *bête noire* of many historians who pursue evidence for Christian 'syncretism' while forgetting that Christians were well aware of the danger and quite capable of distinguishing between acculturation of their message within particular environments, and a combination which would amount to assimilation by that environment.

56 This is the theme of Augustine's major work on the topic, the *De doctrina christiana*; see T. O'Loughlin, 'The development of Augustine the bishop's critique of astrology', *Augustinian Studies*, 30 (1999), 83–103.

57 *Vita*, I. 8: Muirchú signals this with the phrase *oportuno tempore*; I suggest that the significance of this phrase is that it designates a moment chosen by God when all is ready for his purposes, cf. Gal 4: 4.

58 *Vita*, I. 5–7.

59 *Vita*, I. 10.

60 See Matt. 2: 1–10; these scriptural echoes are examined in my 'Reading Muirchú's Tara-event within its background as a biblical "trial of divinities" '.

61 *Vita*, I. 20. 8.

62 The text, as edited, reads *doctrina molesta* and Bieler records no variant readings, but I am emending *molesta* (annoying, burdensome) to *modesta* (gentle). I have three reasons for this emendation. First, *molesta* makes no sense in the context, for it is clear that Muirchú wants to show Christianity as something attractive: 'a multis susceptum, ab omnibus honorandum.' Moreover, Muirchú would have had to reconcile *molesta* with Matt. 11: 28–30. Second, *doctrina modesta* would echo James 3: 17: 'quae autem desursum est sapientia primum quidem pudica est deinde pacifica modesta', which was commonly used as a description for Christian wisdom. Third, the corruption of *modesta* to *molesta* is easily explained by haplography: the loop of the <d> could have been confused with the <o> such that the copyist saw <moolesta> and his eye skipped over the second loop and read <molesta>.

63 Literally: 'all of the works of their craft'.

64   This term is used on three occasions in the *Vita*: I. 1. 15; I. 21.1; and I. 23. 11.
65   *Vita*, I. 11 and 13.
66   Although he does not directly refer to the passage, the structure is that of Acts 17: 23–31.
67   *Vita*, I. 15.
68   *Vita*, I. 22 – it is quoted above.
69   *Vita*, I. 27 – the numeration of the text is confusing, but what is here referred to as I. 27 follows immediately upon I. 22.
70   Muirchú would have read these texts in a different sequence from the modern scholar: the starting-points would have been the preaching of John the Baptist: 'paenitentiam agite adpropinquauit enim regnum caelorum' (Matt. 3: 2); which was then taken up by Jesus: 'exinde coepit Iesus praedicare et dicere "paenitentiam agite adpropinquauit enim regnum caelorum"' (Matt. 4: 17); and this was summarized by Mark: 'impletum est tempus et adpropinquauit regnum Dei paenitemini et credite euangelio' (1: 15); and further explored by Luke: 'non ueni uocare iustos sed peccatores in paenitentiam' (5: 32). This then, it seemed, became the pattern of the Apostles' preaching: 'et exeuntes praedicabant ut paenitentiam agerent' (Mark 6: 12); and 'paenitemini igitur et conuertimini ut deleantur uestra peccata' (Acts 3: 19).
71   It was this notion of a process inherent in the Irish penitentials that marks their major theological break with the patristic understanding of penance as a 'laborious second baptism' where penitence was a one-off event.
72   See T. O'Loughlin, 'Penitentials and pastoral care', in G. R. Evans (ed.), *A History of Pastoral Care* (London, 2000), 93–111.
73   *Vita*, I. 22.
74   For the purpose of understanding the shift in Muirchú's position we can leave aside the notion of 'Original Sin' as it does not figure in the *Vita*, and his shift in position with regard to the cleansing action of baptism is distinct from that question.
75   This is in contrast to the way he presents the baptism of the nation where that first Easter Vigil marks a decisive point in the nation's history.
76   It is often forgotten that the penitentials should not be viewed simply as a change in praxis, for such a change only became possible due to the developments in theological understanding (see my *Celtic Theology*, 48–67) and the extension of Cassian's view of the barriers to the growth in holiness within monasticism to every kind of sin in the wider community (see T. O'Loughlin, 'Penitential Books', in the *Encyclopedia of Monasticism*, 1006–7).

77 This is the great 'dark period' in historical surveys of the Latin theology of sin/forgiveness and is usually bridged only by a section on
penitentials as practical pastoral regulations, cf. B. Poschmann,
Penance and the Anointing of the Sick (trans. F. Courtney, London,
1963) which devotes pp. 122–38 to the penitentials, and K. B.
Osborne, *Reconciliation and Justification: The Sacrament and its Theology*
(Mahwah, NJ, 1990) which devotes pp. 84–94 to them.

7

Incarnate glory: the spirituality of D. Gwenallt Jones

D. DENSIL MORGAN

In a volume on the idea of a Celtic Christianity, it seems wholly appropriate to include a chapter on a modern Welsh poet whose work embodies so many of those themes which characterize the spirituality which many (despite some considerable qualms) equate with Celticism: a Trinitarian vision of reality, a holding together of the motifs of creation and redemption, an incarnational attitude to the material world, and a sense of community which expresses a continuity with an ancient and pre-Christian past. The fact that this collection examines the work of a poet – not a scholar or a theologian, though D. Gwenallt Jones has a claim to have been both – whose function in Wales, even today, is much more social and public than in many places elsewhere, presents another strand in the Celtic pattern wherein the poet as creator expresses an inspiration which, according to the claim, is of God. And just as the renewal of Celtic spirituality is a response to the crises and questions of the late modernity and post-modernity of the twenty-first century,[1] in Gwenallt a holistic Christianity, which is rooted in the apostolic, patristic, medieval and Reformation past, is wholly compatible with the myriad challenges of contemporary life. Whatever the challenges of a new millennium, Gwenallt is still the poet of our present and, I would venture to claim, of our future as well.[2]

D. Gwenallt Jones was born David James Jones in Pontardawe, an industrial village in Glamorgan's Swansea Valley, on 18 May 1899. His family had migrated from neighbouring rural Carmarthenshire, and his links with the ancestral home would remain strong. His education at the local primary school and the Ystalyfera County

School would have taken him straight to the University of Wales, Aberystwyth, had it not been interrupted by the Great War. Rather than volunteering for service or, after the passing of the Military Service Act in 1916, being conscripted into the armed forces, he chose the arduous path of conscientious objection and spent two years at Dartmoor and Wormwood Scrubs. (His novel *Plasau'r Brenin* (The King's Mansions, 1934) and sonnet 'Dartmoor' in his 1942 collection of verse *Cnoi Cil* (Chewing Things Over), recount his experiences at the time.) Having resumed his studies, at Aberystwyth, he graduated and, following postgraduate research and a short time as a schoolmaster, he returned to the University, in 1926, as a lecturer in the Department of Welsh where he spent the rest of his career. He retired, as Reader in Welsh Literature, in 1967. By the time of his death, on Christmas Eve 1968, he was renowned as one of Wales's leading poets and, in literary circles, a seminal twentieth-century influence.

This bald and rather uninspiring précis of his life conceals a poetic and spiritual pilgrimage which was as interesting as it was significant. Gwenallt came to the notice of the public by winning the chair in the National Eisteddfod of 1926 for his *awdl* entitled 'Y Mynach' (The Monk) and two years later he gained notoriety when the Eisteddfod adjudicators refused to award him the chair for what they admitted was the best poem in the competition, his *awdl* 'Y Sant' (The Saint), because it contained sexually explicit material – at least by the very prim and puritanical standards of 1920s Wales! Neither poem was exceptional, though the medievalist Romanticism which permeated them both typified the aesthetic phase which Gwenallt was going through at the time. It was not until 1936, when the strikingly modern five stanzas of 'Ar Gyfeiliorn' (Adrift) were published in the progressive literary magazine *Heddiw* (Today), that it became obvious that Gwenallt's muse had matured, that he had developed a vivid and specific vision of the world and that he had found his poetic voice:

Gwae inni wybod y geiriau heb adnabod y Gair
A gwerthu ein henaid am doffi a chonffeti ffair,
Dilyn yn ôl pob tabwrdd a dawnsio yn ôl pob ffliwt
A boddi hymn yr Eiriolaeth â rhigwm yr Absoliwt.

Dynion yn y Deheudir heb ddiod na bwyd na ffag,
A balchder eu bro dan domennydd ysgrap, ysindrins, yslag:

Y canél mewn pentrefi'n sefyllian, heb ryd na symud na sŵn,
A'r llygod boliog yn llarpio cyrff y cathod a'r cŵn . . .

Woe unto us knowing the words who know not the Word
Having sold our souls for toffee and fairground confetti,
Following every drumbeat and dancing after every flute,
Having drowned the hymn of Intercession with the rhyme of the
    Absolute.

Men in the South have no food or drink, or a fag,
The proud beauty of their land is covered by heaps of scrap, cinders
    and slag;
The village canals are idle, silent and still,
While the big-bellied rats rip open the corpses of cats and dogs . . .[3]

The harsh realism of this picture of industrial south Wales ravaged
by the inter-war recession was novel and raw. Most popular Welsh
poetry of the time was pastoral, Romantic and lyrical, while the
agnostic modernism of T. H. Parry-Williams and others did not
engage with the social realities of the day. But this was different
and, coming from the chaired bard of the 1926 Eisteddfod, quite
unexpected. Moreover, its Christian content, which was devoid of
conventional pieties, was explicit:

Gosod, O Fair, Dy Seren yng nghanol tywyllwch nef,
A dangos â'th siart y llwybr yn ôl at Ei ewyllys Ef,
A disgyn rhwng y rhaffau dryslyd, a rho dy law ar y llyw,
A thywys ein llong wrthnysig i un o borthladdoedd Duw.

O Mary, place Your Star at the centre of the dark heavens,
And show us on your chart the path back to His will,
And climb down through the tangled rigging, and put your hand on
    the helm,
And guide our perverse ship into one of the harbours of God.

The publication of Gwenallt's first volume of verse *Ysgubau'r
Awen* (Sheaves of the Muse) in 1939, which contained this poem
and many others in the same vein, established his reputation as a
poet of the first rank whose voice – uncompromising, severe with a
passion held in check by the trammels of metrical form – was
unique. What is more, this was Christian verse of a stark kind.
  The path of the poet's spiritual journey was revealed in an auto-

biographical essay entitled 'Credaf', the 'I believe' of the Apostles' Creed, which was published in 1942 as an explicit contribution to Christian witness. In it he describes vividly an upbringing immersed in the culture and piety of popular Nonconformity, and the inherent tensions between that culture and the social inequality and industrial unrest of which he became aware in his youth. Adolescent rebelliousness took the form, initially, of the Socialist idealism of Keir Hardie's Independent Labour Party, progressing towards a full-blown Marxism with its dogmas of class warfare and the victory of the proletariat. According to this ideology, Christianity was a capitalist tool used to keep the workers in subjugation to the entrepreneurial class. Being incompatible with the truth of the materialist interpretation of history, there was no choice but to reject it:

> Marxism became our gospel [he recalled], a much better one than Methodism. It was a religion, a social religion, for which we were prepared to live and die and make sacrifices; but we would not have raised a finger to defend Calvinism. Capitalism was something that we knew in our lives. We saw the poverty, famine and near-famine, the hovel-like houses, mothers growing old before their time, the cruelty of soldiers and policemen during the strikes, doctors putting tuberculosis instead of silicosis on death certificates to avoid having to pay compensation to relatives, and the bodies being brought home after accidents. Years later my father's body came home after he had been burnt to death by molten metal, and that unnecessarily. When, in the funeral sermon, the minister said that it was God's will, I cursed his sermon and his God with all the haulier's swear-words that I knew, and when they sang the hymn *Bydd Myrdd o Ryfeddodau* at the graveside, I sang in my heart *The Red Flag*.[4]

It was this revolutionary compulsion, exacerbated by such a traumatic family loss, which led Gwenallt to conscientious objection on political (not religious) grounds during the Great War, and would have marked out the course of his consequent life had it not been for a restless, continually enquiring streak in his nature which drove him on from one form of commitment to the next.

His student years at Aberystwyth were marked by an eclectic mixture of atheism and aestheticism in which political activity was eclipsed for a time by a hedonistic Romanticism. These were the years of his early poetic successes. Two things occurred during this period which were to have a lasting effect: his discovery of the verse of Baudelaire and his disenchantment with Socialist politics (though not with the need for radical political reform). Both were to draw him back to a Christian analysis of reality and, before long, to the discipline of personal faith. Baudelaire, the most decadent of the French Romantic poets of the nineteenth century, had realized that human evil – which was the theme of *Les Fleurs du mal* – was rooted in its rebellion against God; it was this which lent to the human condition a depth of tragedy and guilt which indicated its greatness. (It was Baudelaire, too, who was described by T. S. Eliot as being 'man enough to be damned'.) For him sin was an existential and ontological reality. Sin, of course, was what the Socialists had rejected in favour of humankind's perfectibility and, given the right economic circumstances, the capacity to create a classless utopia, a heaven upon earth. Yet, following the 1924 general election, Gwenallt's experience of Socialism in action and his more general observation of the uncomradely brawls between Communists, Marxists and the rest gave him much pause for thought. 'Marx showed that self-interest lurked behind *bourgeois* ideals', he wrote, 'and he was right, but could not self-interest lurk behind Communist ideals as well?'[5] It was the unique insight of Christianity that humankind was not merely flawed but corrupt at a core level and that this corruption could be perpetually masked by all sorts of ideological evasions. Yet even a corruption as deep as this was not beyond the possibility of being redeemed. Little by little, some time during the mid- to late 1920s, Gwenallt was drawn back to the Christian estimate of reality and, more explicitly, to the practice of Christian faith:

> Anyone who discovers his own sinfulness is half a Christian . . . As Socialists and Communists we wanted to reform everyone and everything, except ourselves. We could not see that the old Adam still lived in Moscow. The Communist revolution is a mere flea-bite beside the Christian revolution.[6]

The doctrinal analysis embodied in the essay 'Credaf' is intuitive and eclectic rather than systematic and considered, yet with its emphasis on sin, redemption and the renewal of creation through God's costly grace, it bears all the marks of a Catholic orthodoxy. It contains not a shred of pietism. The theological synthesis which Gwenallt sought would have to take him *into* the world, not out of it, and whereas he was attracted by the classical

Protestant formulations of Williams Pantycelyn and the Methodist fathers whose inheritance he was now in a position positively to reassess, he could not accept their vision totally:

> Between he [Pantycelyn] and I stood the wilderness of South Wales. The humanism of Dafydd ap Gwilym [the greatest of our medieval poets] and the theology of Pantycelyn, how to reconcile this world and the world to come, time and eternity, human understanding and divine revelation, reason and faith? That was the challenge.[7]

Ysgubau'r Awen (1939), the slim volume *Cnoi Cil* (1942), and to an even greater extent the more tranquil 1951 collection *Eples* (Leaven), contain a theological and artistic vision in which these dualities are, on the whole, reconciled if not totally synthesized and integrated. Their central themes of Wales, flesh and spirit, sin and redemption, and the renewal of civilization through the healing of the cross, comprise a body of work which combines rhetorical strength, a mastery of form and metaphor, with a subtlety which, given the poetry's directness and accessibility, is not always immediately apparent. If the 1959 volume *Gwreiddiau* (Roots), received less critical acclaim than its predecessors, it, too, contained some very arresting and satisfying poems, as did the posthumous *Y Coed* (The Trees), of 1969. Although this body of work predated the contemporary interest in Celtic spirituality, and is ostensibly more indebted to the Augustinianism of the Latin Fathers and the Reformers than to the more immanentist theology of the Christian East, Gwenallt's work displays a catholicity which affirms God's involvement with creation and his sacramental presence within the world as well as his gracious judgement upon it. Mankind is not merely sinful but, as the object of redemption, God's active partner in his work of transforming nature by grace. The vision is Celtic in so far as it is rooted in the Christian praise and worship of a specific community which maintains its continuity with the direct and ancient past in which God, as Father, Son and Holy Spirit, was seen to be a constant participant in the life of the world.

Gwenallt's introduction to experiential and doctrinal Christianity was through the conviction of the reality of original sin. The theme is all-pervasive in the first volume of verse in which he expresses guilt and corruption by using animal imagery. The Twrch Trwyth, the mythical wild boar of Welsh medieval folklore, becomes the symbol not merely of human fallenness but of the primitive evil in which the poet himself shares: 'He was formed of the blind passions / In the soil of our base nature.' No matter how hard he applies his will to pursue the beast in order, he hopes, to destroy it, its wiliness and its beguiling nature, 'the jewels between its ears / Which excite our lust and greed', ensure its perpetual escape. Yet the beast's death is assured, not through the feeble and inadequate willpower of the hunter but through the invincible grace of Christ manifest in and through his Church. The four stanzas of a second poem on the same theme, 'Y Ffwlbart' (The Polecat), are quite virulent in their invective and the description of the animal is even more striking and ugly:

> Gwelais di'n syllu yn haerllug a barus
> Ar fryn ac yn fawr dy frol,
> A'th gorpws drewllyd yng nghanol yr heulwen
> Fel ysmotyn inc ar y rhol . . .

> I saw you staring impudent and greedy
> On a hillside so full of yourself,
> Your wretched corpus in the light of the sun
> Was like a blot of ink on a scroll . . .

Such is the creature's vileness that its eventual destruction can only be a cause for jubilation. The identification of human sinfulness with such stark imagery strikes a generation more attuned to the cause of animal rights and ecological concerns as mildly, and perhaps blatantly, shocking. Yet these harsh poems said something profound about the human condition which was well in tune with the awful realities of inter-war Europe of which Gwenallt's Wales was such an integral part. The animal imagery which he employed in some of his later poems would signify not so much sinfulness as the redemption of the whole of creation, but there is one further poem, this time a sonnet, in which the theme of human evil would reach a memorable crescendo. Its title, quite simply, is 'Pechod' (Sin):

> Pan dynnwn oddi arnom bob rhyw wisg,
> Mantell parchusrwydd a gwybodaeth ddoeth,
> Lliain diwylliant a sidanau dysg,
> Mor llwm yw'r enaid, yr aflendid noeth:
> Mae'r llaid cyntefig yn ein deunydd tlawd,

Llysnafedd bwystfil yn ein mêr a'n gwaed,
Mae saeth y bwa rhwng ein bys a'n bawd
A'r ddawns anwareiddiedig yn ein traed.
Wrth grwydro hyd y fforest wreiddiol, rydd,
Canfyddwn rhwng y brigau ddarn o'r Nef,
Lle cân y saint anthemau gras a ffydd,
Magnificat Ei iechydwriaeth Ef;
Fel bleiddiaid codwn ni ein ffroenau fry
Gan udo am y Gwaed a'n prynodd ni.

When we strip off all our garments,
The cloak of respectability and academic knowledge,
The cloth of culture and the silks of learning,
How bare is the soul, the naked impurity:
The primitive mire in our makeup is revealed,
The beastly slime in our blood and bone,
The bow's arrow held between our finger and thumb
And the barbaric rhythm in our dance.
As we wander through the ancient, primeval forest,
We glimpse through the branches a strip of Heaven,
Where the saints sing anthems of grace and faith,
The *magnificat* of His salvation;
So like wolves we lift our nostrils sky-wards
And howl for the Blood by which we are redeemed.

As the poet was soon to reiterate, 'Anyone who discovers his own sinfulness is half a Christian'.

A second rich and connected motif in *Ysgubau'r Awen* is that of spirit and the flesh. The sonnet 'Cnawd ac Ysbryd' (Flesh and Spirit),

Duw ni waharddodd inni garu'r byd,
A charu dyn a'i holl weithredoedd ef,
Eu caru â'r synhwyrau noeth i gyd,
Pob llun a lliw, pob llafar a phob llef . . .

God has not forbidden us to love the world,
And to love man and all his works,
To love them with all the naked senses,
Every shape and colour, every voice and every sound . . .,[8]

is justly famous as Gwenallt's most rounded description of the incarnational or sacramental principle which banishes all duality between the temporal and the spiritual realms and revels in God's affirmation of his own good creation. Though the flesh has been contaminated by the blight of sin and so shares in the inheritance of death, it is yet capable of being restored to become a vehicle for the true praise of God and for his service within human society and the world. The tremendous crescendo in the closing couplet, which follows the description of the death of the body and its resurrection when immortality renews, rather than ignores, that which belongs to the corporeal realm,

> Dwyn ato'r corff, ei ffroen a'i drem a'i glyw,
> I synwyruso gogoniannau Duw.

> Taking to itself the body, its nostrils, sight and hearing,
> To make sensuous the glories of God.

sums up what was to be the poet's abiding conviction and the key to his Christian philosophy and practice. The same conviction is apparent in a lesser known but very arresting sonnet 'Fenws a'r Forwyn Fair' (Venus and the Virgin Mary), in which transient Hellenistic beauty is pitted against the eternal verities of the gospel, with the poet deciding, unblushingly, in favour of the latter:

> Syfrdenaist fyd pan godaist ti o'r don
> A'i hewyn hi ar groen am gnawd mor goeth,
> Crynai bob calon wrol ger dy fron
> A mynnai'r hen yn ôl eu nwydau poeth;
> Cerfiodd celfyddyd â meistrolaeth cŷn
> Ddelw dy dduwiestod yn y marbl a'r maen,
> Ac yn dy deml ymgrymai gwanwyn dyn,
> Llefai morwyndod a phuteindra o'th flaen.
> Daeth Mam Gofidiau ac Eirioleg Nef
> O Fethlem i'th gynefin ar ei rhawd,
> A throes dy demlau'n demlau iddo Ef
> A phlannu'r Groes lle bu allorau'r cnawd;
> Hi saif hyd byth lle gynt y safet ti
> Ac Iechydwriaeth rhwng Ei breichiau Hi.

> You stunned a world when you rose up from the waves
> Whose spray was skin on flesh so smooth,
> Every heart quickened in your presence
> And even the aged had their tepid passions renewed;

Artistry carved, with chiselled mastery,
The image of your divinity in marble and stone,
And in your temple man's spring prostrated itself,
Virginity and harlotry both cried out before you.
The Mother of Sorrows and Heaven's Intercessor
Came forth from Bethlehem into your world on her journey,
Turning your temples into the temples of her Son,
And planting the Cross where the altars of flesh had been;
She will stand forever where once you stood
With Salvation resting between Her arms.

Just as, during the fourth and fifth centuries, Greek paganism had been swept away by the victory of Christianity, so even the most enticing temporal charm is forced to yield to the gracious compulsion of God made flesh in Christ through Mary, the Blessed Virgin, *Theotokos* or the bearer of the divine.

Surprisingly perhaps, in light of the excerpts which we have quoted, Gwenallt's return to faith had not taken him to the Catholic Church or indeed, at this time, to Anglo-Catholicism either. Despite his robust incarnationalism and his regard for Mary, the Mother of God, his theology was still very eclectic, and the Wales to which he was committed was yet a Protestant, chapel-going Wales, whose culture was overwhelmingly Nonconformist. Along with such themes as human sinfulness, the spirit and the flesh and Christianity's victory over the forces of corruption, another major topic in *Ysgubau'r Awen* is that of Wales itself which, for the poet, always combined the rural *and* the industrial, the harsh economic and political realities into which he had been born as well as the more pastoral ideals of the agrarian past. Wales was, and was to remain, a nation of the people, and the people among whom he had grown up were the steelworkers and coalminers of the Glamorgan valleys for whom the chapel, in the 1930s, was still integral to their lives. His sonnet 'Sir Forgannwg' (Glamorganshire) typifies this theme:

Mor wag dy lowyr yn eu dillad gwaith
A llwch y glo yn fwgwd ar eu pryd,
Arian papur y gyfnewidfa faith,
Allforion ym mhorthladdoedd gwanc y byd:
Codasant yng ngwrthryfel cig a gwaed,
Fandrel a rhaw i daro duw eu hoes,
Ond hoeliwyd hwy'n dynnach, ddwylo a thraed,

A rhoddi mwy o sment wrth fôn eu croes.
Y Sul a rydd amdanynt ddillad glân
Ac yn eu hwyneb olau enaid byw,
Ac yn y cysegr clywir yn eu cân
Orfoledd gwerin bendefigaidd Duw;
Tynnir y caets o waelod pwll i'r nef
Â rhaffau dur ei hen olwynion Ef.

How empty are your colliers in their working clothes
With a mask of coaldust on their faces,
Paper currency in the vast exchange,
Exports from the docks of the world's greed:
In the rebellion of flesh and blood they raised
Pick and shovel to strike the god of their age,
But they were pinned down more firmly, hands and feet,
And more cement was laid at the base of their cross.
Sunday, however, sees them in clean attire,
In their faces shines the light of a living soul,
And in their sanctuary their song is heard,
The joyful hymns of God's royal race;
The cage is wound from the pit's depths to heaven
By the steel ropes of God's sure and ancient wheels.

This sonnet is characteristic of Gwenallt's style, first an octave which sets out in realistic detail the bleakness in which the people, *his* people, find themselves, describing their situation and plight, followed by six lines in which those same people are transfigured and humanized by their faith, the final couplet containing an apt and highly striking metaphorical climax. Even in translation, this inventive and forceful use of metaphor expresses the poem's feel, even if the intricacies of rhythm and rhyme are unfortunately lost. When Saunders Lewis said of Gwenallt in 1940 that he inhabited 'a cosmos, a world which has meaning, a world which has been given an aim and an objective',[9] it was to the artistic verve, theological commitment and moral seriousness of poems like these that he referred.

Though he remained the poet of the industrial south, the aesthetic and doctrinal appeal of Catholicism took Gwenallt, in 1944, into the fellowship of the Church in Wales. He was confirmed by the bishop of St David's in his palace at Abergwili and thereafter became a regular worshipper at the ancient parish church of Llanbadarn near his Aberystwyth home. Given his sacramentalist principles, his rounded view of incarnation and redemption and his feeling for an unbroken tradition between the present generation and ancient Celtic past of the Church in Wales, this move was, in a way, inevitable. Many of the poems in *Eples* contain resonances of liturgical worship and often aspire to integrate grace and nature within the seasons and rhythms of God's good creation. 'Sul y Fferm' (The Farmer's Sunday) is an eight-stanza'd poem with, what was for 1951, an unfamiliar ecological theme:

> A wnei Di gofio, O Grist, am amaethwyr Cymru?
> Hen greaduriaid digon tlawd a balch;
> Ti wyddost, mi wn, fod Dy holl lawogydd
> Yn sugno o'r pridd y ffosffad a'r calch . . .
>
> Maddau inni mewn heddwch am anghofio ein daear,
> Am ddienyddio Dy bridd, am ladd ei lun a'i liw;
> A Thithau wedi rhoddi cymaint o'th gyfoeth a'th brydferthwch
> Yn y cornelyn o'r byd lle'r ydym ni'n byw . . .
>
> Rhaid rhoddi yn ôl i'r ddaear onest
> Am a gawsom o'i dwylo cyfiawn hi;
> Maddau i ni am sarnu Dy greadigaeth;
> Maddau ein materoldeb a'n hunanoldeb ni . . .
>
> Will You remember, O Christ, the farmers of Wales?
> Such mean and proud old creatures, as they are;
> I know that You know that all Your rains
> Suck from the soil the phosphate and chalk . . .
>
> Forgive us in peacetime for forgetting our earth,
> For executing Your soil, for killing its content and colour;
> And You having given so much of your richness and beauty
> In this small corner of the world where we live . . .
>
> We must put back into the honest earth
> That which we have taken from her righteous hands;
> Forgive us for spoiling Your creation;
> Forgive our materialism and our selfishness . . .

The creation-based spirituality of these simple, somewhat whimsical verses, with their culmination in the eucharist which transforms even the agriculture of modernity: 'In the genesis of the world You created the soils, / And from that earth You also created man, /

And restored Nature and husbandry and its tractors / In Your Supper by blessing the bread and the wine', contrasts utterly with another of the *Eples* poems on a rural theme. 'Rhydcymerau', the Carmarthenshire village from which Gwenallt's parents had moved late in the nineteenth century in order to find work, is not typical. Whereas most of his work to date had been in strict metres, sonnets or rhymed stanzas at the very least, this is a prose poem which describes a lost reality bleakly, unencumbered by metrical pattern.

They have planted the saplings for the third world war
On the land of Esgeir-ceir and the fields of Tir-bach
Near Rhydcymerau.

I remember my grandmother in Esgeir-ceir
Sitting by the fire pleating her apron;
Her face was as yellow and wrinkled as a medieval manuscript,
And the Welsh on her aged lips the Welsh of Pantycelyn.
She was a piece of last century's Puritan Wales.
My grandfather, though I never met him,
Was a 'character'; a brisk, twinkling little creature,
Fond of his pint;
He had strayed in from the eighteenth century.
They raised nine children,
Poets, deacons and Sunday School teachers,
Each a leader in his small locality.

My Uncle Dafydd used to farm Tir-bach,
A country poet and local rhymester,
His song to the cockerel was famous in those parts:
    'The little cock goes scratching
    In the garden here and there'.
It was to him that I would go during my summer holidays
To help tend the sheep and fashion lines of *cynghanedd*,
Englynion and eight-line stanzas in the eight-seven measure.
He too raised eight children,
The eldest was a Calvinistic Methodist minister
Who also wrote verse.
Our family was full of poets.
And now there is nothing left but trees,
Their impertinent roots sucking the old soil dry:
Trees where there was once community,
A forest where there were once farms,

Bastardized South Wales English where there was once poetry
  and divinity,
The barking of foxes where there had once been the cries of
  children and of lambs.
And there, in its dark midst,
The lair of the English Minotaur;
And on trees, as though on crosses,
The skeletons of poets, elders, ministers and Sunday School
  teachers
Being bleached by the sun,
And washed by the rain and licked dry by the wind.

The poem is harsh, brutal but exceedingly memorable. It is a
protest against the barbarity of capitalism and the expendability of
tradition and all that is civilized and humane. For Gwenallt it was
a parable of twentieth-century Wales. Yet for all its savagery – and
savagery does not, in the main, characterize *Eples* – it belongs to a
wider vision in which the splendours of the past could in fact be
preserved in order to become part of a contemporary synthesis, a
vision in which the rural ideal is compatible with both modernity
and faith. The Celtic insight, in which ecological wholeness and a
spirituality in which salvation is, in fact, God's gracious renewal of
his own creation, resonates throughout this, his most accom-
plished volume of verse.

As with the earlier poems, certain animals become symbolic of
human pride and iniquity, just as others – doves especially – are
made to express hope and redemption. A hedgehog, spotted one
day on a journey from Gwenallt's home to nearby Nanteos, a
place sanctified in Welsh legend as the resting place of the Holy
Grail and during the medieval centuries a place of pilgrimage,
becomes the symbol for humankind's perpetual rejection of God.
The picture of the creature – putrid, spherical and thorny – is
brutal and typically twentieth-century:

Efe ydyw'r proffwyd ar adfeilion Ewrob,
Cynddelw ei llên a'i chelfyddydau cain;
Efe a lanwodd y gwacter lle bu'r Drindod,
O! belen anfarwol. O! dduwdod y drain.

He is the prophet on Europe's ruins,
Archetype of her letters and fine arts;

It is he who filled the void where once was the Trinity
O! eternal orb. O! thorn-laden deity.

The use of the psychoanalytical term 'archetype' is quite deliberate, as is the allusion to Christ's crown of thorns in the description
of the creatures' spikes. If this admittedly brutal poem has been
heavily criticized for its extreme and unflattering portrayal of
human corruption, there is also evidence in *Eples* of a gentler, less
judgemental strain where human imperfection is met by the divine
pity leading to salvation and wholeness. This is exemplified by the
interesting poem to the so-called 'fatling' of Isaiah's prophecy:
'The wolf also shall dwell with the lamb and the leopard shall lie
down with the kid, and the calf with the young lion and the fatling
together, and a little child shall lead them' (Isa. 11: 6).

> Ni welais i ef erioed yn fy myw,
> Ac ni wn beth oedd ei lun a'i liw,
> Ai du ai llwyd ai coch,
> Beth, Eseia, oedd ei hanes a'i dras?
> Yr anifail bras.
>
> Cerddodd drwy'r canrifoedd i'w ffiaidd ffald
> Yn Siberia, Belsen a Buchenwald,
> Ac uwch Hiroshima goed
> Y gollyngodd ei holl lysnafedd cas;
> Yr hen anifail bras.
>
> Pe gwelai'r bwystfil Ei ogoniant Ef
> A'r Groes yn clymu daear a Nef,
> Gyda'r fuwch a'r ych a'r oen
> Yr âi i bori ei borfa las;
> Yr anifail bras.
>
> Never once did I see him
> Nor do I know what he looked like,
> Was he black, grey or red,
> What, Isaiah, was his background and pedigree?
> This fatling.
>
> He stalked through the centuries to his dire lair
> In Siberia, Belsen and Buchenwald,
> And above the trees of Hiroshima

He left his slimy trail,
That fatling.

Were that creature to glimpse His glory
At the Cross which binds together earth and heaven,
In the company of the cow and the ox and the lamb,
He, too, would graze his lush grass;
The fatling.

There are other poems in the same vein which, although they have
drawn little attention in the past, are nevertheless thought-provok-
ing and stimulating. In 'Yr Eryrod' (The Eagles), he visualizes
those formidable birds first as God's saints soaring down from the
skies and after alighting on the earth being transformed into
wholly unprepossessing creatures walking incognito among its
inhabitants yet doing God's strange work: 'Giving up all to the
poor, a coat to a tramp / And kissing a leper's cheek'. The eagle, of
course, is symbolic not only of the saints but of other aspects of
the Christian tradition. As a worshipping member of the Church
in Wales, Gwenallt would listen week by week to the scriptures being read from the huge brass eagle-shaped lectern in
Llanbadarn church. The eagle was the symbol of John's gospel, the
one New Testament book above all others which emphasizes the
fact of God's incarnation in Christ. Having been redeemed from
metaphysical speculation of a Platonist kind by a Christianity
which takes time, place and human history seriously, the poet
found that the very words of the gospel underlined the essence of
his faith in all its concrete particularity:

Ioan yr Efengylydd; brenin eryrod byd,
Efe a'm cododd uwchlaw'r clyfar gysgodau;
Ei Gymraeg yn fy mwrw i lawr ag ergyd gordd
A chlirio'r dryswch rhamantaidd â bwyall ei adnodau . . .

John the Evangelist; the king of the eagles,
It was he who raised me above the insubstantial shadows;
His Welsh felled me with a hammer-blow
And cleared away the romantic undergrowth with the scythe
    of his words . . .

He mentions too 'Apostolic eagles; my theological eagles, / Staring
at the Logos in eternity, /Who strode from the goal of the far

Trinity / To clothe Himself in flesh', and the 'eucharistic eagles' who presided over that transformation of the elements in the bread and wine which vouchsafed Christ's real presence within his creation.

That other bird which features so poignantly in the Christian story is the cockerel, the symbol not of St John but of St Peter and his betrayal of Christ. In a marvellously evocative poem entitled 'The Weathercock' (Ceiliog y Gwynt), Gwenallt pictures Peter's cockerel having found a place not so much in the church but ever present above it, on its spires, still ready to turn in the prevailing wind.

> 'Rwyt tithau erbyn hyn yn rhan o'r Eglwys,
> Fe'th godwyd o'th domen i'w thŵr;
>   Fe roddwyd i tithau le yn Ei blan
>   Pan genaist ti ddwywaith yn y fan,
> A throi calon yr hen Apostol yn ddŵr . . .

> By now you too are part of the Church
> Having been raised up from your perch to its tower;
>   You were given a place in His scheme
>   When you crowed twice on that night
> And turned an old apostle's heart to water . . .

Despite its fickleness, the cockerel's place is secure. The betrayal of Christ, far from being the cause of the Apostle's perdition, led in fact to conviction, costly repentance and an assurance of forgiveness through the divine mercy. This leads, in turn, to the poet's prayer: 'O Wind, give again his old gift / To raise, as from the heart of hasty Peter, / The violet tears to the eyes of the world.' Brief as it is, there is no doubt that this is one of Gwenallt's finest and most heartfelt religious poems.

Although the author's fourth volume of verse entitled *Gwreiddiau* (Roots) is said to have contributed little that was new to his development as a poet, nevertheless this 1959 collection contains more than a few striking and moving pieces. Some more recent critical appraisals of the work have been surprisingly positive as to its quality and abiding value. The theological content of the book permeates the whole; in fact this was the most obviously religious of Gwenallt's work up to that point. The poet is unashamedly Christian, indeed more than one of the poems refers back to his conversion a generation or more earlier and shows how his spiritual development had subsequently progressed. 'Yr Hen Emynau' (The Old Hymns) is a case in point.

Buont hwy yn canu uwch fy nghrud,
Uwchben fy machgendod a'm hienctid,
Fel côr o adar Cristionogol:
Hwynt-hwy â'u cân oedd yn cario Calfaria
A'r Groes i ganol y gweithfeydd;
Bethlehem a'r crud i ganol y tipiau;
Y bedd gwag i blith y gwagenni,
A dwyn afon yr Iorddonen heb fitrel yn ei dŵr . . .

They would sing above my cradle,
Above my childhood and my youth
Like a choir of Christian birds:
They and their song would carry Calvary
And the Cross to the midst of the works;
Bethlehem and the manger to the middle of the tips;
The empty tomb to among the wagons,
And make present the River Jordan without vitriol in its waters . . .[10]

The next two verses describe how the birds were expelled from the woods with blasts from the young man's 'well-aimed scientific shotgun' and blows from his 'solid, materialist cudgel', but still they sang, their distant echo audible 'beneath the threshold of reason and the doorstep of the mind'. Despite the poet's refusal to heed their song it persisted 'diligently, assiduously, inexorably'.

A phan ddaeth y goleuni yn ôl i'r goedwig
Esgynasant o blith y gwraidd i'r canghennau a'r brig
I ganu eilwaith, a'u cân wedi aeddfedu yn y nos:
Dwyn y crud, y Groes, y bedd gwag a'r Pentecost
Yn ôl o'r newydd, yn danbaid newydd;
Ac o dan y diferion gwaed a'r dŵr
Cusanu Ei fuddugoliaethus draed,
Heb feiddio edrych gan euogrwydd ar santeiddrwydd
    ofnadwy ei wyneb.

And when the light returned to the forest
They rose up from among the roots to the branches and the treetops
To sing again, their song having matured during the night:
They brought the manger, the Cross, the empty grave and Pentecost

Back anew, magnificently new;
And beneath the drops of blood and of water
They kissed His victorious feet,
Without daring, because of their guilt, to gaze on the terrible holiness
  of His face.

The Nonconformist spirituality in which Gwenallt was brought
up had been moulded by its hymns. More even than preaching
and infinitely more than any formal sacramental teaching, it was
through the content and the singing of their hymns – Williams
Pantycelyn, Ann Griffiths, Thomas Lewis and the rest – that
chapel folk would be introduced to spiritual experience and
nurtured in the faith. The unconscious effect of these hymns in the
context of popular communal worship at a receptive age was
seldom less than profound – as any visit to an international match
at Cardiff Arms Park up to the 1970s would have shown! Yet for
Gwenallt their influence, albeit unconsciously, was considerably
more than cultural. It was through them that God's presence had
perpetuated itself in his soul. During his agnostic, unbelieving
phase, the poet's contempt for Christianity, Nonconformity in
particular, was withering, yet the experience which the poem
expresses, so reminiscent of Francis Thompson being pursued by
his 'Hound of Heaven', or that other twentieth-century adult
convert, C. S. Lewis, being followed, cornered and ultimately
overcome by the God whom he had no desire to meet, is powerfully captured. Here spiritual experience, theological conviction,
poetic sensibility and the dreadful consciousness of God's holiness
meet; the context, as it was in *Ysgubau'r Awen*, is the history of
industrial south Wales.

By 1959, when *Gwreiddiau* was published, Gwenallt was sixty
years old, his core convictions were now long established and his
reputation as one of Wales's leading poets secure. Although his
muse was still, on the whole, Catholic, his antipathy to certain
Anglicizing trends within the Church in Wales, along with a
progressive reclamation of all that was best in the Nonconformist
tradition, had taken him back to the Calvinistic Methodism of his
childhood and youth. The church into which he had been born
and baptized would be the one in which he would spend the rest
of his days. The biblical and theological renaissance of the mid-
1930s to the 1950s, linked to such Protestant thinkers as Barth,

Brunner, Niebuhr and their disciples, had convinced Gwenallt that, far from undermining Catholic truth, the Reformation had rediscovered much of the richness of the early Church's faith. If informed by patristic learning and sacramental wholeness, Protestantism was a valid interpretation of apostolic Christianity. It also laid store on evangelical experience, the *experience* of the saved soul, which came to take a more central place in Gwenallt's thinking the older he became. If poems like 'The Old Hymns' recalled the process of his conversion, others like 'Corff Crist' (The Body of Christ) illustrate the way in which his belief in the incarnational principle and sacramentalism was as staunch as ever:

> Dwylo yn debyg i'r rhain
> A bwniwyd ar y Pren:
> Traed fel ein traed ni
> A dyllwyd: pen fel ein pen
> A gariodd y gwaradwyddus ddrain.
>
> Y fath anrhydedd, y fath orfoledd, O Gnawd,
> Oedd cael rhoi corff i Fab Duw;
> Corff Iddew ym Methlehem,
> Corff marwol dynol-ryw:
> Y Corff a weddnewidiwyd yn y bedd
> Yn Gorff catholig byw.
>
> Hands like these hands
> Were hammered to the Tree;
> Feet like our feet
> Were pierced: a head like our head
> Bore the mocking thorns.
>
> Such was the honour, the rejoicing, O Flesh
> In providing a body for the Son of God;
> The body of a Jew in Bethlehem,
> The mortal body of humankind:
> The Body which was transformed in the grave
> Into a living catholic Body.

His was a catholicity of the Word, a faith in which God, in his transcendent otherness, took upon himself all the particularity of time and place. Human mortality, enslaved to sin and under the divine judgement, was yet borne by God in the incarnation of his Son and through the sacrifice of Calvary and the resurrection of the body, transformed into something glorious and new.

The same theme is expressed memorably in a poem entitled 'Catholigrwydd' (Catholicity) in his final volume of verse, *Y Coed* (The Trees) published posthumously in 1969. Here he describes the person of Christ 'imprisoned by his flesh and his Jewish bones / Within the confines of his land'. This was the Christ who gave himself as a living sacrifice to the Father before being raised up anew in the miracle of resurrection. And the result?

> A mwy y mae Caerdydd cyn nesed â Chalfaria,
> A Bangor bob modfedd â Bethlehem,
> Gostegir y stormydd ym Mae Ceredigion,
> Ac ar bob stryd fe all y lloerigion
> Gael iechydwriaeth wrth odre Ei hem . . .

> And since then Cardiff is as near as Calvary,
> And Bangor every inch as Bethlehem,
> The storms are stilled on Cardigan Bay,
> And in every street the afflicted
> Find healing from the touch of His hem . . .[11]

Flesh and spirit, the particular and the universal, the ordinary and the extraordinary are all harmonized in Christ, the incarnation of God's redemptive love, whose reality is forever known anew in the *epiclesis* or making present of the Holy Spirit. If Celtic spirituality represents a living tradition in which the eternal verities of the gospel become incarnate in the everyday lives of ordinary people in Cardiff, Bangor and on the shores of Cardigan Bay, it is to this tradition that the artistry and poetic imagination of Gwenallt belong.

This brief exposition of some of the themes in the poetry of D. Gwenallt Jones has attempted to illustrate the way in which Christian faith can yet provide the inspiration for a spiritually satisfying and intellectually rigorous analysis of the human condition. Gwenallt's Celticism was not forced or contrived but the result of practising his faith in the context of a living tradition of worship, both Catholic and Nonconformist, which refused to divide God's transcendent holiness from his immanent presence within his good, though blighted, creation. As that presence was the presence of God, its holiness was equally real; it was through the gospel of incarnation, atonement, resurrection and renewal that men and women were invited to share in the glories of God's presence within the world. Gwenallt's catholicism was an evangelical catholicism, and his Christianity, though universal, was rooted in the particular mid-twentieth-century experience of the people of Wales. It is this blend of the local and the universal, Wales (and Europe) as representing all of humankind, which gives his vision a potency and depth which can speak to a new generation at the beginning of a new millennium. For Gwenallt, as for Celtic Christianity as a whole, false dualities yield to a true synthesis which is rooted in Christ who is both God and man, creator and creation's redeemer, the eternal Son who is the sacrament and presence of the Father's glory:

> Cydfydd fferm a ffwrnais ar Ei ystad
> Dyneiddiaeth y pwll glo, duwioldeb y wlad:
> Tawe a Thywi, Canaan a Chymru, daear a nef.

> Farm and furnace cohabit His estate,
> The coalpit's humanism, the countryside's piety:
> Tawe and Tywi, Canaan and Wales, earth and heaven.[12]

Notes

All translations of poetry from Welsh in this chapter are by D. Densil Morgan.

[1]   See Donald E. Meek, *The Quest for Celtic Christianity* (Edinburgh, 2000), esp. 23–37.

[2]   This contention is argued at length in Donald Allchin and D. Densil Morgan, *Sensuous Glory: The Poetic Vision of D. Gwenallt Jones* (Norwich, 2000), 1–89.

[3]   My translation. For a full trans. of the poem, see Patrick Thomas in Allchin and Morgan, *Sensuous Glory*, 149–50.

[4]   'What I believe', trans. Ned Thomas and André Morgan, *Planet*, 32 (1976), 3.

[5]   Ibid., 5.

[6]   Ibid., 6.

[7]   Ibid., 7.

[8]   Allchin and Morgan, *Sensuous Glory*, 20.

[9]   Quoted by Robert Rhys, 'Poetry 1939–70', in Dafydd Johnson (ed.),

A Guide to Welsh Literature, 1900–1996 (Cardiff, University of Wales Press, 1998), 89.

10   For a full trans. of the poem, see Patrick Thomas in Allchin and Morgan, *Sensuous Glory*, 107–8.

11   Ibid., 118.

12   'Sir Forgannwg a Sir Gaerfyrddin' (Glamorganshire and Carmarthenshire), *Eples*. See Allchin and Morgan, *Sensuous Glory*, 130–1.

8

The natural world in early Irish Christianity: an ecological footnote

MARY LOW

In the margin of the *Félire Óengusso / Martyrology of Óengus* the following poem appears as a gloss. I quote in translation:

> The skilled lark calls
> You go outside to look at her
> To see the wide-open beak
> In the dappled cloudy sky.[1]

The work is anonymous and there are no clues as to the author's state of life. He or she could have been a monk, a nun or a lay poet. The bird's song attracts, almost summons, the listener, indicated here by the indefinite pronoun *neach:* anyone, someone. It is as if you or I, or anyone, would do the same: recognize the bird by its song, put other activities aside and go outdoors to watch. The verb suggests close observation, not a cursory glance but a good long look, which also takes in a certain quality of the sky. The poem communicates a sense of lightness, an upward lift, mirroring the flight of the lark and the upward gaze and mood of the observer. The spirituality is implicit rather than overt, as it would be centuries later for Patrick Kavanagh with his 'poet's faculty of loving to the heart of any ordinary thing'.[2] It occurs in a religious context, next to a poem about praying the Psalms. Anyone consulting the *Félire* for the 31 March would have come across it. Similarly, the author of the ninth-century *Martyrology of Tallaght* thought it quite appropriate to intersperse information about the saints with notes about what the birds were doing on their feast-days: wild geese, cuckoos, swallows are all mentioned.[3]

The 'green' credentials of Celtic Christianity have often been intuited on the basis of fragments like these. Other commentators have been more critical, drawing attention to exaggerated or anachronistic ways in which medieval Irish texts about nature have been pressed into service, out of context and with a limited understanding of the world-view and purpose of their authors.[4] James Mackey has identified among Celtic enthusiasts, 'time-travellers in search of a quick fix'.[5] This caution is as relevant for ecologists as for others, but I am not convinced that the first intuition about nature was wholly wrong, despite the shortcomings of some of its presenters, including myself. I am not convinced, for example, that fear of thunder and lightning is necessarily incompatible with loving nature.[6] This chapter will review the background to the 'green' hypothesis, look at some of the objections to it, and present a rough guide to a number of texts which do, I believe, have something to contribute. My main focus will be early Christian Ireland, but given the close religious, linguistic, cultural and political connections which existed at this time between Ireland and Scotland, some of the outlooks to be examined here may be common to both. This is certainly the case with texts from Iona, whose influence extended up and down the west coast, east along the Great Glen and south as far as Melrose and Lindisfarne. And of course Columba's followers were not the only group of Irish Christians to leave traces in what is now Scotland.

The makings of the green hypothesis

Love of nature and sensitivity to its beauty were identified as important themes in early Irish literature, at the end of the nineteenth century, by two of the founders of the Gaelic League, Eoin Mac Néill and Douglas Hyde.[7] They pointed to the example of Columba and also to pre-Christian figures like Ossian and Finn. During the first half of the twentieth century, several leading scholars of Celtic languages and literatures, Kuno Meyer, Eleanor Hull, Gerard Murphy and Kenneth Jackson, all produced anthologies in which nature was either an important theme or the main subject.[8] Murphy also contributed 'The origin of Irish nature poetry' (1931) and Robin Flower's famous paper, 'The two eyes of Ireland', was written for a Church of Ireland conference the following year. Flower and Murphy, in particular, saw the monks and hermits of early Christian Ireland as keen observers of the natural world, affectionate towards it and celebrating it in poetry.

For Murphy, this was a response to the doctrine of creation; for Flower, it derived from a purity of vision brought on by 'continuous spiritual exercise'.[9] Flower was mistaken in thinking that many of these poems were actually composed in hermitages, but they do come from a monastic milieu and could well have been composed by people with first-hand experience of the hermit life.[10] Flower also believed that no other European people wrote nature poetry as early as this in the vernacular. As far as I know, this claim still stands. There had been Latin nature poetry in the ancient world; and Augustine of Hippo praised the beauty of creation in typically elegant prose; but Irish poets were the first in post-imperial Europe to celebrate nature in their own language. Indeed, it seems that the earliest nature poetry was written at around the same time as the first poems in Irish on ecclesiastical subjects.[11]

During the nineteenth and early twentieth centuries, scholars with a theological background (for example, William Reeves, Louis Gougaud, John Ryan, Lambert McKenna) contributed to Celtic studies mainly as Church historians or translators. For many, this was an exploration of their own heritage, an important process of reclamation which is ongoing in the work of Diarmuid O'Laoghaire, Martin MacNamara, Thomas Finan, Peter O'Dwyer and a rising generation of younger scholars who bring lay and female perspectives as well as clerical ones.

Students with a more general interest in religious ideas have usually had to make their own way, with the help of the small number of people who saw, in Irish and Hebridean Christianity, something of more than local interest: not some provincial curiosity or exotic 'other' (always a pitfall for visitors) but a faith-experience of relevance to other faith-experiences elsewhere. Some chose to comment on aspects of the natural world. Helen Waddell for example, in her introduction to *Beasts and Saints* (1934), drew attention to a theme of 'mutual charity' between birds, animals and Christians at their best. *Beasts and Saints* contains extracts from the Latin Lives of Welsh, Anglo-Saxon and Irish saints. She presents these in highly accessible form, accompanied by similar examples from the Middle East and linked with the teaching of Jesus that even 'a huddle of feathers on the ground [is] not unregarded by the Father of mankind'.[12]

Waddell and Meyer were among the influences on naturalist and journalist H. J. Massingham.[13] Writing in the middle of the Second World War, Massingham foresaw a future struggle, not between right and left, but between 'earth men' and the forces of economic materialism. Concerned mainly with the English countryside, he hoped to enlist the support of English Church people by showing that love of nature was very much part of their heritage, hence perhaps his rather dubious emphasis on the 'British church'. British and Irish Christianity, he said, escaped the 'Manichean' fear of nature which dogged the faith in the rest of Europe, separating faith and spirituality from care for the earth.[14] He contrasted this with 'pre-Aquinian' and Puritanical beliefs, both Catholic and Protestant. This belief in a more integrated world-view turns up again in the titles of anthologies like Christopher Bamford and William Parker Marsh's *Celtic Christianity: Ecology and Holiness* (1986) and Esther de Waal's *A World Made Whole* (1991).[15]

George MacLeod, founder of the Iona Community, saw nature as a beautiful prisoner, in thrall to death and decay, and longing for redemption. MacLeod's main concern was with people, but love for the rest of the natural world sings from some of his prayers.[16] Around 1967, the Community also took the brave but inspired decision to replace the capitals on the damaged pillars of the cloister, not with replicas of the surviving medieval ones, but with modern carvings of plants and flowers of Iona by Douglas Bissett and Chris Hall. Indeed, since the end of the nineteenth century, churches have often commissioned artwork on a nature theme to underline their Celtic connections. The *Benedicite* ('Bless the Lord all created things'), for example, appears as a mosaic in the Honan Chapel, University College, Cork; as a mural in St Mary's Song School, Edinburgh; and again in the stained-glass windows of Dunblane Cathedral.[17]

Among academic theologians, John V. Taylor was perhaps the first in recent times to discuss a medieval Irish text in the context of comparative spirituality. His brief note on parallels between African world-views (including views of nature) and those encountered by the author of 'St Patrick's Breastplate' first appeared in 1963.[18] Nine years later, John MacQuarrie was proposing Celtic Christianity as an antidote to the 'spiritual crisis of the West' which he saw as characterized by an acquisitive-aggressive attitude to other men and women and to the rest of the natural world. Linking the ecological crisis with the spiritual one, he attributed both to theologies 'which exaggerate the transcendence of God to such an extent that the world is conceived as purely external to God, as wholly profane and dedivinised *and therefore as entirely given over to human exploitation*'.[19] MacQuarrie describes these destructive theologies as Calvinistic, though there are of course, similar strands in other traditions.

It is interesting to note that MacQuarrie sees the Edinburgh theologian John Baillie (1886–1960) as holding a basically Celtic view of immanence.[20] Whether by accident or design, it was on Baillie's home territory of New College, from 1985 to 1999, that two Irish philosophers, Noel O'Donoghue and James Mackey, pioneered an interest in Celtic Christianity as a Divinity Faculty subject, with studies of nature and immanence among the first doctoral theses to be produced there.[21]

O'Donoghue is strongly influenced by what outsiders call the modern Irish folk tradition. This everyday faith of the people was learned from his father, Dan Jerry, a small hill-farmer in Glen Flesk, Co. Kerry, in the early decades of the twentieth century. In one of his later essays, O'Donoghue takes the image of the sanctuary lamp in the chapel in Glen Flesk, symbol of Christ's presence in the Church, and the image of the midsummer (St John's Eve) bonfires which his father used to light on the hills above. There, 'in the deepest part of his being', says his son, 'he met with God in the ancient way'. Dan Jerry was a regular Mass-goer who knew and respected the meaning of the sanctuary lamp. But God was also present for him in the hills outside. What he expressed through lighting the St John's fires, his son would later express in theological terms: that 'the Word through which all things were made, is first and always present as creative, and only consequently present as redemptive'.[22] This is not to minimize the agony of the cross or the need for deliverance, but it does mean that nature is not just the setting, far less the distracting or irrelevant background, to more important spiritual events. God is, and always has been, at work there.

It is now possible to study Celtic Christianity as theology or religious studies in a number of academic centres, while religious texts continue to be examined, with a different kind of expertise, in Irish, Welsh and Celtic Studies departments. As more literature has become available, in popular and academic forms,

MacQuarrie's 'antidote' has been seized upon by students, parish groups, religious orders, school chaplains and retreat-givers all over Europe, North America and Australia, as well as by lapsed Christians and people with no church connection at all. It has also been invoked in connection with green politics.

In 1995, James Hunter claimed early Irish (or in his terms, 'Gaelic') nature poetry as evidence for an 'indigenous green consciousness' only waiting to be nudged awake.[23] The phrase came originally from Christopher Smout, vice-chair of Scottish Natural Heritage, but was taken up and developed by Hunter, formerly of the Crofters' Union, now director of Highlands and Islands Enterprise, as part of an argument in favour of local Highland communities handling their own environmental affairs. One might argue over the details, but the poems which he chooses are Scots as much as they are Irish, and Hunter contrasts them with what he sees as the more adversarial approach to nature found in most of the rest of Europe before the eighteenth century.[24]

Not all of these poems are obviously monastic. Some are more closely associated with the Finn Cycle, but there is common ground between the two traditions.[25] The lifestyle of those who inhabited the beehive cells of Skellig Michael and Eileach an Naoimh also suggests to Hunter a 'less exploitative, less utilitarian attitude' towards nature, though he remains oddly resistant to the idea that mystical experience might have had anything to do with this.[26]

Celticity, diversity and other considerations

Celticity

Questions about the greenness or otherwise of Celtic Christianity are inextricably linked with the debate about Celticity itself. This is discussed elsewhere in the present volume and the arguments need not be rehearsed again here.[27] Suffice it to say that while some now question the very existence of Celts in Britain and Ireland,[28] others continue to find the term useful.[29] Oliver Davies, for example, recommends a soft use of the term 'Celtic' as an accurate description of a certain set of cultural and linguistic affinities.[30] These are clearly in evidence where nature poetry is concerned. Though there are differences between the Irish and the Welsh traditions, there are also clear affinities, and some Irish poetry can also be described, quite accurately, as Scottish.[31] It is true that people living in different parts of Ireland, Scotland and Wales did not generally, if ever, refer to themselves as Celts. They used clan and dynastic names instead. But the term has long since been appropriated by their descendants (cf. 'Scots') many of whom hold fast to their Celtic identity. Indeed, no less a person than the Gaelic poet Somhairle Mac Gill-eain (Sorley McLean) could write without apology about Celtic characteristics, including a love of nature, as recently as 1996.[32] Where Celticity is accepted, it tends nowadays to be defined mainly in terms of language and culture. Most Celticists (*pace* McLean) would be wary of assigning to it any distinctive outlook or racial predisposition and (on the evidence of papers offered at the Eleventh International Congress of Celtic Studies in 1999) treat it as a continuing phenomenon which is still with us today.

Diversity within the tradition

If we were to apply this definition to Celtic Christianity, it would become the Christianity of people whose mother-tongue is or was one of the Celtic languages, and/or who identify with the cultural heritage of one of these traditional language areas in a recognizable way. If some church people are still inclined to view it as a moment in the distant past, a 'golden age' followed by a series of 'revivals', this has much to do with the old idea of the 'Celtic Church' which came to an end, allegedly, at the synod of Whitby in 664. This is misleading, not just because of arguments over the existence or otherwise of the 'Celtic Church', but because the vast majority of the surviving texts of Ireland, Scotland and Wales, the Lives of Saints, hymns, nature poetry and so on, had yet to be written in 664. The same is true of high crosses and illuminated gospels. Enculturated expressions of, and responses to, Christianity flourished in Ireland in the sixth, seventh and eighth centuries, gathered momentum in the Middle Irish period, survived the Anglo-Norman invasions (as evidenced by the bardic poetry of Giolla Brighde Mac Con Midhe and Philip Bocht Ó Huiginn, to name but two) and persisted into Irish and Hebridean folk traditions and beyond.

Freed from the ghost of the 'Celtic Church' and reunited with language and culture, Celtic Christianity can be seen as expressing itself differently in different times and places, and embracing a range of theological positions, on nature as on other matters. As early as 1911, the Benedictine scholar Louis Gougaud implied a degree of diversity in the title of his study, *Les Chrétientés celtiques.*[33] He was thinking mainly of variations within the medieval world, but perhaps we need to go further than that. There are after all, Irish and Gaelic speakers whose faith (Catholic, Reformed, Nonconformist) now has closer ties with Rome or Lowland Scotland than with medieval Glendalough or Iona. General statements about Celtic Christianity can only appear nonsense from their point of view, though whether they would want their own faith to be described as 'Celtic' is another matter. Perhaps Celtic Christianity is more varied than has been generally acknowledged. And perhaps something survives through shifting emphases of homilies and catechisms, changing at its own pace and keeping its counsel. Either way, attitudes to the natural world cannot be assumed to be the same throughout.

Problems of interpretation

Even within medieval Ireland, there are different points of view, and newcomers with 'green' expectations are likely to experience a kind of culture shock as they encounter a wider range of primary texts for themselves. A brief case study on animals will serve to illustrate the point for other aspects of nature as well. The idea that 'Celtic Christians' were kind to animals needs to be set against a pervasive love of hunting and meat-eating, certainly among the laity: 'Three deaths that are better than life: the death of a salmon, the death of a fat pig, the death of a robber.'[34] This late ninth-century saying, with its brutal sense of humour, comes from a courtly background. It is in sharp contrast to the late seventh-century story of Columba and Molua's knife, as told by Adomnán, abbot of Iona, in his Life of St Columba.

Molua goes to Columba and asks him to bless his knife. Columba is busy copying and does not look up. He reaches out his hand with the pen still in it, makes the sign of the cross and goes back to work. Later, he asks his servant Diarmait what it was that he blessed. 'A knife', says Diarmait, 'for the slaughtering of bulls or cattle.' Columba is taken aback. 'I trust in my Lord', he says, 'that [it] will not harm man or beast.' And so it turns out. Molua goes to slaughter a bullock, but the knife will not pierce the skin. It is taken to the blacksmiths' shop, melted down and used to coat all the other iron tools in the monastery so that, from then on, they are 'unable to harm any flesh'.[35] This story is clearly intended to glorify Columba, but a message of non-violence towards animals (and other humans) is also present.

That this message was not applicable in all instances is illustrated in an earlier part of Adomnán's Life, where Columba curses a wild boar so that it drops dead at his feet. Since he was on his own 'no little distance from the brethren' and seems to have got caught up inadvertently in a hunt, his motive can perhaps be interpreted as self-defence, but the tension remains.[36] In all the wildlife stories, we need to be alert for symbolic meanings and covert commentaries. We also need to recognize that there is, in parts of the hagiographical tradition, a lingering admiration for dramatic displays of power, even violence.[37] Some kind of ideal is being reflected in Columba's tenderness towards animals, but it is often mixed with other considerations.

The boar tradition does not invalidate the story of Molua's knife or Adomnán's other well-known stories of the heron blown off course and tended by Columba till it recovers and the white workhorse who mourns for Columba on the evening of his death, nuzzling against his chest.[38] Nor does it eclipse the admiration of the author of the *Félire* for a different Molua, St Molua mac Ocha, and his colleague St Mael Anfaid who refuses to eat till he knows what is distressing a certain little bird. He is told that it is because of the death of Molua mac Ocha who 'never killed a living thing, great or small' and 'that is why the living things bewail him'.[39] There may well be other things going on in these passages, other references and levels of meaning: but neither author has any problem with the idea that animals suffer and have feelings. Both portray the saintly person as one who is affectionate towards them, concerned for their well-being even when there is no profit to be made from it, who does not cause them unnecessary hurt and may choose not to kill them for food.[40]

Adomnán goes so far as to suggest that animals have their own kind of communication with God. After telling us that Columba ascribed the horse's foreknowledge to a revelation by the Creator, he adds his own personal belief that God reveals something of himself to every creature. All this is told without embarrassment. It is not presented as a major part of the Columban ethos, but neither is it brushed aside. On the contrary, the servant who tries to drive the horse away from Columba is reprimanded in words which recall Jesus's rebuke to Judas, while the animal is blessed.[41]

Pre-ecology: some basic texts and attitudes

The idea that humans could do serious permanent damage to the rest of the natural world is entirely foreign to early Christian Ireland. But there are texts which can be used to support modern concerns. If it is legitimate to approach contemporary situations by way of early Christian writings from the Mediterranean world, then appropriate works of Irish Christians, clergy and laity, can surely be used in the same way. The decision as to what is appropriate has to be negotiated in both instances. Thomas Charles-Edwards's image of Celtic Studies as a big house in whose basement different teams of chefs are preparing a variety of dishes, implies that contemporary needs (the people waiting hungrily upstairs) are also very much part of the picture.[42] This was certainly the way in which early Irish writers worked, taking what they needed from the materials and techniques at their disposal in order to stir emotions and shape opinions.

Selecting texts on grounds of usefulness risks a charge of 'cherry-picking' and will not yield a detailed historical understanding of the whole tradition. It will also be misleading if the cherry-picker is not aware, or does not make clear, that there are, as it were, other trees in the orchard. Another difficulty is that many of these authors studied theology and used sources in ways which their modern European counterparts find difficult to accept. They were bold in their approach to 'salvation history', inventing whole new episodes and rewriting familiar ones to link themselves, culturally and historically, with the Bible. They also preserved more apocryphal texts than anywhere else in Western Europe.[43] Like their neighbours in the Mediterranean world, they grafted their Christianity on to earlier beliefs which have not become invisible to us through long familiarity, unlike many Graeco-Roman and Semitic ones.[44] This ordinary process of synthesis allowed them to adapt and carry forward into Christianity, from Irish primal religions, insights and practices which they considered valuable and compatible with the new faith. O'Donoghue places the natural world at the very heart of this conversion process: 'Just as Christianity became wedded to *logos* in Hellenism, and to authority and law in Romanism, it became wedded to nature and the natural world, in all its various levels and regions, in the Celtic world.'[45] Approving of this is easier for those of us who admit to there being 'good spiritual and moral elements'[46] in non-Christian religions than for those who do not; and synthesis is often mistaken for syncretism, which may also sometimes be present. Getting to know early Irish Christianity takes the skills of a good listener. Engaging with it theologically can also become an exercise in historical ecumenism. Cherry-pickers will have to be prepared for all of this.

In the right situation, however, cherries may be exactly what is required. This chapter cannot be anything more than a rough guide and makes no claim to be comprehensive or definitive. It recognizes that beliefs about nature were only a small part of the faith-world of early Irish Christians, and presupposes a close familiarity, on their part, with canonical scripture and Christian writings from other parts of Europe. What follows is offered, by way of orientation and resource, under six overlapping headings: power, presence, a gift to be shared, kinship, love and sacrifice.

Power

The first thing to say about the natural world in early Christian Ireland is that people were aware of it. They were in direct daily contact with it, even if their normal activities were indoors, in the scriptorium or the kitchen. The rest of the natural world constantly impinged on them in terms of heat and cold, diet, health, mood. It had an immediacy which is rare in the 'developed' world today. The kind of urban environment described by Albert Camus, in which the seasons are noticeable only through changes in air quality and different goods for sale in the shops, was unimaginable in early Christian Ireland.[47] Travellers would have seen cities abroad and settlements around royal and religious centres were growing, but the non-human natural world was still underfoot, overhead and on the doorstep. It was real, it was powerful and living close to it was not so much an ideal as a matter of necessity. Some, of course, lived closer to it than others, but everyone realized their dependence on it for the raw materials of survival. Being on good terms with it was a matter of life or death and every day brought new reminders of the fact. Stewardship may seem like a suitable model for today, but up until the eighth century, perhaps longer, the task was closer to community relations than estate management.

This experience had, over generations, given rise to a healthy respect. This is not to claim a perfect ecological sensibility, but the natural world had been accorded the highest possible value. It is possible to discern traces of pre-Christian myth in which the land itself was experienced as divine. This 'sovereignty myth', which involved the marriage of a local goddess to the king, saw the relationship between humans beings and the rest of the natural world as an alliance or partnership in which the land retained a power and integrity of its own. If the king ruled wisely and justly, land and people would flourish, otherwise there would be floods, famines and general disorder.[48] A good leader enjoyed the support of the goddess and probably also of her Otherworld relatives, the *áes síde* who were believed to inhabit the underground regions of the earth, air, rivers, sea, forests and so on.[49] These could withdraw their support from leaders who acted unjustly (ignoring the lawlessness of powerful friends, breaking the limits set on them by their *gessi* or taboos) with disastrous consequences.[50] Land and people are inseparable in the sovereignty myth. They stand or fall together. But the non-human natural world is recognized as foundational, an essential partner in human thriving.

With the adoption of Christianity, life began to be seen differently. We do not know enough about Irish primal religions to understand the appeal of the new faith, but judging by the relative ease with which it spread, it must have seemed to offer an improvement on the old ones. The sovereignty myth was not easily discarded, however. The issues with which it dealt were too important. It persisted in modified form, in stories, ceremonies and seasonal activities. Recognizing the importance of the land, people expected an answering recognition from the clergy and, gradually, Christian leaders (usually abbots) became involved in the inauguration ceremonies of kings, and in seasonal fairs like those named after Carmun, Tailtiu and Macha who were probably once goddesses.[51] In one account of Carmun fair, Patrick, Brigit, Kevin and Columba are invoked as guarantors; and the closing act of worship consists of 'mass, genuflection and chanting of psalms'; Carmun was still remembered, with a mixture of fear, admiration and nostalgia, but fertility was now entrusted to the Christian God.[52]

It has been suggested that by destroying 'pagan animism', Christianity cleared the way for exploiting nature in a mood of indifference.[53] There is probably something in this, though greed has gnawed away at other religions as well. Features of the natural world which had previously been associated with guardian spirits or tutelary deities did eventually come to be viewed as material resources. It took a long time, however, for Irish Christians to accept the idea that water, air and earth, for example, were simply inert substances for their use. A belief in sacred places (holy mountains, wells, islands, trees, the graves and 'beds' of saints) survived the adoption of Christianity in Ireland. Indeed, there are signs of continuing resistance. In the 1990s, planning applications for a gold mine in the valley behind Croaghpatrick and a large-scale tourist development on Mullaghmore in the Burren were both opposed on spiritual as well as environmental grounds. At one stage, the language of holiness even entered the Dáil debate over Mullaghmore, with one minister describing the process as an 'unholy mess'.[54]

Back in the eighth century, the powers of nature were still, to a degree, personal. The evidence is there in texts like *Fáeth Fiada,* usually translated as 'The Deer's Cry' or 'St Patrick's Breast-plate';[55] in the spiritual guarantor list at the beginning of *Cáin Adomnáin* (Adomnán's Law of the Innocents); in Blathmac's poem on the crucifixion and in the popularity of the canticle, *Benedicite.* It seems that, like the first generations of Christians in the Mediterranean world, some Irish Christians found themselves unable to ignore the 'elemental spirits' but found a way of coming to terms with them, by enrolling them in the household of heaven, as 'the elements of God'.[56] The use of titles such as *Dé Dulig* (God of the elements) and *Dia dúilech* (Creator God or God imbuing everything) point in the same direction,[57] as does the early Latin 'credo' attached to the story of how Patrick won over the two sisters, Ethne and Fedelm, daughters of Loegaire, by describing the Creator to them. Ethne had asked what God was like; whether he was in the sky, the earth, water, rivers, mountains or valleys. Patrick, in what looks like a brilliant application of Ephesians 4: 5, describes to her a God who is not confined to any one place or element, but who is in all and over all and through all:

> God of heaven and earth, sea and rivers
> God of sun and moon, of all the stars,
> God of high mountains and low valleys,
> God above heaven, and in heaven, and under heaven.
>
> He has his dwelling in heaven
> And earth and sea
> And in everything that is in them.
>
> He breathes in all things
> Makes all things live,
> Surpasses all things
> Supports all things . . . .[58]

The conversation is imaginary, of course, but it is not impossible that Patrick, with his fingertip knowledge of scripture, would have communicated like this. Even if he did not, the poem shows the kind of arguments which the author, writing around 600, thought would be effective.[59]

Patrick's God might 'surpass all things' but one does not have to read very far into the wider body of literature to discover the ambivalence which many people continued to feel about the natural world. These honest complaints never really go away, as the delights of May Day are described side by side with the miseries of winter. 'Son of God the Father, with mighty hosts', writes an eleventh-century poet, 'save me from the horror of fierce tempests.'[60] A line from 'St Patrick's Breastplate' also asks for protection against some worrisome aspect of nature: *ar foirmthech-taib aicnid* – translations vary from 'tendencies' to 'assaults' and 'failings', though it expects help from that other aspect of nature, the elements.[61] Broccán's Old Irish hymn to Brigit assures us that: 'Victorious Brigit did not love the world; she perched in it like a bird on a cliff.'[62] So we are not dealing here with a naïve view of the natural world as unreservedly gentle and trouble-free. An awareness of danger and precariousness offsets the expressions of pleasure and appreciation found elsewhere. Different voices, moods, and rhetorical devices exist in early Irish literature as in other parts of the Christian tradition and, indeed, in the Bible.[63]

But even as they prayed to be saved from thunder, lightning and storms, there is sometimes a kind of admiration as well, like the admiration of an outclassed team for a dazzling opponent: 'Wild winter has slain us, it comes across the sea . . . what is there indeed more wonderful than the incomparable tremendous story?'[64] This is not intended as a response to serious natural disasters, but for ordinary winter weather it shows courage and generosity. In another poem, the storm is protective, keeping the Viking raiders at bay.[65] But more often there are complaints: 'the wind has broken us, it has crushed us, it has drowned us, O King of the star-bright kingdom.'[66]

There is no sign in any of this that the natural world was regarded as evil, though some texts describe it as inhabited by demons and monsters.[67] Fear of nature is linked in some modern theologies to fear of the body and its needs. This may be so in parts of the ascetical tradition, but here the natural world is frightening because it is bigger and stronger than human beings and ultimately beyond their control. Irish poets could be lyrical in its praise, but their relationship with nature also called for a certain mental and physical toughness.

Endurance was a quality they admired. They did not believe, however, that nature should always be allowed to 'take its course'. When there were droughts, they prayed for rain. When they were ill, they prayed for healing. Saints were seen as men and women who could, by the power of prayer, influence the way in which the rest of the natural world impinged upon human beings. They were credited with being able to dispel bad weather, prevent fires, improve yields and banish the demons which caused disease.[68] Furthermore, some hagiographers recount, threateningly, how people who criticized the saint or made him or her unwelcome could expect the rest of the natural world to turn against them too.[69] Bad weather, illness and death were sometimes seen as punishments for sin.[70] There were both biblical and native grounds for these negative traditions: the cursing of the ground in Genesis, for example, and the chaos of kingly misrule in the sovereignty myth. Both can be seen as attempts to explain natural ills, though the threats are less innocent. In the positive examples, the natural world, under the authority of God, supports the saint as once it supported the righteous king – or prophets like Elijah. Throughout the hagiography, a large body of compassionate miracles echo miracles of Jesus in the gospels where they are signs of God's way for the world ('the kingdom of God'). Through all of this, the suggestion seems to be that nature can and sometimes should be manipulated to suit human needs.

At a time when people had so little control over their environment, this must have seemed reassuring to those who could feel confident of God's favour. They could not have envisaged that the same attitude, harnessed to technology, would become such a key ingredient in the environmental crisis. But if we set aside those miracles which seem purely concerned with power and threat (and these are a minority) we are left with multiple instances of compassion. Miracle stories in which people are protected from destructive forces (storms, droughts, fevers, blights, murrains) can be seen as legitimating the human need to survive amid what has been called the 'reckless vitality' of a million rivals.[71] Other ethical tools may be needed to distinguish between needs and wants, but miracles in which power is in the service of compassion bear witness to a belief in a sheltering God who is favourably disposed towards humans and entrusts to some of them the ability to set limits on the power of creatures to destroy each other.[72]

Presence

There is, among Christians, a mental habit of jumping from creation to the Creator with barely a pause. We consider the lilies and the birds just long enough to draw a lesson about providence. John O'Donohue, in his essay, *Stone as the Tabernacle of Memory*, draws attention to this restless preoccupation with elsewhere and begins his meditation on presence with an invitation to settle down and notice what is before our eyes.[73] O'Donohue's concerns are with the present, but here he seems to be in touch with that earlier world in which anyone might stop and listen to a lark. I shall return to this kind of attentiveness in the section called 'love'.

For early Irish Christians, the natural world, in both surface and depth, was intimately connected with the presence of God. They saw this as a belief which had always been present in Ireland among the wise. It was claimed, for example, that the pre-Christian king Cormac Mac Airt 'would not worship stones or trees but would worship the one who had made them and was Lord behind every created thing'.[74] In one ninth-century poem he says: 'I was a listener among woods, / I was a gazer at stars.'[75] Cormac has his eyes and ears open. But to see his attentiveness purely in terms of physical observation is to set up barriers and distinctions which did not yet exist. The world, in ninth-century Ireland, was not just a physical place. It had hidden depths and was inhabited by spiritual presences, normally hidden, but real none the less: from the more familiar members of the household of heaven (angels and saints, Mary, souls of the faithful departed) to the *áes síde* who were so much part of the landscape that many Christians continued to believe in them.

Nature was not a sacrament in the traditional sense, but it had a sacramental quality which appears already in Patrick's *Confession*: in his night-time experiences on the mountain, and in a powerful later experience which took place at sunrise.[76] If the *Confession* is autobiographical, as it appears to be, the sun in the second example is more than just a metaphor for the victory of light over darkness. It is also, as Noel O'Donoghue suggests, the visible means by which Patrick is rescued from the evil one. Patrick is keen to distance himself from 'sun-worship' and goes on to assert, rather forcefully, that Christ is 'the true sun'. None the less, he has no difficulty with the idea that God's help can be encountered in and through nature. This had been his own experience as a young man and he saw no need to hide it, though he does not present this as normative or ideal.

There was also the fictional character Suibne *geilt*, who comes to an experience of God almost in spite of himself. Poems and stories about him, set in the sixth century, were already being written in the eighth, but the most complete surviving version of the Suibne Cycle was written in Middle Irish, probably during the twelfth century. The story is well known and need not be repeated here. Suibne lives out in the wilds, cursed by St Rónán, bereft of his family and his peace of mind. He is never completely reconciled with Christianity as it is presented to him. To the end, he prefers ivy leaves to book-leaves, birdsong to the chanting of psalms, but the monastic author also endows him with a kind of feral spirituality.[77] St Moling later recognizes a kind of holiness in him and when he dies, one of the monks describes him as 'the saintly madman'.

There are strong parallels between the Suibne Cycle and hermit and ascetical traditions in which nature was deliberately sought out as part of a spiritual exercise. One thinks of Colmán Mac Duaich spending the forty days of Lent in a cave in the Burren; or Cuthbert getting up before dawn to stand chest-deep in the sea at

St Abb's.[78] Similar activities were sometimes prescribed as a penance. The idea seems to have been that close encounters with the elements could bring one closer to God.[79]

A gift to be shared

The integrity of creation appears in the *Catechism of the Catholic Church* under the heading of the seventh commandment: 'You shall not steal.' The earth and its fruits, we are told, are destined for the common good of present and future humanity.[80] In early Irish literature, avarice is closely associated with shame. Kings, in particular, were expected to be generous and those who were tight-fisted could expect to be satirized. No doubt the desire of poets to be paid and churchmen to collect taxes contributed to this ethos, but it was there none the less. There were similar expectations of ordinary men and women:

> The grudging which women practise
> empties the pantries –
> The grudging which men practise
> leaves the ground without corn.[81]

It is as if meanness breeds meanness on a cosmic scale. The generosity of the King of Heaven was to be emulated by all his people. One of Brigit's character traits as a young woman is to be always giving things away: bacon to a dog, butter to the poor, her father's sword to a beggar.[82] Sometimes the things she gives away are miraculously replaced or multiplied, as if God were both rewarding her and egging her on.

A slightly less mythological treatment of the subject is found in the anonymous *Life of Cuthbert*, written on Lindisfarne in Northumbria *c.*700. Cuthbert was almost certainly Anglian but he was strongly influenced by Irish Christianity. Melrose, where he trained, was a daughter-house of Lindisfarne, which in turn was founded from Iona by St Aidan in 634. Both monasteries were, in some sense, part of the Columban *familia*. Celtic and Anglo-Saxon traditions meet in the person of Cuthbert, as they do in the Lindisfarne Gospels created in his honour, but if Bede is to be believed, his mentor (Boisil) and his role model (Aidan) were both Irish.[83] We know nothing of the ethnic background of the anonymous writer.

The story is as follows. Cuthbert is on a pastoral journey along the banks of the River Teviot. There is a boy in his company and Cuthbert asks the child whether he thinks he will get any dinner that day. It appears that Cuthbert sometimes travelled without food like a mendicant friar or a Hindu sadhu. The boy tells him that he has no relatives along that way and does not expect any sort of kindness from strangers. Cuthbert promises him that God will provide: 'Seek ye first the Kingdom of God . . .' he says, 'and all these things shall be added unto you.' Soon afterwards, they see an eagle flying overhead. Round the next corner, they see it again, this time on the ground. It flies off, leaving a large fish behind. The boy brings it to Cuthbert. 'Why did you not give our fisherman a part of it?' he asks, 'since he was fasting?' The boy divides the fish and gives half of it back to the eagle. They roast the other half, eat some of it themselves and share the rest with some strangers who happen to be passing. 'They ate', says the anonymous writer, 'and were satisfied, worshipping God and giving thanks.'[84]

As usual, we should be alert for symbolic meanings, but providence remains an important theme: God provides food from the natural world, as a gift. He provides it generously – there is more than enough for several people in only half the fish. The boy, by contrast, wants to keep the gift for himself and Cuthbert. He does not expect any sort of kindness from strangers and seems to have had little experience of sharing. Cuthbert turns the whole episode into a lesson in giving and receiving. Not only does he share the gift with strangers, but he prompts the boy to give part of the fish back to the eagle. This story goes further than theologies which concentrate on human use of natural resources. It endorses the view that humans have a call on them, but specifically enjoins sharing with non-human creatures as well. Nowadays, with ospreys and white-tailed eagles rare and persecuted as a result of human non-sharing, one might wish that the whole fish had been left with the fisherman.

Kinship

Some early Irish texts convey a strong sense of human beings as part of nature. The famous poem 'I am Wind on Sea' can certainly be interpreted this way.[85] Attributed to Amairgen, chief poet of the mythological ancestors of the Gaels, it survives only in Middle Irish, a primal-looking hymn written at least five centuries after the beginnings of Christianity in Ireland. This raises all kinds of questions. Did it reflect a purely antiquarian interest or did 'I am Wind on Sea' still appear true in some way? The speaker claims kinship with (literally, claims to *be*) the wind, a wave on the ocean, various birds, fish and animals, a dewdrop, the fairest of flowers, a lake, a mountain, a skilful word, a weapon and finally even God. It is probably this last arresting claim which has led most Christian commentators to disown it, though Christian mystics have also envisaged the unity of all things in God. They can sound equally shocking when taken out of context: for example: 'In God all things are equal and are God himself.'[86] It is generally assumed that the composer of the Amairgen poem lacked the philosophical sophistication of these later writers. This may be so, though we know very little about its background. As it stands, however, it celebrates the interrelatedness of the natural world in a way which modern Western Christianity is only now rediscovering.[87]

Similar ideas underlie the tenth- or eleventh-century apocryphon known as *In Tenga Bhith-Nua Annso Sis* (The Evernew Tongue Here Below).[88] This may go back ultimately to a lost *Apocalypse of Philip* from fourth- or fifth-century Egypt but it has been 'transformed in the crucible of the author's imagination' into a thoroughly Irish document.[89] Human beings are made, it says, not just from the dust of the earth, as in Genesis, but from wind, air, fire, sunlight, stars, salt, stones, clay and flowers. Poetry and theology combine here with ancient ideas of physiology, for example, the theory of the four elements – fire, water, earth and air – which gave rise to the different temperaments and in some cases to illness.[90] This is not modern medicine but it knows intuitively what ecologists are still trying to convey: that human beings are not separate from the rest of creation but belong to the earth, utterly and completely, for as long as they are in it. They also believed, of course, that there were other worlds, but this one was not a godforsaken place which Christians should be in a hurry to leave. On the contrary, it had been blessed, in every part of it:

> Every material and every element and every nature which is seen in the world were all combined in the body in which Christ arose, that is in the body of every human person. . . . All the world arose with him, for the nature of all the elements was in the body which Jesus assumed.[91]

Through the incarnation, God had become one, not just with human flesh, but with the wind and air, fire, the sun and the stars, salt, bitterness, stones, the earth and flowers. 'Every material and every element in nature' rose from the grave with him and was freed from the power of death. I am not sure that Western theology has ever really got to grips with this, though it is reminiscent of Irenaeus's doctrine of recapitulation and St Paul's prophecy: 'The creation itself will be set free from its bondage to decay and obtain the glorious liberty of the children of God.'[92] Clear enough, though, is the sense of kinship between human beings and the rest of creation – with both taken up into God.

Love

Marina Smyth finds 'a surprising interest in the physical world for its own sake' in the early Latin writings of Irish scholars. Comparing two Hiberno-Latin texts from the mid-seventh century (*On the Miracles of Holy Scripture* by the writer known as the 'Irish Augustine' and the anonymous *Book of the Order of Creatures*) with similar works by Gregory the Great, Augustine of Hippo and Isidore of Seville, she finds that, while the latter were interested in nature, they looked to it mainly for allegorical signs and 'higher' truths. The Irish Augustine, she suggests, is far more curious about its internal workings.[93] It is possible to overstate the differences, but the Irish Augustine does puzzle at length over how a bush could burn without being consumed, how a baby could be born without intercourse, how water could bear the weight of one person (Jesus) but not another (Peter). Indeed, questions like these form the basis of his entire book. The African Augustine was deeply sensitive to the beauty of the natural world, more so perhaps than his Irish counterpart, but he frequently moves on quickly to praise of the Creator, lest he be ensnared by 'the lust of the eyes'. The natural world is an allurement to him, and he warns that curiosity about it is a waste of time since it is of no use in reaching blessedness.[94]

Augustinus, the Irish Augustine, by contrast, gives free rein to his interest, believing that the whole of the natural world would be glorified at the end of time. His 'explanations' may be outlandish by today's standards, but he argues from observation and from the work of 'natural philosophers' as well as from scripture, and is delighted with the idea that if he ever gets to heaven, he will understand everything there is to know about all creatures.[95] Is he in love with nature or with knowledge? It is hard to tell. Even the nature poets declare themselves only indirectly. Perhaps they were embarrassed by 'the blather of love'.[96] Perhaps, like the skilled *literati* they were, they knew how to evoke a thing without resorting to the bald statement or the abstract noun.

The American theologian Sallie McFague describes two ways of looking at the natural world: with an arrogant eye which views nature as an object; or with a loving eye which looks on nature as another subject. To look on nature with a loving eye, she suggests, is to see it as God sees it.[97] This has made me look again at those passages of early Irish nature poetry which can otherwise seem purely descriptive. Could it be that the spiritual quality sensed by Flower and Murphy among others has to do with the loving quality of the observation? It is present even in the earliest poems, but many of the best examples are in Middle Irish. Take, for example, the poem known in English as 'Marbán's Hermitage'. On one level, this is a poet's flight of fancy, but it can also be seen as a celebration of the natural world in all its beauty and biodiversity. Written probably in the tenth century, it describes the idealized life of a Christian hermit. The following extracts are typical:

> I have a shieling in the wood, none knows it but my God. An ash tree on the hither side, a hazel bush beyond, a huge old tree encompasses it . . .
> A choice pure spring and princely water to drink. There spring watercresses, yew berries, ivy bushes thick as a man.
> Around it, tame swine lie down, goats, pigs, wild swine, grazing deer, a badger's brood.[98]

The poet is concerned to show that God provides for Marbán, so there is a strong theme of nature as gift, particularly the gift of food and drink (apples, strawberries, ale, mead) but self-interest is not the only factor at work here. The unnamed virtue is infectiously present as he describes 'the music of the dark torrent' and the colour of the feathers on a bird's back. The poet names at least twenty-two different plants and some fourteen different species of wild birds as well as mammals, fish and insects. These are Marbán's companions at the court of the King of Heaven; indeed, on one level, the whole poem is a witty comparison between the hermit's hut and the court of his brother, King Guaire; but there is more here than just literary skill. The poet has observed nature closely and presents the saint as someone who did the same, looking upon it, not only with self-interest, but with a loving eye.

This is found not only in summer idylls, but also in poems about the miseries of winter: 'The eagle of brown Glen Rye gets affliction from the bitter wind; great is its misery and its suffering, the ice will get into its beak.'[99] The same poem tells how the deer cannot get at their food, the wolves are too cold to sleep, and the wrens and blackbirds shiver in their nests: 'woe to the company of little birds for the keen wind and the cold ice'. This is just one of a number of winter poems from Ireland at this period. Like exercises in mindfulness, they pay attention to what is rather than what should be, bearing to look when others might turn away. Here is another, full of harshness and brutality, but still with a note of compassion as we see the drooping wings, share the hunger and the drudgery:

> In the black season of deep winter a storm of waves is roused along the expanse of the world. Sad are the birds of every meadow plain, except the ravens that feed on crimson blood, at the clamour of harsh winter; rough, black, dark, smoky. Dogs are vicious in cracking bones; the iron pot is put on the fire after the dark black day.[100]

This is part of a 'four seasons' set, each carefully observed. The eleventh-century poet ascribes this to Amairgen; that it was also seen as the attitude of a good Christian is evident from near-contemporary poems like 'Manchán's Wish' and 'St Columba's Island Hermitage'. Religious references are quite explicit in these, and there is the same quality of loving attentiveness towards the natural world: 'a beautiful wood close by . . . for the nurture of many-voiced birds' ('Manchán'); the 'heavy waves over the glittering ocean . . . the shallow waves against the rocks' ('Columba').[101] This is not the only voice or attitude in the tradition. By contrast, there is the extreme asceticism of 'The Hermit' ('making holy the body with good habits, treading it boldly down . . . desires feeble and withered, renunciation of this poor world') who is so anxiously preparing for death that he can hardly bear to look around. Yet even he cannot help noticing the 'fair-coloured hillside' where he goes for water.[102]

Ernst Sieper once claimed that 'Celtic nature poetry is interested in nature objectively and for its own sake alone, not subjectively for its relation to the poet's own, more important feelings.' Jackson took the opposite view: that the poet's feelings were everything.[103] I do not believe that subjectivity and objectivity can be separated in this way, but Sieper was surely right in identifying an objective quality in them just as he was wrong if he saw in them only dispassionate description. Most of these poems do have an emotional charge, but they also show an interest which is not *entirely* bound up with what humans can get out of the situation, materially, emotionally or even spiritually. They also have to do with knowing the natural world in 'the dignity and glory of its pure otherness'[104] and in all its moods.

Sacrifice

It may seem a little dour to suggest that asceticism might have something to offer the green movement. Even to mention it in the company of some creation-centred Christians is to risk being associated with all the old life-denying impulses which have driven some of the most dedicated men and women to despise nature in themselves and in the world around them. It is possible to find examples of this world-fleeing asceticism in the Irish tradition: in some of the Rules and Penitentials and in poems like 'The Hermit' and 'Building a Wall'.[105] This is not the asceticism that I mean. It is certainly possible to interpret the gospels in an otherworldly sense, as these texts do, but the teaching of Jesus that the two greatest commandments are 'love God and your neighbour as yourself' and his own example of self-giving 'for the life of the world' place at the heart of Christianity the idea that hardship and limits are sometimes to be accepted voluntarily for the sake of 'the kingdom of God'.[106] Asceticism can be seen as a training (*ascesis*) in this fertile kind of renunciation, a striving to be released from narrow self-interest. The relevance of this to voracious consumerism is obvious enough. The Irish tradition provides numerous examples of people who were admired for their asceticism. Their motives were probably varied but saints like Patrick and Adomnán are portrayed as enduring discomfort for the benefit of other people.[107] The Glendalough tradition goes further: another creature benefits.

We are told that St Kevin of Glendalough went to his hermitage for the forty days of Lent, as was his custom. His hut was so small that in order to pray in cross-vigil he had to put one arm out of the window. One day, a blackbird came and laid her eggs in the palm of his hand: 'and so moved was the saint that in all patience and gentleness he remained, neither closing nor withdrawing his hand' till the chicks had hatched.[108] This story, like that of St Columba and the horse, is easily swamped by sentimentality, but in fact it illustrates something which is really quite unsentimental and challenging: a human being giving up something of his own comfort, for the sake of something as 'insignificant' as a bird.

This is, of course, a miracle story. Exaggeration is a normal part of its idiom, as is the glorification of the saint, in this case by claiming for him a heroic capacity for cross-vigil. But the emphasis on 'patience and gentleness' suggests that there is more going on here than just spiritual machismo. It might be objected that the blackbird story comes to us from a source written six centuries after the event by Gerald of Wales, but Gerald does seem to be repeating something which he had heard in Ireland, and which Irish Christians admired. It may not be reliable information about Kevin himself, but it does reveal something of the values and ideals of the Glendalough community and is very much in keeping with earlier traditions about the saint.

His Latin Life, probably written during the seventh or eighth century, describes how 'a crowd of birds perched on his shoulders and his hands' and flitted about him as he stood still, praying under a tree; how 'the wild things of the mountains and the woods came and kept him company and would drink water from his hands like domestic creatures'; how a cow used to visit him in his hermitage; a boar took refuge from huntsmen in his oratory while the hounds remained respectfully outside; and a doe came to the monastery to be milked. There are harsh moments as well: women are much less welcome than animals; there is a case of divinely inspired panic among cattle and on one occasion Kevin loses his temper with some rooks; more often, however, he is on good terms with other creatures and takes their well-being into account. When God offers to move mountains for him, literally, by changing the hills around Glendalough into gentle meadows to support a larger number of the monks, Kevin declines, for the sake of his non-human neighbours:

I have no wish that the creatures of God should be moved because of me . . . and moreover all the wild creatures on these mountains are my house mates, gentle and familiar with me, and they would be sad of this that thou hast said.[109]

These stories repeatedly link holiness with positive, considerate relationships towards other creatures and the rest of the natural world. It may be significant that Kevin, kneeling in cross-vigil, is not just an icon of himself, but of Christ crucified. In a world where saints were seen as people united with, and manifesting, God, Kevin's sacrificial care for the blackbird has a quality which is both this-worldly and divine:

> Kevin feels the warm eggs, the small breast, the tucked
> Neat head and claws and, finding himself linked
> Into the network of eternal life
>
> Is moved to pity . . .[110]

Summing up

I would like to finish with another lark poem, this one bearing a heavy weight of anxiety. It comes to us from the Isle of Skye, a place which was once within the orbit of Iona[111] but which has long since gone its own way in matters of religion. The poet, Aonghas MacNeacail, gives no clue as to his own religious convictions, but love, language and a sense of kinship connect his lark poem with earlier traditions:

uiseag uiseag anns na speuran	skylark skylark soaring high
seachain duslach dubh an dadaim	beware the dark atomic dust
thig e ort gun fhios gun chumadh	which comes with neither shape nor warning
thig e ort gun fhuaim gun bholadh	which comes with neither sound nor savour
uiseag uiseag anns na speuran	skylark skylark soaring high[112]

MacNeacail wrote this in the aftermath of the Chernobyl nuclear accident in 1986. The image of a lark soaring into a radioactive sky has a powerful emotional impact and the childlikeness of the chant 'Uiseag uiseag' gives it added poignancy, a warning to lark and reader alike, out of the mouths of babes and sucklings. The confession comes a few verses later: 'mise leig an urchair nimheil / ó mo nàire ó mo ghuineadh' (it was I who pulled the trigger / now my guilt is my own wounding) and as the poem ends, we realize that the speaker has been blinded by a nuclear explosion and can no longer see whether the lark is rising or falling. He realizes too late his complicity in the disaster, and the interconnectedness of things. The nuclear threat is not so much in the headlines these days but there are still concerns about global warming, genetic modification, species extinction. Recent figures for the south-east of England show a 60 per cent decline in skylarks since 1972 and in some urban areas house sparrows have declined by over 90 per cent – an indicator of what is happening with other components of the environment as well.[113]

Early Irish Christianity was never designed to meet this situation. Its capabilities and its outlook were very different from our own and its faith world, when allowed to speak for itself, presents some fundamental challenges. Nor is it uniformly helpful. There was, however, a greater awareness of the natural world and of being dependent on it for the raw materials of survival. We find ideas of partnership with it, in which nature has its own integrity and is not endlessless malleable for human purposes. It is seen as a gift to be shared and a place of encounter with God who was believed to have entered into and hallowed every part of it. God's care for non-human creatures is also expressed in some lives of saints. There is an interest it for its own sake and numerous examples of looking at it with a loving eye. The Marbán poem ends: 'I am grateful for what is given me from my good Christ . . . the prince who gives every good to me in my shieling.'[114] Saying thank you acknowledges the goodness of the gift, as well as of the giver, and this is also very much part of the tradition.

Notes

[1] From the Lebor Brecc version of the *Félire*, ed. Whitley Stokes, *On the Calendar of Oengus*, Transactions of the Royal Irish Academy (Dublin, 1880), I. 1. lxvi, my trans. Kenneth Jackson, *Studies in Early Celtic Nature Poetry* (Cambridge, 1935), 5 (henceforth *ECNP*). The Lebor Brecc is an early fifteenth-century collection from the area around Clonmacnoise. Most of the material in it dates from the twelfth century or earlier. The *Félire* itself was written around AD 800 but the poem occurs uniquely in the Lebor Brecc version.

[2] From 'Moment on the Canal Bank', in *Patrick Kavanagh: The Complete Poems* (Newbridge, 1992), 310. See also 'Cool Water Under Bridges', 'What To Offer' and 'Our Lady's Tumbler', ibid., 296–7, 300–2.

[3] R. I. Best and H. J. Lawlor (eds.), *The Martyrology of Tallaght*, Henry Bradshaw Society, 68 (London, 1931), 94–7. In other parts of early Irish literature, birds are often described singing God's praises or even reciting the liturgical hours. See my *Celtic Christianity and Nature*,

(Edinburgh, 1996), 95, 107, 118 (henceforth *CCN*). Cf. Alexander Carmichael, *Carmina Gadelica,* ed. James Carmichael Watson (Edinburgh, 1940), iii. 25.

4 Ian Bradley, 'How green was Celtic Christianity?', *Ecotheology,* 4 (Jan. 1998), 58–69. Thomas Owen Clancy and Gilbert Markus, *Iona: The Earliest Poetry of a Celtic Monastery* (Edinburgh, 1995), 90–3.

5 Mackey, 'Religionists and other Celtic scholars', paper presented at the first Celtic Christianity Study Day, Divinity Faculty, Edinburgh University, 1993.

6 In their commentary on the early Irish hymn *Noli Pater*, Thomas Owen Clancy and Gilbert Márkus give this as an example of fearing rather than loving nature, but their intention is to show a range of attitudes towards nature, including love. *Iona: Earliest Poetry*, 92.

7 Eoin Mac Néill, 'Characteristics of Irish literature', *Gaelic Journal,* 5 (1894), 76. Douglas Hyde, *The Story of Early Gaelic Literature* (London, 1895), 148.

8 Kuno Meyer, *Selections from Ancient Irish Poetry* (London, 1911) (henceforth *AIP*). Eleanor Hull, *The Poem Book of the Gael* (London, 1912). K. Jackson, *A Celtic Miscellany* (London, 1951) (henceforth *CM*). Jackson, *ECNP*. Gerard Murphy, *Early Irish Lyrics* (Oxford, 1956) (henceforth *EIL*).

9 G. Murphy, *Studies,* 20 (1931), 87–101. Robin Flower, ' "The two eyes of Ireland": religion and literature in Ireland in the eighth and ninth centuries', in W. Bell and N. D. Emerson (eds.), *The Church of Ireland AD 432–1932: The Report of the Church of Ireland Conference held in Dublin, 11th–14th October, 1932* (Dublin, 1932), 73. Flower makes a similar point in *The Irish Tradition* (Oxford, 1947), 47 and in his 'The Irish high crosses', *Journal of the Warburg and Courtauld Institute,* 17 (1954), 90–1.

10 Low, *CCN*, 14–51. D. Ó Corráin, 'Early Irish hermit poetry?', in D. Ó Corráin, L. Breatnach and K. McCone (eds.), *Sages, Saints and Storytellers* (Maynooth, 1989), 251–67.

11 James Carney dates *Cétamon* ('Finn's Poem on May Day') to around AD 600, overturning earlier datings by Meyer and Jackson: 'The dating of archaic Irish poetry', in S. Tranter and H. Tristram (eds.), *Early Irish Literature, Media and Communication* (Tübingen, 1989), 40. This makes it contemporaneous with the oldest religious poem in the vernacular, *Amra Choluimb Chille* ('Eulogy of Colum Cille'). For some of the problems and possibilities of continuity with Irish primal religions, see my *CCN, passim,* esp. 13–16.

12 Helen Waddell, *Beasts and Saints* (London, 1934), xix, re-edited with introduction by Esther de Waal (London, 1995). Matt. 10: 29. Luke 12: 6.

13 H. J. Massingham, *The Tree of Life* (London, 1942), 40.

14 Ibid., 6–7, 33–72.

15 C. Bamford and W. P. Marsh, *Celtic Christianity: Ecology and Holiness*, 2nd edn. (Edinburgh, 1986). Esther de Waal, *A World Made Whole* (London, 1991).

16 See, for example, 'Nature is not Enough', in Ron Ferguson (ed.), *Daily Readings with George MacLeod* (London, 1991), 42–3.

17 The *Benedicite*, from the Septuagint version of Daniel 3, was a much-used canticle in early Christian Ireland. See Low, *CCN*, 173–4.

18 John V. Taylor, *The Primal Vision* (London, 1963), 195–7. Joseph Renan (1823–92), the Breton philosopher, theologian and scripture scholar had also been interested in Celtic Christianity at the end of the nineteenth century. See René M. Galand, *L'Ame celtique de Renan* (Paris, 1959).

19 John MacQuarrie, *Paths in Spirituality* (London, 1972), 122; my emphasis.

20 'When Baillie argues that God is known as presence rather than by inference, and when he tells us that this presence is a "mediated immediacy", mediated, that is, by persons, things and events within the world, then he is stating in theological language the basic conviction underlying Celtic spirituality. Also Baillie was one of the few theologians to uphold the doctrine of divine immanence at a time when all of the stress was on transcendence.' Ibid., 124.

21 See Laura Sugg, 'The experience of God in everyday life in Alexander Carmichael's *Carmina Gadelica*' (Edinburgh Ph.D. thesis, 1997), and my own 'Aspects of nature in early Irish religion' (Edinburgh Ph.D. thesis, 1993).

22 Noel O'Donoghue, *The Mountain behind the Mountain* (Edinburgh, 1993), 19–21.

23 James Hunter, *On the Other Side of Sorrow* (Edinburgh, 1995). Christopher Smout, *The Highlands and the Roots of Green Consciousness, 1750–1990* (Battleby, 1993), 7–8. Smout uses the term in relation to a verse from *Moladh Beinn Dobhrain* ('In Praise of Ben Dorain') by Donnchadh Bàn Mac An t-Saoir, Duncan Ban MacIntyre (1724–1812): 'It is from roots like these that an indigenous green consciousness can perhaps be traced', but as Hunter points out there are earlier examples.

24 The poems in question are those trans. by Jackson as 'Arran', 'St Columba's Island Hermitage' and the slightly later 'Deirdre Remembers a Scottish Glen'. *CM*, 70–2, 279–80. Hunter, *Other Side*, 41–68.

25 Jackson, *ECNP*, 121.

26 Hunter, *Other Side*, 42, 57.

27 See the chapters by Davies, Wooding and Atherton.

[28] For example by Simon James, *The Atlantic Celts: Ancient People or Modern Invention?* (London, 1999).

[29] Ruth and Vincent Megaw, 'Celtic connections past and present: Celtic ethnicity ancient and modern', in Ronald Black, William Gillies and Roibeard Ó Maolalaigh (eds.), *Celtic Connections: Proceedings of the Tenth International Congress of Celtic Studies* (East Linton, 1999), i. 19–81.

[30] Oliver Davies, *An Introduction to Celtic Spirituality* (New York and Mahwah, NJ, 1999), 3–12; see also his essay in the present volume.

[31] For examples of the Welsh and Irish traditions side by side, see Jackson, *ECNP* and *CM*. For poems springing from the common ground between Ireland and Scotland, see *CM*, 70–2, 279–80.

[32] 'Chan eil e soirbh Ceilteach a sgaradh bho dhuine eile, ach tha briathras agus ceòl agus gaol Nàduir a' Cheiltich ga chur air leth ann an ealain cò-dhiù' (It is not easy to distinguish a Celt from someone of another background; but the Celt's verbal virtuosity, music and love of Nature set him apart in art at least). Black et al. (eds.), *Celtic Connections*, pp. xxiv, xxi.

[33] Louis Gougaud, *Les Chrétientés celtiques* (Paris, 1911). Trans. as *Christianity in Celtic Lands*.

[34] Kuno Meyer (ed.), *Triads of Ireland* (Dublin, 1906), 12–13, §92. Meat was also enjoyed in some monasteries, for example, at Glendalough, where St Kevin's feast-day seems to have been celebrated with 'much preparing of beef'. Waddell, *Beasts*, 133, from the Latin Life of Coemgen, in *Vitae Sanctorum Hiberniae*, ed. Charles Plummer, 2 vols. (Oxford, 1910), ii. However, the fact that it is mentioned at all suggests that this was not their everyday diet.

[35] Adomnán, *VSC*, II. 29

[36] Ibid., 26. For other boar traditions, see n. 108 below and S. Connolly and J.-M. Picard (eds.,) 'Cogitosus, Life of Brigit', *Journal of the Royal Society of Antiquaries of Ireland*, 117 (1987), 18.

[37] This is not just a characteristic of Irish and Hiberno-Latin Lives. It is also present in some of their sources. For example, the death of Lochru the druid in Muirchú's Life of Patrick in Ludwig Bieler (ed.), *The Patrician Texts in the Book of Armagh* (Dublin, 1979), (16) 6, pp. 88–91, seems to be based on the flight and fall of Simon Magus in *The Acts of Peter*, II. 32 (3), ed. W. Schneemelcher (London, 1965), 315–16; cf. also less edifying parts of the Bible, including the New Testament, such as Acts 5: 1–11, a passage quoted approvingly by Augustinus Hibernicus, *De Miraculae*, §17, cited in John Carey, *King of Mysteries* (Dublin, 1998), 74.

[38] Adomnán, *VSC*, I. 48, III. 23.

[39] *Félire Óengusso / Martyrology of Óengus*, ed. Stokes, 56; Jackson, *Celtic Miscellany*, 296; Low, *CCN*, 13.

40 For the belief that animals do not suffer, see Ruth Page, 'God, natural evil and the ecological crisis', *Studies in World Christianity*, 3/1 (1997), 72.

41 'Let him alone' may echo 'Let her alone' in Mark 14: 6 (to Simon the Leper) and John 12: 7 (to Judas). Other parallels include tears and a presentiment of death.

42 Plenary paper delivered at the 11th International Congress of Celtic Studies, Cork, 1999.

43 Carey, *King of Mysteries*, 22, 75.

44 For a valuable external perspective on the enculturated nature of European Christianity, see Kwame Bediako, *Theology and Identity: The Impact of Culture upon Christian Thought in the Second Century and in Modern Africa* (Oxford, 1992).

45 O'Donoghue, *Mountain behind the Mountain*, 15.

46 Second Vatican Council, Declaration on the Relation of the Church to Non-Christian Religions (1965), §2.

47 Camus described his home-town of Oran in Algeria as follows: 'A town without pigeons, without trees, with neither the flutter of wings nor the whisper of leaves, a neutral place, in fact. The changing of the seasons can be read only in the sky. Spring makes itself known only by the quality of the air or by the baskets of flowers which small traders bring in from the suburbs.' *La Peste* (Paris, 1947), 1. My trans.

48 For a selection of texts relating to these beliefs, see *CCN*, 25–35, 43–5.

49 T. Ó Cathasaigh, 'The semantics of *síd*', *Éigse*, 17 (1977–9), 135–54.

50 See, for example, the downfall of Conaire Mór in *Togail Bruidne Da Derga / The Destruction of Da Derga's Hostel*, ed. W. Stokes, *Revue Celtique*, 22 (1901), and in J. Gantz (ed. and trans.), *Early Irish Myths and Sagas* (London, 1981). See also the death tale of Muirchertach Meic Erca, in Stokes, *RC*, 23, 395–431. Low, *CCN*, 34–5, 177–80.

51 Low, *CCN*, 98.

52 E. J. Gwynn (ed.), *The Metrical Dindshenchas*, Todd Lectures Series (Dublin, 1903–35), iii. 2–25. Low, *CCN*, 29–32.

53 Lynn White, 'The historical roots of our ecologic crisis', *Science*, 155/3767 (10 March 1967), 1205.

54 Dáil Debates Official Report (15 October 1998).

55 J. H. Bernard and R. Atkinson (eds.), *The Irish Liber Hymnorum*, Henry Bradshaw Society, 14 (London, 1897–8), ii. 50. Meyer, *AIP*, 25–7. Carey, *King of Mysteries*, 127–135. Kuno Meyer, *The Law of Adomnáin / Cáin Adomnáin* (Oxford, 1905), §23–4. A similar, but later, guarantor list backs up the protection of the saints of Carmun fair. Gwynn, *Metrical Dindshenchas*, iii. 2–25. Low, *CCN*, 30. J. Carney, *The Poems of Blathmac* (Dublin, 1964), 23–5, §§61–70. Low, *CCN*, 169–75.

56 Gal. 4: 8–11; 2 Peter 3: 10–11. Low, 'Henotheism: the One and the

many in early Christian Ireland', paper delivered at the Tenth International Congress of Celtic Studies, Edinburgh, 1995. Cf. William Sayers, '*Mani Maidi an Nem* . . .: ringing changes on a cosmic motif', *Ériu*, 37 (1986), 99–117.

57 Low, *CCN*, 177–80, 184–5; 215 n. 51.

58 Tírechán, 26. 5, Ludwig Bieler (ed.), *The Patrician Texts in the Book of Armagh* (Dublin, 1979), 142–3. James Carney, *Medieval Irish Lyrics* (Portlaoise, 1985), 2–7.

59 Ibid., pp. xv–xvi. It is perhaps a measure of our distance from those times that Ethne's questions, always attractive, now have almost as many supporters as Patrick's answer. See, for example, Mary Condren, *The Serpent and the Goddess* (London, 1989).

60 Meyer, *Otia Merseiana*, ii. 76. Meyer, *AIP,* 51–2. Jackson, *ECNP,* 31.

61 Carey, *King of Mysteries*, 133. David Greene and Frank O'Connor, *A Golden Treasury of Irish Poetry* (Dingle, 1990), 31. Noel O'Donoghue, 'St Patrick's Breastplate', in James Mackey (ed.), *An Introduction to Celtic Christianity* (Edinburgh, 1989), 48. Meyer, *AIP,* 26, omits the line altogether. The manuscripts also vary.

62 Carey, *King of Mysteries,* 164.

63 For example, on the theme of loving/not loving the world, compare 1 John 2: 15 with John 3: 16.

64 Jackson, *ECNP,* 30–1. Cf. Meyer, *AIP,* 51–2. The poem is said to have been sung by Rumann mac Colmáin to the Vikings of Dublin in the eighth century. Meyer dated it to the eleventh century. Jackson, *ECNP,* 46. For a prayer against thunder and lightning, see *Noli Pater,* in Clancy and Markus, *Iona,* 84–5. The commentary there provides a view different from my own.

65 Jackson, *ECNP,* 32.

66 Ibid., citing Kuno Meyer, *Bruchstücke der älteren Lyrik Irlands* (Berlin, 1919), 67; context unknown. See also Jackson, *CM,* 127.

67 For examples, see Low, *CCN,* 74–6, 108, Clancy and Markus, *Iona,* 57–8.

68 Examples from the traditions of Brigit, Patrick and Columba would include: Cogitosus, 'Life of Saint Brigit', ed. S. Connolly and J.-M. Picard, *Journal of the Royal Society of Antiquaries of Ireland,* 117 (1987), §§1, 3, 4, 31; *Bethu Brigte,* ed. D. Ó hAodha (1978), §46; Life of Brigit from *Lives of Saints from the Book of Lismore,* ed. W. Stokes (Oxford, 1890), 1412–24; Muirchú, Life of Patrick, *The Patrician Texts,* ed. Ludwig Bieler, i. 20 (19) 3–7, 92–5; Adomnán, *VSC,* II. 44–6. Colic demons appear in *Chronicum Scotorum,* ed. W. M. Hennesy (London, 1866), 231, and pestilence demons in the *Annals of Tigernach,* ed. Stokes, *Revue Celtique,* 17, 417.

69 See, for instance, *Bethu Brigte,* ed. D. Ó hAodha (Dublin, 1978), §32;

and Muirchú, Life of Patrick, *The Patrician Texts,* ed. Bieler, I. 26(25) 112–13.

70 'I am Eve', Meyer, *AIP,* 34. Cf. Adomnán, *VSC,* II. 44.

71 Austin Farrer, *Love Almighty and Ills Unlimited* (New York, 1961), 50.

72 For a challenging discussion of some of the theological problems involved in such an optimistic view, see Page, 'God, natural evil and the ecological crisis', 68–86.

73 John O'Donohue, *Stone as the Tabernacle of Memory* (Galway, 1994), 6–7.

74 *Senchas na Relec / The Lore of Burial Places, Lebor na hUidre,* ed. R. Best and O. Bergin, 50a–50b. Kim McCone, *Pagan Past, Christian Present* (Maynooth, 1990), 73.

75 Kuno Meyer, *The Instructions of King Cormac,* Todd Lectures Series, 15 (Dublin, 1909), 346b.

76 Patrick, *Confession,* 16, 20. O'Donoghue, *Aristocracy of Soul: Patrick of Ireland* (London, 1987), 57–8. Low, *CCN,* 41–2, 141–3.

77 J. G. O'Keeffe (ed.), *Buile Suibne / The Frenzy of Suibne,* Irish Texts Society, 12 (Dublin, 1913), §§23, 34–5.

78 'Three legends from the Brussels Manuscript 5100–4', ed. W. Stokes, *Revue Celtique,* 26 (1905), 372–7. Bede, *Life of Cuthbert,* §10.

79 For example, the penance of Macuil Moccu Grecae in Muirchú's Life of Patrick: A. B. E. Hood (ed.), *St Patrick: His Writings and Muirchú's Life* (London, 1978), 93–4, §23. Bieler, *The Patrician Texts,* I. 23(22) = B. II. 4, 102–7. See also the discussion of this incident by T. O'Loughlin in Chapter 6 of the present volume. For other examples, see *Cáin Adomnáin, an Old-Irish treatise on the Law of Adomnán,* ed. Kuno Meyer, *Anecdota Oxoniensia* (Oxford, 1905), §45, where it is a woman's penance for murder, and *The Voyage of Snedgus and MacRiagla,* ed. W. Stokes, *Revue Celtique,* 9 (1888), 14–25, §§7–10, 21–3, where a whole community is cast adrift for murdering their king. For further discussion, see P. L. Henry, *The Early English and Celtic Lyric* (London, 1966), 181–94.

80 Exodus 20: 15. *Catechism of the Catholic Church* (London, 1994), §2415.

81 J. G. O'Keeffe, 'Mac Dá Cherda and Cummaine Foda', *Ériu,* 5 (1911), 18–44, at 25.

82 Cogitosus, 'Life of Saint Brigit', *Journal of the Royal Society of Antiquaries of Ireland,* 117 (1987), §§1, 3. *Bethu Brigte,* ed. Ó hAodha, §§10, 12, 13.

83 For Boisil see Bede, *Ecclesiastical History of the English People,* trans. Leo Sherley-Price and revised R. E. Latham (London, 1990), IV. 27 (hereafter *HE*), and Colin Ireland, 'An Irishman hidden in the works of Bede', *Peritia* 5 (1986), 400–3. Examples of Cuthbert taking Aidan for his role model include entering the monastery (Bede, *Life of*

Cuthbert, §4), living as a hermit on Farne (ibid., §17; *HE* III. 28), and accepting the bishopric (*HE* IV. 28). Low, *St Cuthbert's Way: A Pilgrims' Companion* (Glasgow, 2000), 27–50, 140–4.

84   Anonymous, II. 5, in *Two Lives of St Cuthbert*, ed. Bertram Colgrave (Cambridge, 1940).

85   R. A. S. Macalister (ed.), *Lebor Gabála Érenn / Book of the Takings of Ireland*, part 5, Irish Texts Society, 44 (Dublin, 1956), 110–13. It can also be interpreted as a divine utterance, as I have pointed out elsewhere; Low, *CCN*, 10–11.

86   Meister Eckhart, Sermon on Ecclesiasticus 24. 30, quoted in David Fleming (ed.), *The Fire and the Cloud: An Anthology of Catholic Spirituality* (London, 1978), 166.

87   For modern illustration of the same principle, see 'Carbon' in Primo Levi's *The Periodic Table* (London, 1985), 224–33.

88   W. Stokes (ed.), *Tenga Bhith-Nua Annso Sis / The Evernew Tongue Here Below*, *Ériu*, 2 (1905), 98–99, §§11–13. Màire Herbert and Martin McNamara, *Irish Biblical Apocrypha* (Edinburgh, 1989), 109–18, 163–4 (*IBA*). John Carey, *King of Mysteries*, 75–96.

89   Carey, *King of Mysteries*, 75.

90   This tradition was known in Ireland from apocryphal works like 2 Enoch. The Irish 'Creation of Adam' is closely related to it. See Herbert and McNamara, *IBA*, 163–4.

91   From *Tenga Bhith-Nua Annso Sis / The Evernew Tongue Here Below*, ed. Stokes, 98–9, §§11–13; Herbert and McNamara, *IBA*, 109–18.

92   Rom. 8: 21. Irenaeus, *Adv. Haereses*, II–V.

93   Marina Smyth, 'The physical world in seventh-century Hiberno-Latin texts', *Peritia*, 5 (1986), 201–34; Carey, *King of Mysteries*, 51–74.

94   Augustine of Hippo, *Confession*, 10. 34–5; *De Genesi ad litteram / On the Literal Meaning of Genesis*, II. ix. 20. For an unusually long appreciation of the beauties of nature, see *De Civitate Dei / On the City of God*, 22. 24.

95   *De Mirabilis sacrae scripturae*, I. 7; Smyth, 'Physical World'; Carey, *King of Mysteries*, 23.

96   The phrase is from Seamus Heaney, 'The Cleric', *Station Island* (London, 1984), 107, though there scorn is for hypocrisy as much as from embarrassment.

97   S. McFague, *Super, Natural Christians* (London, 1997).

98   Meyer, *AIP*, 47–50. See also Murphy, *EIL*, 10–19; Jackson, *ECNP*, §5, *CM*, 68–70; Carney, *Medieval Irish Lyrics* (Dublin, 1967), §27. Ruth Lehmann, 'Guaire and Marban', *Zeitschrift für Celtische Philologie* (*ZCP*), 36 (1978), 96–111. Low, *CCN*, 134–7.

99   Jackson, *CM*, 64–5; Jackson dates this to the eleventh century; see also Meyer, *AIP*, 57–8.

100 Jackson, *CM*, 66–7 and *ECNP,* 45–6. Meyer, *Ériu*, 7, 2–4. Greene and O'Connor, *A Golden Treasury*, 140–3.

101 Jackson, *CM*, 279–80; Meyer, *Ériu*, 1, 39–40; Murphy, *EIL*, 28–31; Greene and O'Connor, *Golden Treasury*, 35–150. Low, *CCN*, 132–3, x.

102 Jackson, *CM*, 281–2. Jackson dates this to the eighth or ninth century. Murphy, *EIL*, 18–23.

103 *ECNP,* 79–80, quoting E. Sieper, *Die Altenglische Elegie* (Strasbourg, 1915), 65.

104 O'Donohue, *Stone as the Tabernacle of Memory*, 1.

105 Ludwig Bieler, *The Irish Penitentials* (Dublin, 1963). Jackson, *CM*, 281–2, and Murphy, *EIL*, 18–23. R. Best and H. Lawlor (eds.), *The Martyrology of Tallaght*, Henry Bradshaw Society, 68 (London, 1931), 104, quoted in Peter O'Dwyer, *Céli Dé, Spiritual Reform in Ireland 750–900*, 2nd edn. (Dublin, 1981), 142.

106 Mark 12: 28–33; John 6: 51. Cf. John 10: 10; Mark 8: 34–6.

107 W. Stokes (ed.), *Tripartite Life of Patrick* (London, 1887), ii. 475–9. Low, *CCN*, 48–52. Meyer, *Law of Adomnáin / Cáin Adomnáin*, §§6–27.

108 Helen Waddell's trans. from Giraldus Cambrensis, in *Beasts and Saints*, 137. Gerald of Wales, *History and Topography of Ireland*, trans. John J. O'Meara (London, 1988), 78, §61. Cf. Cogitosus, 'Life of Saint Brigit', *Journal of the Royal Society of Antiquaries of Ireland*, 117 (1987), §21.

109 Waddell, *Beasts and Saints*, 123–36, from the Life of St Coemgen in *Vitae Sanctorum Hiberniae*, ed. Charles Plummer. The Life of Coemgen was probably written during the seventh and eighth centuries, the heyday of Latin learning in Ireland; see R. Sharpe, *Medieval Irish Saints' Lives* (Oxford, 1991), 17–22, 234.

110 Seamus Heaney, 'St Kevin and the Blackbird', in *The Spirit Level* (London, 1996), 20. Thanks to Faber & Faber Ltd. for permission to quote this.

111 Adomnán, *VSC,* I. 33, II. 26.

112 Aonghas MacNeacail, *A Proper Schooling / Oideachadh Ceart* (Edinburgh, 1996), 38–41. With thanks to Polygon for permission to quote this verse.

113 David Summers-Smith, 'Decline of house sparrows in large towns', *British Birds*, 93 (May 2000), 256–7. The information on skylarks was supplied by the British Trust for Ornithology whose Common Bird Census shows a 60 per cent decline between 1972 and 1996.

114 Based on Meyer, *AIP*, 47–50. For other translations, see Murphy, *EIL*, 10–19; Jackson, *ECNP*, §5, *CM*, 68–70; Carney, *Medieval Irish Lyrics* (Dublin, 1967), §27; Ruth Lehmann, 'Guaire and Marban', *ZCP*, 36 (1978), 96–111.

Index